European Financial Markets

Tony F. Southall

European Financial Markets

The Effects of European Union Membership on Central and Eastern European Equity Markets

Physica-Verlag
A Springer Company

Tony F. Southall
Fröhlichstrasse 39
8008 Zürich
Switzerland
Tony_Southall@monitor.com

ISBN 978-3-7908-2565-7 e-ISBN: 978-3-7908-2074-4

DOI: 10.1007/978-3-7908-2074-4

Softcover reprint of the hardcover 1st edition 2008

Cover design: WMXDesign GmbH, Heidelberg

Printed on acid-free paper

9 8 7 6 5 4 3 2 1

springer.com

Abstract

European Union (EU) accession involves both political and economic reforms which suggest changes with regard to financial markets. This study contains empirical tests of four research questions relating to the effects of EU accession. The initial question relates to effects on the level of integration between equity markets in European transition economies and those in global as well as European economies. The second research question explores changes in the level of influence of global and local macroeconomic factors on equity market performance. The last two questions explore the impact of EU accession on equity market volatility and return levels. The study is based on data samples taken from eight markets which accessed the EU in May 2004.

The study provides evidence of a significant increase in the level of equity market integration, measured by co-movement between equity indices in transition economies and global reference indices. This implies that while successful market liberalisation involves an increase in the level of co-movement, as is concluded in existing academic research, further equity market co-movement can be expected as a result of EU accession. With regard to the co-movement with European reference indices, the results of the study suggest that increases occur at stages prior to the actual EU accession announcement and that no statistically significant change occurs in association with EU accession.

The study also provides evidence suggesting that the influence of macroeconomic factors shifts from local to global factors in association with the EU accession. Global factors demonstrate a significant increase in explanatory power after the accession, while a corresponding decline is found for local factors.

Finally, the study provides evidence of a significant decline in equity market volatility coupled with limited changes in the return levels in most markets. This implies that while there is only some evidence of changes in the return levels which are not adjusted for risk, there is clear evidence of increasing risk-adjusted returns in association with EU accession.

About the Author

Tony Southall is a strategy consultant with Monitor Group. Since 1999, Tony has served global clients across Europe, the Middle East and Africa on topics relating to corporate strategy, acquisition and divestiture support, post-merger integration, marketing and operational improvement. More recently, Tony focuses on serving investment companies and other clients in emerging markets.

Tony received his Ph.D. in Economics from the University of St. Gallen. He also holds an M.Sc. in Finance from the Stockholm School of Economics and a CEMS M.Sc. in International Management from the Stockholm School of Economics and the HEC School of Management Paris.

Contents

List of Figures

List of Tables

Chapter 1
Introduction

1.1 Context of Study

Subsequent to the dismantling of the Soviet Union in the 1990s, improved political stability and reforms have substantially changed the economic environment in the Central and Eastern European economies. The political transition has resulted in improved conditions which in turn have led to real economic growth superior to that in Western Europe as well as to a continuous flow of capital into the region.

An event that has had significant political impact on a group of Central European economies is the accession to the European Union (EU) on the 1st of May 2004. As of this date, ten additional states joined the EU, bringing the total number of member states to 25. Eight of these ten new member states are former Soviet Union satellite states located in Central Europe and the Baltic region. The accession process is likely to have affected not only the development and integration of the Central European region but also the perception of the respective markets by international investors.

Market integration theory (Bekaert and Harvey, 2003) suggests that emerging markets go through a dynamic change process prior and subsequent to the liberalisation stage. The change involves phases of both increasing and decreasing cost of capital and volatility. Understanding the implications of market liberalisation and integration on financial markets is important not only from the perspective of specific assets but also from the perspective of portfolios of assets. Modern portfolio theory (Markowitz, 1952) states that equity markets in emerging economies could constitute an attractive complement to investments in developed markets given the low level of covariance between the two types of markets.

While the process of determining the date of liberalisation and the analysis of effects of market integration have been conducted in earlier research, the assessment of effects of accession to an established free-trade economic union on financial markets has received limited attention from an academic point of view. Given the importance of the EU accession in terms of political, economic as well as potentially financial integration, this study aims to further expand the understanding of market integration processes in the context of financial markets in European transition economies.

T. Southall, *European Financial Markets*,

More specifically the focus is on expanding the understanding of the effects of EU accession and related accession events in terms of equity market integration and performance in the eight most developed European transition economies. These eight economies were successful in the negotiations with the EU over the course of the decade leading up to May 2004 when they all accessed the EU. The eight economies, in order of largest population size, include Poland, the Czech Republic, Hungary, the Slovak Republic, Lithuania, Latvia, Slovenia and Estonia.

This study focuses on several distinct research areas directly or indirectly related to market integration. The first focus area relates to complementing extant knowledge in the area of market integration by empirically testing the impact on integration levels in the financial markets as a result of EU accession among European transition economies. Previous research (Bekaert and Harvey, 2000) suggests changes in degree of integration as a result of successful liberalisation. Given the political and economic integration characteristics of EU accession, it is feasible to expect a certain level of positive impact on the integration of financial markets of the accessing economies. As part of the integration analysis, estimates of the timing of the market liberalisation in the eight markets are explored.

Under the assumption that market liberalisation in the studied economies occurred in the 1990s and that significant effects on financial markets can be determined, EU accession would constitute an additional stage in a lengthy market integration process. This research would thereby contribute to the existing research on market integration and the dynamics of the integration process.

The second and third focus areas relate to understanding whether there are any significant effects on volatility and return of equity markets in emerging economies as a result of the EU accession. This involves exploring the rate of return before and after the accession to determine any significant differences. As the accession process towards becoming an EU member involves requirements of economic reforms and measures as well as financial support from the EU, it is reasonable to presume that a resulting shift in the perceived level of uncertainty of these markets among investors should have an impact on the volatility and return characteristics. In the case of significant effects on volatility and return measures as a result of EU accession this research would contribute to the understanding of how to incorporate emerging markets in global portfolios during periods of integration.

1.2 Scope of Study

The scope of this study is limited in terms of geographies, time horizon and types of financial markets covered. The delimitations do not only narrow down the analyses to the most relevant markets, they also focus the study in a way that enhances the potential for relevant research findings. Figure 1.1 illustrates the areas of delimitations.

In terms of geographic scope, the study is limited to a specific type of economy in a certain geographical region in which the particular integration effects are likely to appear. The economies included in this study are all Central and Eastern European

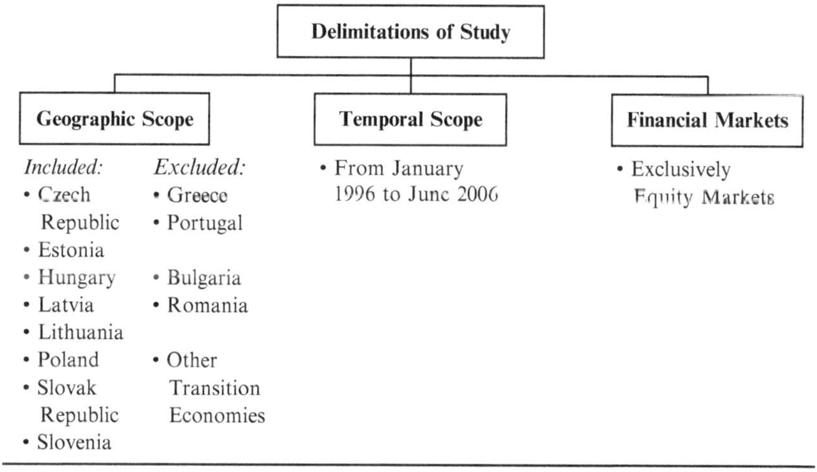

Fig. 1.1 Delimitations of study

transition economies as defined by the World Bank. The term transition economy will be discussed in further detail in Sect. 1.4. At this stage suffice it to say that the World Bank distinguishes between emerging, or developing, economies and transition economies although it includes the latter category in the former category (Soubbotina, 2004). The distinction is based on the political legacy of transition economies which requires them to make significant reforms to transition from closed political and economic systems into open market economies representative of developed countries.

By applying the World Bank definition of transition economies in this study, the probability of identifying relevant market integration effects is improved despite the consequent reduction in sample size. While the focus markets are similar in the sense that they were all highly influenced by the Soviet planned economy and that they accessed the EU in 2004, they are different in many dimensions including size and industrial mix. These differences imply that the analyses and results of this study can be viewed as more generic than if the analyses had been based on a single economy or on a group of nearly identical economies.

The application of the definition also implies that two nations, Cyprus and Malta, of the ten that joined the EU in 2004 are excluded from the analysis on the basis that they are already defined as developed countries and are therefore already likely to be largely integrated with world markets.

In terms of temporal scope, the study is limited to the period covering the ten years subsequent to 1996. The time period is selected to provide sufficient time series data for the periods both prior to and after the EU accession. The exact length of each time series sample is, however, dependent on data availability. Given that the financial markets in the European transition economies were launched in the 1990s, there is limited opportunity to extend the time horizon further back in history. The consequence of this temporal limitation is that Greece and Portugal are not included in the study although they were defined as emerging markets at the time of their respective EU accessions in the early and mid 1980s. Also Bulgaria and Romania are excluded as they joined the EU in January 2007.

Finally, the scope of the study is limited in terms of financial market components. While there are potentially valuable insights to be generated from the study of bond, derivative and real estate markets as well as other financial markets, this study focuses exclusively on equity markets. This limitation of scope is partly based on absence of relevant data, but also driven by the aim to build on and complement existing market integration research using equity markets in other emerging economies as the foundation for analyses and conclusions.

1.3 Contribution of Study

The recent enlargement of the EU offers a unique opportunity to study the impact on performance characteristics of emerging equity markets under a specific and clearly defined event that theoretically should affect both the performance and the level of integration with world markets. Although this enlargement process could be characterised as a rarely reoccurring event it is relevant to study for a number of reasons.

First, EU accession of transition economies continues to occur. In January 2007 Bulgaria and Romania accessed the EU as a result of meeting the accession requirements in a timely manner over the course of 2006. In addition, Turkey is already in discussions with the EU and Croatia aims to begin detailed talks (Cottrell, 2005). Furthermore, other countries on the Western Balkans, including Albania, Bosnia, Macedonia, Serbia and Montenegro have been promised EU membership although no timetable has yet been provided and countries like Ukraine, Moldova and Georgia are hoping to join one day although this is predicted for the long rather than short or medium term perspective (Cottrell, 2005). With some of these economies succeeding in the negotiations, the EU may grow to over 35 member states in the coming decade and thereby increasing the relevance of this research in understanding effects of this enlargement on equity markets.

In the context of up to ten additional economies potentially accessing the EU in the coming years, an understanding of the effects of EU accession on the performance and level of integration of financial markets is important not only for individual investors but also for portfolio managers and policy makers at the EU as well as the national level and for financial exchange authorities (Fig 1.2).

Second, this study is relevant as it addresses the more general topic of the impact on financial markets as a result of the inclusion of an emerging economy into an established economic free-trade union which indirectly implies a continued process of transitioning from segmented to integrated market status. Certain findings from this study could be generalised to economies and economic trade unions outside of Europe, which in turn could lead to an improved understanding of how risks related to investment in emerging markets can be reduced during a transition into an economic union. This in turn could lead to the availability of cheaper capital for governments and

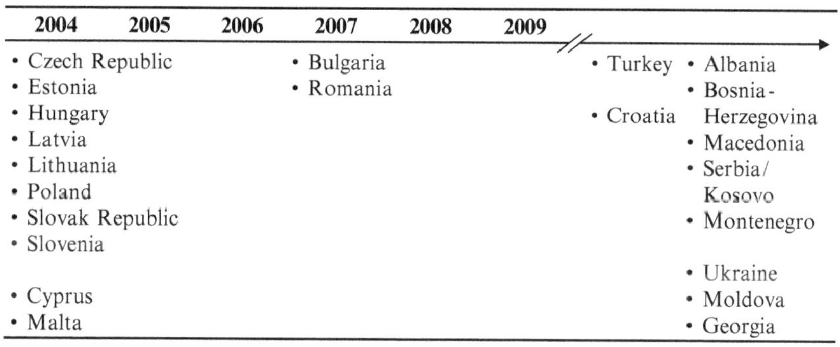

Source: Cottrell, 2005

Fig. 1.2 Recent and potential EU candidates

corporations in these markets. From this perspective the study is relevant for policy makers and corporate managers far beyond the EU and Central Europe.

Third, understanding how the integration of emerging markets affects equity markets in emerging economies could provide valuable information to investors and portfolio managers on how to best incorporate emerging markets in their international investment portfolios.

Fourth, while not explicitly studied within the scope of this work due to a lack of sufficient empirical foundation, insights can be derived with regard to the effects on corporate performance of implementing corporate governance guidelines in markets where such frameworks are either not available or not enforced. As part of the accession, these markets have been requested to bring their corporate governance guidelines closer in line with the standards prevailing in Western Europe. The transition has resulted in a substantial increase in the level of awareness of governance issues particularly since the inflow of international capital has increasingly put pressure on all players in the market to introduce and abide by stricter governance measures. These findings would be of interest to investors, decision makers at financial exchanges as well as policy makers.

In addition to providing insights relevant for investment practitioners and policy makers, this research contributes to the academic knowledge base in two distinct ways. First, it contributes to the understanding of the effects on equity return and volatility associated with emerging market EU accession, an important event that ties an economy closer to other economies within an economic free-trade union. In this context, the research can be described as providing predictions for how equity markets in other transition and emerging economies will behave as a result of accessing the EU or potentially a similar economic trade union. Thereby the study helps clarifying important dimensions of regional market integration research.

Second, the research also contributes to the understanding of the market integration process. Market integration constitutes a highly complex and dynamic process which has received limited attention. Previous market integration research

(Bekaert, 1995, 2000; Bekaert and Harvey, 2001; Bekaert et al., 2002) has focused on the early stages in the transition from segmentation to integration with a focus on the effects of successful liberalisation. Later stages in the integration process have received little academic focus. By evaluating whether there are important events that can significantly change the level of integration after the successful occurrence of market liberalisation, this study contributes to a more complete understanding of the integration process.

1.4 Definition of Key Terms

Prior to entering into the review of the theoretical and empirical research which provides the foundation of this study, it is useful to introduce the key terminology which reoccurs throughout this study. While most of the terms below are discussed to a certain extent in other parts of this study, this section offers a compilation that aims to facilitate the reading.

1.4.1 Definition of European Transition Economies

The term emerging economy has been broadly used since its inception by the International Finance Corporation (IFC) of the World Bank in 1981. Despite the broad use, the definition is somewhat unclear as the term is based on a combination of criteria rather than a single parameter such as market size or national wealth.

Originally, the World Bank defined emerging countries based on the level of gross national product (GNP) per capita and the share of a market being investable for foreign investors (Soubbotina, 2004). Investability is measured as the share of market capitalization as a percentage of the gross domestic product (GDP) that is available to foreign investors. Non-investable holdings include large block holdings and parts of companies that are inaccessible due to investment limitations for foreigners.

However, in the early 1990s, the IFC identified a number of limitations with using the above described two criteria in defining emerging markets (International Finance Corporation, 1999). First, exchange rate fluctuations caused significant variations in the US Dollar (USD) denominated GNP per capita measure. Second, as the GNP per capita data is tedious to calculate, it is often outdated by the time data become available. Third, fluctuations in currency and market valuations also caused the investability criterion to be unstable.

Consequently, in 1996 the IFC revised its old definition and introduced two new criteria to conclude whether an economy can be characterised as developed. First, GNP per capita must exceed the World Bank's upper income threshold for at least three consecutive years. Second, the investable market capitalisation-to-GDP ratio must approach the average of that in developed markets during three consecutive years (International Finance Corporation, 1999).

Furthermore, there are additional factors that determine whether an economy is defined as an emerging economy. Nations with stock markets containing investment restrictions such as foreign limits, capital controls, extensive government involvement and other legislated restraints on market activity tend to fall into the emerging market category. In addition, there are qualitative features to consider such as operational efficiency, quality of market regulation, supervision and enforcement, corporate governance practices, minority shareholder rights, transparency and level of accounting standards which are all important characteristics for investors to consider in their tolerance for any specific emerging market exposure (International Finance Corporation, 1999).

As discussed in Sect. 1.2, the World Bank applies the same criteria to transition economies as for emerging economies. However, the distinguishing factor of a transition economy is the additional presence of political and economic legacy involving the absence of free markets. In addition to countries in Central and Eastern Europe, transition economies include China, Mongolia, Vietnam, and former Soviet Union countries in Asia (International Finance Corporation, 1999). These markets, however, are not included in this study.

1.4.2 Definition of European Union Membership

The EU is a political and economic union established in 1993 after the ratification of the Maastricht Treaty by the 12 member states of the European Community. The history of the European Community goes back to the Treaty of Rome of 1957 when six European nations agreed to pool resources across borders to preserve and strengthen peace and liberty in Europe (European Commission, 2006).

Over time, the EU has continued to expand in terms of member states and in the beginning of 2004 the total number of members was 15, commonly referred to as the EU15. In May 2004, ten additional member states accessed the EU bringing the total number of member states to 25.

While the most extensive form of EU involvement is membership, there are additional ways for nations to be associated with the EU. One such agreement is the Stabilisation and Association Agreement which is typically concluded with countries on the Western Balkan in exchange for commitments on economic, political, trade and human rights reforms (European Commission, 2000). Another related agreement is the European Neighbourhood Association Agreement which targets non-member states around the Mediterranean Sea and the Central and Eastern European states neighbouring the EU. While both of the association agreements can imply tariff-free access to some or all EU markets, the depth of the harmonisation is not as extensive as that associated with full membership (European Commission, 2007).

In 1992, the EU also established an agreement with the European Free Trade Association (EFTA) to allow for some of the EFTA members including Iceland, Liechtenstein and Norway, to participate in the European single market without

Table 1.1 List of EU members and states with EU association agreements

EU 15 members	EU members joining in 2004 and 2007	EU Stabilisation and Association Agreement States	EU Neighbourhood Association Agreement States	European economic area members
Austria	*2004*	Albania	Algeria	All EU members
Belgium	Cyprus	Bosnia-Herzegovina	Armenia	Iceland
Denmark	Czech Republic	Croatia	Azerbaijan	Liecthenstein
Finland	Estonia	Montenegro	Belarus	Norway
France	Hungary	Macedonia	Egypt	
Germany	Latvia	Serbia Kosovo	Georgia	
Greece	Lithuania		Israel	
Ireland	Malta		Jordan	
Italy	Poland		Lebanon	
Luxembourg	Slovak Republic		Libya	
Netherlands	Slovenia		Modova	
Portugal			Morocco	
Spain	*2007*		Palestinian Authority	
Sweden	Bulgaria		Russia	
United Kingdom	Romania		Syria	
			Tunisia	
			Ukraine	

Source:
The Council of the European Union

actual EU membership. The remaining current EFTA member, Switzerland, does not participate in the European Economic Area and has instead negotiated a set of bilateral agreements to control the relationship between the markets (EFTA, 2004). Table 1.1 provides an overview of the EU states as well as the state with the respective EU association agreements.

This study focuses exclusively on states having joined the EU in 2004. The study disregards any country with limited harmonisation derived from association agreements. Further details on the EU and the accession criteria are provided in Sect. 5.1.3.

1.4.3 Definition of Effects on Equity Markets

As discussed in Sect. 1.2, the scope of this study is limited to the equity part of the financial markets. This implies studying the trading prices of listed company shares in the financial markets of the selected economies. However, in order to measure the overall market trends, as large a sample as possible of the local markets must be collected. This is likely to be best facilitated by using indices of the local markets which incorporate the effects of both dividend payments and capital gains.

While there are several potential effects that could be studied, this study comprises four particular effects which are all highly relevant from both practical and academic perspectives. Each effect is carefully detailed in Chap. 3, where the research hypotheses are derived. At this point, the effects are only briefly detailed before entering into the review of existing research literature.

The study comprises two equity market effects related to integration and two effects related to performance. More specifically, the integration effects include the level of co-movement between local and global equity market indices and the level of influence on local equity markets derived from local as well as global macroeconomic factors.

The effects related to performance are associated with the level of returns and the level of volatility in local market indices. The definition of return applied within this study is in line with several other academic studies (Bekaert et al., 1997; Bekaert and Harvey, 1997) and does not involve any adjustment to the risk level in the initial stage. The return is measured at the total return level which includes return generated both directly from dividends and indirectly from capital gains over time. In a second stage, however, the return levels are adjusted to the associated volatility levels to provide a more relevant measure of return. A commonly used measure for risk-adjusted performance in academic research as well as in the investment community is the Sharpe ratio (Sharpe, 1966, 1994). The Sharpe ratio is therefore applied in this study.

The second performance-related equity market effect studied is volatility which can be seen as a measure of overall market risk from the perspective of the investor. As with the return, there are several alternative measures of risk including credit ratings, credit spreads, and country risk estimators incorporating a range of qualitative and quantitative parameters affecting risk. In this study, credit ratings and country risk estimators are reviewed and incorporated in the analyses but the main focus remains on the volatility of the local equity market indices.

1.5 Structure of Study

The study is structured into seven complementary chapters that together introduce the derivation of the hypotheses and describe the research methodology as well as the analyses, conclusions and contributions of this study.

This introductory chapter includes a background as well as an introduction to the topic of the study. This chapter also includes a description of how and for whom the research is relevant as well as how it contributes to the current academic knowledge base. Finally, this chapter introduces definitions of key terminology applied within the scope of this study.

Chapter 2 provides a review of the relevant existing academic research. The review covers four topical areas of research ranging from characteristics of emerging financial markets and general market integration research to areas related to regional market integration focusing on the European markets as well as related corporate governance research. The review introduces both theoretical frameworks and empirical tests and findings.

Chapter 3 incorporates the derivation of the four research hypotheses. The derivation is based on existing academic research and identifies how the research hypotheses fit into the existing knowledge base and how the insights can help fill gaps in what is currently known.

Chapter 4 contains an introduction to the research methodology and selected analytical approaches applied in testing the research hypotheses. Each approach is described in detail and links to previous empirical research where these approaches have been applied are presented.

Chapter 5 presents and critically reviews the empirical data used in the analyses of the research hypotheses. Sources and characteristics of the different data are scrutinised and links to similar data applied in previous empirical research are presented.

Chapter 6 includes a presentation of the analyses and the empirical results of each of the test approaches. The statistical relevance of the results is discussed in each case to understand how the particular empirical findings contribute to the test of the research hypotheses.

Chapter 7 describes the overall contribution of this study in the context of the existing knowledge base and introduces how the findings of this research can be applied. Furthermore, the chapter includes an interpretation of the results along with a discussion of the limitations that should be considered when interpreting the empirical findings. Finally, a presentation of associated areas that have fallen outside the scope of this study but nevertheless would deserve further research attention is provided.

In addition to the seven chapters there is an appendix which contains further details of data applied within the study but have not explicitly been introduced elsewhere in the text.

Chapter 2
Literature Review

This chapter offers a review of the relevant theoretical foundation and existing empirical evidence upon which this study is based. The chapter is divided into four topical sections.

The first section introduces the performance characteristics of emerging equity markets, which help explain the subsequent theoretical review relating to market liberalisation and integration. While findings from several emerging markets are included, the focus remains on equity markets in European transition economies. In addition to a review of definitions and theories around market liberalisation and market integration, section two also describes the main conclusions on liberalisation and integration effects on financial markets. The third section reviews the area of regional market integration and introduces studies relating to the macroeconomic effects of the EU enlargement. The fourth section explores theory and associated empirical evidence of an area linked to the EU accession preparations, namely corporate governance and how it is linked to equity performance characteristics.

2.1 Performance Characteristics of Emerging Markets

Prior to discussing market liberalisation and integration theory and what this theory implies for emerging equity markets, it is useful to introduce some general research on the characteristics of emerging equity markets. This is particularly important since emerging financial markets tend to differ from those in developed economies. Furthermore, the strong evolution of emerging markets around the world in the last decades triggered a wave of empirical research that jointly contributes to the understanding of the foundations of market liberalisation and integration.

This section aims to present some of the empirical findings that illustrate similarities and differences of emerging equity markets compared with developed equity markets.

2.1.1 Return and Volatility Characteristics

Equity markets in emerging economies have been the focus of extensive academic research in the last decades (Aggarwal et al., 1999; Aydogan and Gursoy, 2001; Barry et al., 1998; Basu et al., 2000; Bekaert et al., 1997; Bekaert and Harvey, 2003). Returns and risks were under particular attention in the 1990s when emerging markets offered attractive returns compared to those in developed markets during certain periods but also demonstrated significant volatility during for example the Mexican crisis of 1994, the Thai crisis of 1997 and the Russian crisis of 1998.

A wide range of empirical research suggests that emerging equity markets offer a combination of higher returns and higher volatility compared to developed markets (Bekaert and Urias, 1999; Divecha et al., 1992; Gottschalk, 2005; Price, 1994; Stanley, 1995). These findings contribute to the common perception, also supported by financial theory, that the additional risk associated with emerging markets is rewarded with higher expected returns. Asset pricing theory, in the form of the capital asset pricing model (CAPM), suggests that assets associated with higher levels of sensitivity to volatility must offer superior expected returns in order to attract capital from the market (Lintner, 1965; Sharpe, 1964).

Bekaert and Harvey (1997) suggest that standardised univariate volatility models offer only limited insights into the nature of volatility in emerging markets. Instead, models adjusted to better represent the characteristics of emerging market data might have to be applied. First, as emerging market data have been shown to contain both skewness and excess kurtosis, they apply models that account for these higher moments. Second, the models also allow for time-varying conditional means to compensate for the predictability characteristic in emerging market data. Finally, their models allow for variation over time in the importance of both local and global information to reflect shifts in the level of market integration. Based on these models they conclude that volatility is more likely to be influenced by global factors in fully integrated markets whereas segmented markets tend to be affected by local factors. Furthermore, they conclude that more open emerging economies have lower volatility than less open economies.

However, other empirical research raises concerns about these conclusions. The conclusions of superior returns in emerging markets run the risk of being biased due to the fact that returns tend to be higher soon after the emergence compared with the time horizon prior to emergence and the time horizon long after emergence. As recently emerged markets tend to be included in most analyses while markets that have not emerged are excluded, empirical findings on returns tend to receive an unnatural boost (Goetzmann and Jorion, 1999).

The importance of choices around time horizon in determining emerging market returns are further underlined by empirical research based on longer time series of emerging market return data (Barry et al., 1998). Barry et al. (1998) compare a composite index comprised of 26 emerging markets against the Standard and Poor's (S&P) 500 index, the NASDAQ index as well as United States (US) treasury bills (T-Bills) and concludes that while volatility remained higher for the composite index over all time horizons, mean return for the composite index in the 20-year period ending in 1995 was actually lower than that for the S&P 500 index.

Another important factor questioning the conclusion that emerging markets offer superior returns compared to assets in developed markets relates to the fact that costs might not be appropriately reflected in the return calculations (Bekaert and Urias, 1999; Masters, 2002). The most frequently applied source of calculating emerging market returns is the S&P/International Finance Corporation (IFC) Emerging Market Data Base (EMDB) Global Index (Bekaert and Urias, 1999), which does not reflect the true and often significant costs of investment compared to developed markets. While this effect has a negligible impact on the volatility of emerging market performance, it does result in an inappropriate augmentation of the actual emerging market returns when compared with that of investments in developed markets.

While there is general consensus that volatility in emerging market returns is higher than that in developed markets, there are different opinions on what the main causes for this fact are. One cause suggested in research is that rapid shifts in flows of international capital driven by perceptions of relative market conditions in developed and emerging markets largely contribute to the volatility (Frenkel and Menkhoff, 2004). It is also possible to assume that large and rapid changes in the political and economic environments translate into higher levels of volatility in emerging financial markets.

Furthermore, as indicated above, despite suggestions of economic theory (Lintner, 1965; Sharpe, 1964) that higher levels of sensitivity to volatility should imply higher levels of return, empirical evidence indicating the opposite exists. Given uncertainties around the superiority of equity returns in emerging versus developed economies, the question whether emerging markets can offer any attractive investment opportunities arises. The subsequent sub-section introduces empirical evidence that suggests that emerging equity markets do have an important role to play from an investment perspective when considering overall portfolio volatility, even if superior performance relative to developed markets is uncertain.

2.1.2 Co-movement Between Emerging Markets and World Markets

Both theoretical and empirical evidence suggests that emerging equity assets have attractive attributes in terms of reducing portfolio risk when combined with assets in developed markets. The benefit stems from the fact that partially segmented emerging markets tend to be influenced by a set of local factors rather than the global factors which influence the world markets (Bekaert and Harvey, 1997; Fifield et al., 2002; Johnson et al., 1999). Furthermore, emerging and developed markets have different industrial mixes which implies that markets are influenced by different market factors (Harvey, 1995b). The following sub-section introduces a theoretical framework as well as empirical evidence that highlight the diversification potential of emerging equity as an asset class.

From a theoretical perspective, the issue of co-movement among asset returns is explained by the fact that the asset prices are influenced by a few pervasive factors as is proposed in the arbitrage pricing theory (APT) (Ross, 1976). APT suggests that the expected return of a financial asset can be modelled as a linear function of macroeconomic factors for which the sensitivity to changes is represented by a factor-specific beta coefficient. The identification and testing of relevant macroeconomic factors have been the topic of much empirical research (Bodurtha et al., 1989; Chen et al., 1986; Fifield et al., 2002; Roll and Ross, 1980).

The macroeconomic factors can be divided into global and local factors. The global factors refer to generic factors not specific to a single national economy. Examples of the global factors include the price of oil and other commodities, returns of world stock and bond indices as well as growth in world industrial production (Bodurtha et al., 1989). The local factors, on the other hand, are specific to a country and could include anticipated inflation, international reserves, term premium, industrial production index, export and import indices as well as interest rates and exchange rates (Bodurtha et al., 1989; Fifield et al., 2002).

When markets are influenced by the same macroeconomic factors, the co-movement between them is expected to be high. In the case of emerging markets, influence on asset prices is largely derived from local rather than global macroeconomic factors and since the local factors are different from the global factors, co-movement is significantly reduced. The lower level of co-movement opens up for attractive portfolio combinations that allow for a reduction in volatility without an equivalent reduction in returns.

The effects of combining emerging and developed markets have been analysed in much research. Barry et al. (1998) explore the minimum variance portfolio of a combination of the S&P 500 index and an emerging market composite index for the period 1985–1995. The conclusion is that a portfolio containing 20% composite index and 80% S&P 500 offers both higher return and lower volatility than a pure investment in S&P 500. Similar results were achieved for both shorter and longer time horizons during which the emerging market composite index even underperformed the S&P 500. Furthermore, benefits of diversification are also found in portfolios combining American depositary receipts (ADR), open-ended mutual funds and closed-end mutual funds from 13 emerging markets with developed markets for the period 1993 to 1996 (Bekaert and Urias, 1999).

Several empirical studies offer similar conclusions on the low correlation levels between emerging and developing markets and the corresponding diversification benefits (Gottschalk, 2005; Jorion, 1985; Solnik and Noetzlin, 1982).

Also between emerging markets, empirical evidence suggests a low level of correlation across countries (Barry et al., 1997). This suggests that including several emerging markets in a portfolio reduces volatility of returns and improves the risk-return characteristics of the portfolio.

However, some empirical evidence indicates that not all emerging markets and not all time horizons offer positive risk-return benefits to a portfolio. For example, in a study of time horizons that include crises such as the Mexican devaluation in 1994, it was found that a basket of Brady bonds from nine emerging markets did not yield any significant risk-return benefits when added to a portfolio of US stocks and bonds (Dahiya, 1997). Similarly, while offering appealing portfolio diversification over longer time horizons, empirical evidence suggests that emerging markets offer only limited diversification benefits in times of crisis, when the reduction of volatility would be needed the most (Barry et al., 1998).

The phenomenon of strong co-movement across individual markets under extreme market settings is referred to as international financial contagion. A clear example of financial contagion occurred in the late summer of 1998 when several banks, hedge funds and security firms simultaneously tried to reduce their exposure to a number of financial instruments leading to a global decline in trading volumes and a broadening of spreads across a wide range of markets (Kyle and Xiong, 2001; Lowenstein, 2000).

While emerging market equities have been proven to have low correlations with developed markets, the distributional characteristics of emerging market returns might not be fully described by the standard mean-variance approach to portfolio management theory as suggested by Markowitz (1959). An empirical study of higher moments within emerging market return data indicates that returns of several emerging markets demonstrate both skewness and excess kurtosis (Bekaert et al., 1998). In the same study it is also found that the characteristics of the skewness and kurtosis changes over time. Bekaert et al. (1998) suggest that as emerging markets experience the dynamic transition from segmentation to integration, skewness and kurtosis may decrease to levels where the central limit theorem can be applied to approximate samples from non-normal return distributions with the normal distribution.

As will be discussed in the next section, the market integration process does not only affect skewness and kurtosis dimensions but rather potentially changes the entire risk and return characteristics of a market.

2.2 Market Integration

The transition from segmented, national financial markets to globally integrated financial markets began in the 1970s when developed countries initiated the dismantling of restrictions on international capital flows. These restrictive obstacles included limitations of foreign exchange transactions, disintegrated taxation legislations and limitations on foreign ownership (Stulz, 1999). While developed markets are largely integrated by now, many emerging economies across Central Europe, South America and Asia, initiated the process later and are still not considered fully integrated.

This section provides a definition of market integration as well as a description of the process and the effects of market integration. It also reviews empirical evidence relating to the effects of integration in emerging economies.

2.2.1 *Distinguishing Between Market Integration and Market Liberalisation*

Over the last decades, a number of emerging economies have taken steps to facilitate the removal of barriers on international financial transactions. These liberalisation steps constitute one level in the broader market integration process.

Market liberalisation is defined as regulatory changes that remove laws limiting access to domestic capital markets for foreign investors and access to international capital markets for domestic investors (Bekaert et al., 2003). However, not all market liberalisations are effective in the sense that they lead to increased openness. Although legal barriers are removed, investors might not perceive the liberalisation as sustainable or effective and might therefore be reluctant to engage in any transactions. Consequently, it is important to distinguish between market liberalisation and market integration.

Market integration implies that the capital market of a country is de facto open for foreign trade and is normally the result of an effective liberalisation process. However, market integration can occur without liberalisation when financial instruments, such as depositary receipts or country funds, provide access to a country's capital market (Bekaert et al., 2003).

A more detailed definition of market integration is that markets are integrated if assets are priced the same, independently of where the claims to the cash flows are made (Karolyi and Stulz, 2003). In other words, markets where there are no additional risks for foreign investors compared to those for local investors and where there are no barriers to capital flows would be defined as fully integrated markets. At the other extreme, markets where local investors are unable to invest in foreign assets and foreign investors have no access to local markets are defined as fully segmented. An economy can also be partially segmented with the level of segmentation being determined by two categories of conditions; the risks borne by foreign investors and the barriers facing foreign investors when investing in a market (Karolyi and Stulz, 2003).

While a liberalisation process can result in a higher level of integration of emerging markets, there are a number of barriers to global equity market integration that limit the possibilities for full integration. One of these barriers relates to the fact that domestic investors might favour domestic assets to foreign assets in what is commonly defined as home bias (Tesar and Werner, 1992, 1995). Other barriers to market integration include poor credit ratings, high and variable inflation, exchange rate controls, the lack of a high-quality regulatory and accounting framework, the lack of sufficient country funds or cross-listed securities, and the limited size of a stock market (Bekaert, 1995).

2.2.2 *Theory of Market Integration*

Market integration is a complicated process influenced by several domestic and international factors. While there are economic models describing general equilibrium for economies in both segmented and integrated states, there are no established economic models that predict the dynamics of these processes between the two states. However, a number of attempts have been made to theoretically model parts of this process.

One largely simplified model is presented by Bekaert and Harvey (2003) based on the standard static integration/segmentation model (Alexander et al., 1987; Errunza and Losq, 1985; Errunza et al., 1998; Eun and Janakiramanan, 1986). The model is based on a quadratic utility framework and examines a three-period scenario for equity prices based on dividend payouts in an emerging market that is either segmented for the entire time horizon, or fully integrated with the world market in the second time period. A set of simplifying assumptions are made in the model. First, the risk-free rate is set to zero. Second, there is only one share in each asset class. Third, the dividend payouts occur only in period three during which no trading takes place. Fourth, currency considerations are ignored. Fifth, market integration decisions can only be taken and implemented in period two. Finally, the weight of the emerging market in the world market is negligible.

The random payoff of equity assets in the world market in the third period is defined as $D_M^W = \sum_{i=1}^{Nw} D_i^W$ and the random payoff in the emerging market is $D_M^E = \sum_{i=1}^{Ne} D_i^E$. Focusing on the equity prices in the emerging market for the second period, the prices under perfect integration (P_2^I) and under perfect segmentation (P_2^S) will be

$$P_2^I = E\left[D_M^E\right] - \bar{C}ov\left[D_M^E, D_M^W\right]$$

$$P_2^S = E\left[D_M^E\right] - \bar{V}ar\left[D_M^E\right]$$

Where ρ is the risk aversion coefficient and the price in the segmentation scenario will be lower than that in the integration scenario since variability of local cash will be high and covariance with the world markets will be low. Given that there are only two scenarios for the price in period two and that the probability in period one of integration in period two is defined as λ, the price in period one is defined as

$$P_1 = \lambda P_2^I + (1 - \lambda) P_2^S$$

Based on the above model, Bekaert and Harvey (2003) argue that the price will jump in period one if liberalisation is announced for period two. The size of the jump will be determined by a combination of credibility of the announcement, the level of price adjustment for the expectation already built into the formula in the form of λ and finally, the level of diversification benefits to be gained from integrating the market. As the integration occurs in period two, a further price increase is expected as uncertainty is completely eliminated.

Although this model is largely simplified and ignores several relevant aspects in the integration process, it illustrates that permanent price changes could appear as a result of integration. These are, however, not the only effects that can be expected from market integration.

Effects have also been explored in the context of other research fields. Researchers in the field of international economics focus on how welfare gains can be generated for countries sharing consumption risks through the trading of equity claims in foreign market outputs. While economists tend to agree on the benefits generated from free trade of goods, views are more diverse regarding the benefits of free mobility of capital flows. Research suggests that international capital mobility generates negative effects particularly for developing economies (Bhagwati, 1998; Tobin, 2003) or that abrupt shocks in market return largely stem from the supply side of capital flows and thereby make the risk of financial crises in developing economies highly dependent on yield curves in the developed markets (Harris, 2000). However, Stulz (1999) points out that free trade in goods is, to a large extent, dependent on free mobility of capital.

Even if welfare gains of market integration concluded in field of international economics are rather limited, additional dimensions are identified within another research field, the field of international finance, which suggests that potential benefits are numerous and considerable (Bekaert and Harvey, 2003; Bekaert et al., 2002; Obstfeld, 1994; Stulz, 1999). Standard international asset pricing models suggest that the cost of capital is reduced as a result of the risk sharing potential associated with market integration (Alexander et al., 1987; Errunza and Losq, 1989; Eun and Janakiramanan, 1986; Stapleton and Subrahmanyam, 1977). The benefits are interlinked and include lower cost of capital in the form of lower expected returns as well as more efficient markets which ultimately may lead to higher investment levels and increased economic output (Bekaert and Harvey, 2003). Market integration should also imply broader investment opportunities for domestic and foreign investors which result in benefits associated with international risk-sharing.

The link between the benefits is well described by Stulz (1999). In a completely segmented market, local companies can only seek capital from investors within the local economy and local investors are equally limited to investing in local companies only. This limitation on investors' diversification opportunities reduces the willingness to provide capital to the market, which in turn might force companies to engage in inefficient diversification activities to be able to attract capital.

The risk-sharing benefits arise from a reduction of portfolio risks achieved through diversification opportunities for domestic and foreign investors when an economy becomes increasingly integrated and access to new sources of capital from outside the domestic market is allowed. The diversification opportunities reduce the required risk premium and the subsequent cost of equity capital by allowing domestic investors to access investments that are counter-cyclical to those available in the domestic market.

The implication of this reduction in cost of capital is twofold. First, given unchanged expected future cash flows, the equity price index of a market experiencing integration should increase as information about liberalisation and corresponding expected integration is announced (Henry, 2000). Second, as the risk premium and capital costs decline, additional investment projects become economically feasible which should lead to higher growth and welfare generation in the economy as a whole (Henry, 2000; Stulz, 1999).

While expected returns are likely to decline as markets go from segmentation to integration, the price shares of companies that offer attractive diversification potential are likely to increase during the actual integration process (Bekaert and Harvey, 2003).

Another predicted effect associated with integration is a higher level of co-movement between the domestic market returns and those in world markets. This is based on the fact that returns in segmented markets are affected by local factors of volatility whereas common global factors increasingly influence the formerly segmented markets as the level of integration rises (Harvey, 1995b). This argument is countered by the fact that emerging markets tend to have different industrial mixes compared to those in developed markets and therefore are less susceptible to macroeconomic shocks originating from developed countries (Bekaert and Harvey, 2000). This would imply that even with a higher level of integration, co-movement with global markets might be limited. Under any circumstance, some change in the level of co-movement is expected due to the increase in international capital flows (Harris, 2000).

Modern portfolio theory (Markowitz, 1952, 1959) suggests that investment decisions should be made based on the overall risk-reward characteristics of portfolios rather than on attractive risk-reward characteristics of individual assets. Under the assumption of risk aversion and with the mean representing expected reward and variance representing expected risk, the mean-variance approach to selecting a portfolio implies minimizing the variance for any given mean or, alternatively, maximizing the mean for any given variance. As correlation between two asset classes decreases, the more attractive the asset combination becomes. Despite the high levels of volatility and limited return premiums compared to leading US indices over certain time horizons, emerging markets play an important role for investors with a global investment perspective.

With the theoretical dimensions of market integration and its effects introduced, the focus is now shifted towards empirical studies that have tested the theoretical predictions.

2.2.3 Empirical Market Integration Research

The expected effects of market integration suggested in the preceding sub-section are largely founded on theoretical grounds. Given the level of complexity of the market integration process and the fact that predictive models often are incomplete and highly simplified, there is a need for empirical testing of the predicted effects of market integration. Political and economic reforms in emerging markets in the last decades have provided ample opportunity for empirical integration analyses. This sub-section discusses some of the challenges associated with empirically analysing the market integration process and reviews the empirical evidence of the effects of integration of emerging markets.

While market liberalisation and integration processes are easy to describe theoretically when simplified models are applied, empirical analyses of the processes and their effects incorporate a number of challenges.

First, liberalisation is not determined by a single event but rather by a range of different occurrences that either in isolation or in combination can lead to liberalisation. The events include, but are not limited to, relaxation of currency controls, reduction of foreign ownership restrictions, access to depositary receipts or country funds allowing for a circumvention of prevailing restrictions (Bekaert and Harvey, 2000).

Second, the timing of some of these events is not distinct. Rather, market liberalisation takes the form of a process increasing over time which makes it difficult to determine an exact point when liberalisation actually is achieved. In fact, the process of liberalisation is also not uni-directional. Emerging financial markets have been shown to transition between segmentation and various levels of integration over longer time horizons (Goetzmann and Jorion, 1999).

Third, even with liberalisation in effect, foreign investors are faced with investment barriers such as legal regulations relating to differences in status between domestic and foreign investors, particular risks associated with emerging markets such as liquidity risks, political risks, economic policy risks, and finally indirect barriers in the form of different availability of local information, varying accounting standards and limited corporate governance measures (Bekaert, 1995; Bekaert and Harvey, 2000). Bekaert (1995) finds that the indirect barriers, in the form of poor credit ratings and limited regulatory framework, show significant relationships with a return-based quantitative measure of market integration while no significant relationship could be found for the direct barriers. This highlights that indirect barriers, including corporate governance regulation, should not be ignored in the analysis of market integration.

2.2.3.1 Measures and Dates of Market Liberalisation and Integration

A key component in conducting empirical market integration research is to define the timing of market liberalisation and integration. Without a particular point in time, it is challenging to measure any effects of either liberalisation or integration. However, neither liberalisation nor integration occurs at a unique point in time which can easily be identified. Instead, as discussed in the previous sub-section, the process occurs over time and must be considered bi-directionally dynamic.

Consequently, before any analysis of liberalisation dates can be initiated, a definition and appropriate empirical proxies for liberalisation must be established. Different approaches to measuring liberalisation and the degree to which an emerging market is integrated have been suggested in research. Some of the indicators allow for a gradual measuring of liberalisation or integration while others are defined as static indicators. In terms of determining a specific date for market liberalisation, different indicators jointly contribute to specifying an official date. These parameters include the date at which regulatory investment barriers for foreign investors are removed as well as the introduction of investment vehicles that allow for circumvention of investment barriers, such as country funds (Bekaert et al., 2002; Errunza et al., 1998) and depositary receipts traded in other markets (Bekaert and Urias, 1999;

Table 2.1 Emerging market liberalisation dates

Market	Liberalisation date-official	First ADR introduction	First Country fund	Increase in US capital flows
Argentina	Nov-89	Aug-91	Oct-91	Apr-93
Bangladesh	Jun-91	NA	NA	NA
Brazil	May-91	Jan-92	Oct-87	Jun-88
Chile	Jan-92	Mar-90	Sep 89	Jan 88
Colombia	Feb-91	Dec-92	May-92	Aug-93
Ivory Coast	1995	NA	NA	NA
Egypt	1992	Nov-96	NA	NA
Greece	Dec-87	Aug-88	Sep-88	Dec-86
India	Nov-92	Feb-92	Jun-86	Apr-93
Indonesia	Sep-89	Apr-91	Jan-89	Jun-93
Israel	Nov-93	Aug-87	Oct-92	NA
Jamaica	Sep-91	Jun-93	NA	NA
Jordan	Dec-95	Dec-97	NA	NA
Kenya	Jan-95	NA	NA	NA
Korea	Jan-92	Nov-90	Aug-84	Mar-93
Malaysia	Dec-88	Aug-92	Dec-87	Apr-92
Mexico	May-89	Jan-89	Jun-81	May-90
Morocco	Jun-88	Apr-96	NA	NA
Nigeria	Aug-95	May-98	NA	NA
Pakistan	Feb-91	Sep-94	Jul-91	Apr-93
Philippines	Jun-91	Mar-91	May-87	Jan-90
Portugal	Jul-86	Jun-90	Aug-87	Aug-94
South Africa	1996	Jun-94	Mar-94	NA
Sri Lanka	May-91	Mar-94	NA	NA
Taiwan	Jan-91	Dec-91	May-86	Aug-92
Thailand	Sep-87	Jan-91	Jul-85	Jul-88
Trinidad & Tobago	Apr-97	NA	NA	NA
Tunisia	Jun-95	Feb-98	NA	NA
Turkey	Aug-89	Jul-90	Dec-89	Dec-89
Venezuela	Jan-90	Aug-91	NA	Feb-94
Zimbabwe	Jun-93	NA	NA	NA

Note: NA represents not available

Source: Bekaert et al. (2003) based on data and research findings from Bekaert and Harvey (2000), Miller (1999) and Bank of New York (www.adrbny.com)

Karolyi, 1998). Large increases in capital flows could constitute another indicator of liberalisation (Bai et al., 1998; Garcia and Ghysels, 1998).

Applying a combination of the above indicators, official liberalisation dates in the last two decades have been determined for 31 emerging markets (Bekaert and Harvey, 2000) (Table 2.1). The research covers Asian, Latin American as well as two European countries, Portugal and Greece, which are no longer considered as emerging markets by the World Bank. No Central European markets are included.

Although official liberalisation dates have been defined, the degree of actual market integration remains undetermined. Different indicators and approaches to empirically evaluate the degree of integration have been suggested. One indicator, which allows for a gradual measurement of integration is the ratio of the market capitalization of the constituent firms comprising the S&P/IFC EMDB Investable Index (S&P/IFCI) to those that comprise the S&P/IFC EMDB Global Index (S&P/IFCG) (Bekaert and Harvey, 1995). Constituents of the S&P/IFCI are derived from the S&P/IFCG based on the criterion of legal and practical accessibility to foreign institutional investors.

Other gradual indicators of integration are the share of foreign ownership, the amounts of bilateral capital flows (Bekaert and Harvey, 2000) or a structural break test applied to these indicators to determine a particular date of integration (Bekaert et al., 2002). There are also static measures indicating liberalisation as either incomplete or complete. One example is the International Monetary Fund's (IMF) Annual Report on Exchange Arrangements and Exchange Restrictions which has been concluded as less suitable as a measure since it contains a large number of variables and is therefore considered too broad (Bekaert and Harvey, 2003).

Using a time-varying measure based on a parameterised model of integration to test the level of integration associated with liberalisation, Bekeart and Harvey (1995) conclude that while integration coincides with liberalisation in some countries, it is not the case for all emerging markets.

In conclusion, empirical research examining whether liberalisation measures have any effect on the level of market integration involves all the challenges described above including determining the timing of the liberalisation and applying a reliable measure of market integration. The empirical evidence regarding the relationship between liberalisation and integration suggests that market liberalisation can be a driver for integration but is neither a sufficient sole driver nor a prerequisite for market integration to occur. Instead, actual market integration occurs at different occasions in different markets.

2.2.3.2 Effects of Liberalisation and Integration on the Character of Equity Returns

Empirical research exploring the effects of market integration is extensive and covers several areas. The following sub-section aims to introduce major evidence in fields directly related to the scope of this study. More specifically, areas covered include the effects of market integration on the characteristics of equity returns as well as the level of co-movement with world markets.

Effects on Rate of Return

As discussed in Sect. 2.2.2, post-integration required return rates, or cost of capital, are expected to be lower than pre-integration cost of capital if a diversification potential is present. However, prior to and at liberalisation as well as during the actual integration phase, returns are expected to increase as foreign investors bid up asset prices to benefit from the liberalisation. These effects have been empirically tested in various studies which will be introduced and discussed below.

Attempts have been made to measure the discrete price change during the liberalisation period based on estimated abnormal returns (Henry, 2000; Kim and Singal, 2000). In a sample of 12 emerging markets in Asia and Latin America, Henry (2000) explicitly controls for several confounding events and finds a statistically significant abnormal return of 3.3% per month during the 8-month window leading up to the country's initial liberalisation date. While this is in line with the predictions of the international asset pricing models suggesting effects at announcement rather than at implementation, the empirical results also indicate that the largest monthly abnormal return occurred in the implementation month itself, when the change had been known for months but when all uncertainties of liberalisation were finally removed.

Other approaches to measuring effects on returns have been applied. Based on a sample of 20 emerging markets, Bekaert and Harvey (2000) use aggregate dividend yields to measure the cost of capital. Dividend yields are argued to be appropriate as they are closely linked to the cost of capital, directly measurable and less susceptible to disturbing shocks on prices. However, it is also mentioned that lower dividend yields may stem from better growth opportunities resulting in lower payout ratios. Controlling for potentially confounding events with a proxy variable in the form of credit ratings, Bekaert and Harvey (2000) find that liberalisation tends to decrease dividend yields.

Effects on Volatility and Higher Moments of Returns

There are theoretical arguments stating that integration of emerging markets allows for speculative international investors to steer large flows of capital in and out of the market in a way that not only causes significant volatility in financial markets but that can also lead to a higher likelihood of financial crises (Harris, 2000; Tobin, 2003). Other researchers argue that international capital flows are crucial in ensuring efficiency in the emerging markets (Stulz, 1999).

With theoretical arguments suggesting changes in several directions, empirical evidence could be applicable in determining actual patterns. Several studies of volatility effects of liberalisation have been conducted applying a wide range of methods. Results are unfortunately not homogeneous.

Successful market integration has empirically been found to imply lower volatility in some studies (Bekaert et al., 1998; Bekaert and Harvey, 1997). More specifically, Bekaert and Harvey (1997) apply two different tests to conclude that volatility decreases as a result of capital market liberalisation. First, they map the average conditional variances 2 years before market liberalisation against those 2 years after. Of 17 emerging markets included in the survey, of which Greece and Portugal constitute the only representatives from Europe, four markets indicate a fall in the variance and one market shows an increase. Second, a cross-sectional analysis based on dummy variables representing different time periods prior to, recently after and significantly after the liberalisation is conducted. The results indicate that post-liberalisation volatility is lower than the pre-liberalisation for all of the 17 markets.

Other empirical research suggests that, although returns increase temporarily at market liberalisation, no equivalent adjustment is found with regard to volatility (Kim and Singal, 2000). In a more recent study, Bekaert and Harvey (2002) compare average annualised standard deviations for 19 emerging markets before and after 1990. While 10 out of 19 countries show increased volatility, the remaining nine indicate declining volatility.

With evidence pointing in both directions, the conclusion from empirical work is that liberalisation and integration can not be said to continuously affect levels of volatility in a single, pre-determined way.

With regard to effects on higher moments, there is empirical evidence that suggests that both skewness and excess kurtosis in emerging market returns increased in the 1990s compared to 1980s (Bekaert et al., 1998). Given that the liberalisation and integration processes were initiated in the beginning of the 1990s for many of the emerging markets included in the studied sample, it is possible that these results could be tied to market integration and thereby suggesting that liberalisation and integration imply increased, or at least, changing skewness and kurtosis.

Effects on Co-movement with World Markets

As the term market integration suggests, the theoretical expectation is that emerging markets which are liberalised effectively so that capital can flow freely across its borders, should start moving in a more integrated way with the global market trends. Understanding the effects of co-movement with world markets is important as it influences investment decisions of portfolio managers and individual investors who aim to achieve a global portfolio that maximises return under a given risk level.

Empirical evidence supporting the theoretical predictions is available although less abundantly. In their study of 20 emerging markets, Bekaert and Harvey (2000) find that correlation with the MSCI World market increases by 0.045 as a result of market liberalisation. The empirical findings are in line with theoretical predictions based on the fact that the two markets become increasingly dependent on the same world factors.

With the effects of the general market liberalisation and integration explored, the focus of the subsequent section is shifted toward an area of market integration that relates to a specific region in general and Central Europe in particular.

2.3 Regional Market Integration

The liberalisation and integration research discussed in the text so far has taken a global perspective on market integration in the sense that it has focused on the effects of effective emerging market liberalisation where liberalisation has referred to market access by global investors. However, integration can be defined somewhat differently and refer to the level of dependency or interaction between a limited number of economies or regions. This type of integration is often referred to as regional market integration.

2.3.1 Welfare Effects of Regional Market Integration

One particular branch of recent regional market integration research aims at understanding the macroeconomic welfare effects associated with different forms of integration and falls largely outside the scope of this study. However, given the EU's structure as a regionally integrated area, it is relevant to briefly introduce some of the main findings in this research field. In addition, macroeconomic effects can play a potentially important role in describing equity market returns and volatility.

While the concept and benefits of economic free-trade has been discussed in academia for centuries, modern regional integration research was initiated as a separate research field by Viner (1950) in the middle of the 20th century. His research focused on understanding the theoretical basis for trade-creating and trade-diverting effects in customs unions. He concludes that customs unions can lead to the substitution of high-cost domestic production by low-cost imports but that welfare costs derived from trade diversion are carried by the consumers in the member states (Viner, 1950). Viner's work sparked a range of additional research which expanded on and adjusted some of his simplifying assumptions (Lipsey, 1957; McMillan and McCann, 1981; Meade, 1955).

A core part of the regional market integration research relates to different regional market integration agreements (RIA) and the effects of each of these on one or several economies. Three different RIAs are traditionally identified (Baldwin and Venables, 2004).

A free trade area constitutes the least integrated RIA and represents a group of member states among which tariffs on trade are removed but where tariffs vis-à-vis non-members are not harmonised or standardised among the respective members.

A customs union implies a somewhat higher level of integration by representing a free trade area where the members' tariffs are harmonised both within and outside the area. Finally, a common market constitutes an area within which the goods, services as well as human and capital factors are allowed to move freely between the states.

The EU and its enlargement will be presented in detail in a later part of this study and at this stage it suffices to indicate that the EU is defined as a single, or common, market with certain exceptions and that the new 2004 members are given restricted access to the common market through the establishment of free-trade agreements for a specific range of goods that will transition into full common market membership over time (Baldwin and Venables, 2004).

2.3.2 *Market Integration Effects of the EU Enlargement*

The importance of the effects of the Central and Eastern European EU enlargement for both incumbent and new members has resulted in several academic studies dedicated to analysing this field. Many studies addressing the macroeconomic effects of the enlargement focus either on a particular economy (Brown et al., 1997; Keuschnigg et al., 2001; Keuschnigg and Kohler, 2002) or a particular dimension of the effects (Burda, 1998; Sinn, 2004; Sinn and Werding, 2001; Sohinger, 2005). Other studies have addressed broader geographic regions as well as several effects (Baldwin et al., 1997; Breuss, 2002, 2001).

The analyses of potential welfare gains have indicated that the effects of EU enlargement will be strongly positive for the new accession states despite an expected increase in emigration to the incumbent member states. Models have predicted real gains in GDP for the largest new members, Poland, the Czech Republic and Hungary, of 5–9% over a 10-year period (Breuss, 2002, 2001).

The effects for the new member states origin from several sources (Breuss, 2002). First, the abolition of existing trade barriers and import tariffs implies a positive effect in terms of cross-border trade. Estimates for the original cost of the border barriers range from 5% to 10% (Baldwin et al., 1997; Kohler, 2000).

Second, factor movements in the form of foreign direct investment (FDI) from the incumbent members to new members impact European transition economies in several positive ways (Sohinger, 2005). A primary consequence of FDI is that it fosters an economic restructuring process. Furthermore, Sohinger (2005) concludes that FDI also contributes to the implementation of institutional and regulatory reforms and influences both economic and political change through its institution-building process. It is possible that FDI entails a transfer of expertise and capabilities that result in indirect effects leading to increases in productivity and efficiency. This fact is supported by findings indicating that countries in which the FDI was directed more towards export-oriented manufacturing sectors rather than service sectors, showed a stronger increase in export competitiveness (Sohinger, 2005).

Third, budget transfers from incumbent members to new members as part of financial support in the transition period imply funding for economic reforms and investments promoting economic and political stability.

All of the above described market integration effects are factors that stimulate growth in the new member states. As a consequence, holding all else constant, the EU accession involves an overall positive effect for the Central and Eastern European economies.

Although outside the scope of this study, it is interesting to note that research also suggests real GDP gains for the incumbent EU member states despite the fact that they will have to face higher net contributions to help develop the new member states. The benefits will, however, be unevenly distributed with the bulk of the gains expected to reside within countries with historically established trade with the new member states and with geographic vicinity so as to benefit from migration benefits. The gains are therefore expected to be concentrated to Austria, Germany and Italy whereas Spain and Portugal are expected to encounter macroeconomic losses as a result of the enlargement (Breuss, 2002, 2001; Heijdra et al., 2002).

2.4 Market Integration and Corporate Governance

One particular dimension that is tightly linked to the process of market liberalisation and integration is that of implementing and enforcing appropriate corporate governance measures as a method to further reduce risks for domestic and, in particular, foreign investors. The call for corporate governance reforms has been frequent across most emerging markets where financial crises and poor governance have affected risks and returns for foreign investors. One region where the topic has received particular attention is in the transition economies covered within the scope of this study. This is due to the fact that accession to the EU involves requirements of aligning corporate governance regulations to the EU norm.

Corporate governance encompasses a vast field relating to a range of internal controls and procedures under which a firm is operated and supervised. According to the Organisation for Economic Corporation and Development (OECD), corporate governance "involves a set of relationships between a company's management, its board, its shareholders and other stakeholders" (OECD, 2004). Functioning mechanisms of corporate governance constitute a cornerstone in today's business world where shareholders and other stakeholders largely rely on appointed managers to operate their enterprises for them.

While the research hypotheses within the scope of this study do not address corporate governance directly, the influence of these factors on the performance characteristics of equity market return in the studied markets is potentially substantial and selected corporate governance theory and empirical research will be introduced briefly to facilitate the understanding of the subsequent analysis.

The aim of this section is therefore to provide a brief introduction to existing theory and empirical evidence around how corporate governance measures can influence emerging equity markets. Given the early development stages of corporate governance measures in emerging markets, the following section will include an overview of empirical research from developed markets as well. Findings from these more developed markets are likely to offer guidance on what is expected when effective measures are implemented also in the less developed markets.

2.4.1 Theoretical Link Between Corporate Governance and Asset Pricing

The main theoretical foundation for the rationale of introducing governance regulations at the corporate level stems from agency theory (Berle and Means, 1932). According to this theory, boards containing the owners themselves would be best incentivised to exercise effective monitoring over the management as a result of the direct ownership. However, this is not feasible for the vast majority of publicly listed companies in either developed or emerging markets. Instead directors are elected as representatives for the owners at the annual general meeting and might in fact not own a single share in the company they manage.

Agency theory illustrates the potential effects of asymmetric information existing between owners and the assigned managers. If both owner and agent are utility maximizing individuals, it is possible that the agent acts in a sub-optimal way from the perspective of the owner (Jensen and Meckling, 1976).

The sub-optimal behaviour of management can be addressed by various mechanisms related to monitoring of management and the subsequent reduction of agency costs. Research suggests a range of mechanisms to control agency problems (Agrawal and Knoeber, 1996; Gompers et al., 2003). First, managerial shareholdings would align management's incentives with those of the shareholders. Second, outside representation on the corporate board would offer improved independence and performance of monitoring duty. Third, concentrated shareholdings by institutions or by block holders would imply increased incentives for monitoring. Fourth, higher use of debt financing would result in increased monitoring by the lenders. Fifth, the presence of an efficient labour market for managers would motivate managers to attend to their reputation among prospective employers. Another mechanism is shareholdings by directors as analysed by several researchers (Bhagat et al., 1999; Hambrick and Jackson, 2000; Morck et al., 1988).

2.4.2 Empirical Evidence Linking Governance and Asset Pricing

Significant research has been conducted with regard to the impact of corporate mechanisms on equity returns. Gompers et al. (2003) conclude in a study of 1,500 large US companies that firms with better corporate governance, based on a basket of 24 governance rules, offer higher firm value. Other research has found that more outside board members, more debt financing, and greater corporate control activity result in lower firm performance while greater insider shareholdings lead to higher firm performance when analysed in isolation (Agrawal and Knoeber, 1996). Based on current empirical evidence, there appears to be no consistent conclusion with regard to the financial impact of corporate governance mechanisms in developed markets.

While there has been extensive research with regard to how corporate governance influences asset pricing, it has primarily been focused on the US market and the amount of research involving emerging markets is limited. However, a few areas relating to emerging market corporate governance have been covered in recent research. The implications of concentrated corporate ownership, a common characteristic in emerging markets, have been evaluated. The conclusion is that expropriation of minority shareholders by controlling shareholders constitutes a significant corporate governance problem (Claessens et al., 2002; La Porta et al.,

1999). This implies that even in the case of effective market liberalisation, foreign investors might be susceptible to additional risk in case they take a minority stake in an emerging market company that contains controlling shareholders.

In terms of effects of corporate governance in European transition economies, findings from the Czech Republic indicate that firms with concentrated or foreign ownership as well as ownership by non-bank investment funds are more profitable and have higher labour productivity (Claessens and Djankov, 1999). This conclusion once again raises concerns for foreign investors relying on minority stake investments based on investment funds.

In association with the liberalisation process, guidelines and regulations protecting foreign minority investors tend to receive significant attention. Lack of governance has been blamed for financial crises in emerging markets (Johnson et al., 2000) and for negatively affecting the willingness for foreign institutional investors to invest (Engardio, 2002).

2.5 Concluding Remarks on Literature Review

The area of emerging market finance has been subject to significant theory-building and empirical research in the last decades. The impact of market liberalisation measures on the level of market integration is increasingly mapped and understood along with the performance characteristics of emerging equity markets in general and during the liberalisation and during the early stages of the integration processes in particular.

However, in part due to limitations of data availability, the bulk of emerging market performance analyses has been based on data from emerging markets in Asia, South America and two European countries, Greece and Portugal, which subsequently have moved into the group of developed markets. In fact, only limited empirical evidence has been based on empirical data from transitioning economies in Central Europe. Furthermore, actual integration experiments such as the accession of emerging markets to the EU are not explored. It is possible that important insights of the actual character of the integration process have not been discovered in earlier research due to the intense focus on the liberalisation dates rather than later events that in their nature suggest a change in the level of market integration.

While the impact on equity markets as a result of EU enlargement into Eastern Europe has received limited focus in previous literature, the enlargement has been studied in the light of macroeconomic welfare effects. With findings suggesting significant macroeconomic gains for the new members due to a combination of a reduction in trade barriers, an increase in FDI and the provision of budget transfers from incumbent to new member states, certain effects on equity markets should be expected.

Chapter 3
Definition of Research Questions and Hypotheses

As discussed in the previous chapter, the areas of emerging market finance and market integration have received attention in previous research. Despite this existing research, there are areas which have not been fully explored. This section serves to introduce the unexplored research questions and associated research hypotheses that will be empirically tested within the scope of this study. The research questions are derived from the current basis of theory and empirical evidence.

Both theoretical and empirical research has been conducted to better understand the impact of the early phases related to the transition from segmented to integrated economy (Bekaert and Harvey, 1995). The focus has largely been on defining and applying official market liberalisation dates based on events of financial market deregulation or events implying improved access for foreign investors and subsequently evaluating the effects around these dates. This is an appropriate research approach when the aim is to understand the effects of market liberalisation and the initial phases of market integration. However, when trying to understand the later stages of the market integration process, this approach risks providing few, if any, relevant insights.

This study aims to extend the existing market integration research by applying an approach that focuses on an event which occurs at a later stage in the market integration process but that is nevertheless likely to have a significant impact on the level of market integration. Understanding the effects on emerging equity markets as a consequence of accession to the EU provides an important complement to the existing academic findings. If it can be shown that emerging economies where liberalisation has already occurred, experience additional integration as a result of accession to an established economic trade union, conclusions about the market integration process in general can be derived.

The effects of an event in which an emerging market accesses an economic union of developed market economies, are worthy of study since they could have an impact on the development of the economy as a whole. Greece and Portugal, countries that accessed the European Economic Community as emerging markets in the beginning of 1981 and 1986 respectively, transformed into developed countries within a 20-year period subsequent to the accession. This transition highlights the potentially important impact EU membership can have on an economy. As additional emerging markets are set to access the EU in the coming years, the effects of this stage in the market integration process are important to understand in preparation for the enlargement.

Furthermore, predicting effects of integration in the form of accession to an economic union is also valuable in a more generic context as such economic free trade unions exist in other parts of the world, including both Asia and Latin America.

In the subsequent sections, the background, logic and scope of each of the research questions will be introduced and discussed. Furthermore, the relevant research hypotheses will be derived and formulated.

3.1 EU Accession and Equity Market Integration

For new members, the accession to the EU implies a substantial increase in the level of political and economic integration with the incumbent EU members. Given the scope and extent of this political and economic integration, it is reasonable to assume that the level of integration between financial markets is also affected.

This section introduces the first research question, which aims to determine whether there is an impact of EU accession on the level of integration between equity markets in European transition economies, also referred to as local markets, and global equity markets. The research question is divided into two distinct but related research hypotheses addressing the level of co-movement between local and global markets on the one hand and the level of influence of global as well as local macroeconomic factors on the other.

From a political perspective, EU accession constitutes a significant event for the Central and Eastern European transition economies. Not only does accession imply that the EU acknowledges the success of recent reforms aiming to improve political stability, it also implies the surrender of a certain degree of national political sovereignty. EU accession involves the transition of national decision power regarding a range of political and economic issues from locally elected national authorities to EU institutions where only a small minority of the participants represents the national interest of any one member state. Furthermore, EU accession implies the loss of the right to an independent, national voice in certain international organisations such as the World Trade Organisation (WTO). In concurrence with the loss of national sovereignty, the EU accession offers new member states the possibility to influence the direction of the entire EU in critical political questions based on the status as a fully integrated member. This centralisation of political influence is likely to lead to a larger degree of political integration and, as a result, a higher degree of dependence on pan-European rather than local political trends.

From an economic perspective, there are a number of factors associated with EU accession which suggest an impact on the level of integration. First, the removal of trade tariffs increases the level of integration in the sense that companies will have a more harmonised level of competition within the economic region.

Second, the inclusion of the new member states into the European customs union implies integration in the form of companies facing an increasingly standardised business background also in terms of factors outside the customs union. More explicitly, the EU accession implies that trading terms of new members with partners outside the EU have to be harmonised with those in the incumbent EU member states.

Third, FDI by Western European companies implies a transition towards harmonised efficiency levels. Furthermore, an increasing presence of multinational corporations (MNCs) in the form of production or service units integrated into global supply chains is likely to further integrate the local economies with those in other countries. While these MNCs also serve the local markets, a large portion of the output is often targeted at markets outside Central and Eastern Europe which implies a higher level of dependence on dynamics in the global economy.

The combination of easier exports within the EU, more harmonised domestic and international business environments, an increased presence of MNCs and rising flows of FDI to the acceding states, suggests that local transition economies will be increasingly influenced by economic factors outside the local market. Assuming that components used in the manufacturing of export products are partly sourced from local companies in the domestic market, the influence of global rather than local factors on the local economy is further magnified as the success of local suppliers becomes increasingly dependent on the demand of the locally present MNCs which in turn are highly dependent on world factors for the demand of their products.

In addition to integration measures related to political and economic dimensions, there are also harmonisation measures implemented on the financial market level. Corporate governance rules and recommendations at the financial exchange level were largely non-existent in the Central European transition economies during the 1990s. However, as negotiations on EU accession approached conclusion in 2002, several Central European transition economies introduced both mandatory and voluntary corporate governance rules and guidelines at the exchange levels which were largely harmonised with those in the EU.

An example is Poland where an initial compilation of wide-ranging corporate governance recommendations was implemented in the autumn of 2002 and subsequently updated based on recommendations from the European Commission and relaunched in 2004 (Best Practices Committee at the Corporate Governance Forum, 2004). The recommendations are voluntary and while only a small portion of the listed companies follow all recommendations and thereby qualify to a special listing category, the introduction of the guidelines have raised both the awareness and the standard across all companies (Best Practices Committee at the Corporate Governance Forum, 2004).

Similar trends can be found in Hungary and Slovenia. Hungary launched the development of corporate governance recommendations based on international principles in mid-2002. The recommendations were phased in and became mandatory for companies listed on the A-list in 2005 (Budapest Stock Exchange et al., 2004). In Slovenia, corporate governance recommendations adjusted to those prevailing in Western Europe were introduced in late 2005 (Ljubljana Stock Exchange, 2005).

3.1.1 Impact of EU Accession on Level of Co-movement

As discussed in Chap. 2, the correlation between developed and emerging financial markets has traditionally been low (Barry et al., 1998; Bekaert and Harvey, 2000). Empirical evidence suggests a correlation coefficient of no more than 0.33 when comparing a basket of emerging markets with the MSCI World Index over the period 1994–2002 (Barry et al., 1998). This coefficient should be compared with a correlation coefficient of 0.57 found within developed countries for the same time horizon. This low level of correlation relative to that between developed markets has provided global investors with an opportunity to further diversify their portfolios.

Consequently, from the perspective of a well-diversified investor considering assets on a global basis, changes in the level of correlation between emerging and developed markets could affect the relationship between expected returns and risk of the portfolio. Modern portfolio theory (Markowitz, 1952) states that assets with low level of co-movement, quantified by the covariance, can be combined to generate a portfolio that generates higher levels of return without increased volatility. As discussed in Chap. 2, there is strong empirical evidence to support this theoretical statement in the context of emerging markets (Barry et al., 1998; Bekaert and Urias, 1999).

Under the assumption that the political and economic dimensions of integration described earlier in this section affect the performance of equity markets, it is reasonable to also expect a higher level of co-movement between equity market return levels in the new member states and those in the incumbent EU members. The explicit hypotheses tested within the scope of this study are therefore

HO_1: EU accession has no impact on the level of co-movement between local and world equity market returns

HA_1: EU accession has an impact on the level of co-movement between local and world equity market returns

3.1.2 Impact of EU Accession on Influence by Macroeconomic Factors

The above hypotheses explore the level of co-movement between local emerging equity markets and world equity markets. As discussed in sub-section 2.1.2, one theoretical explanation for co-movement among asset returns is suggested in the APT (Ross, 1976) which states that asset prices are influenced by a set of economic factors. If the level of influence of a certain set of factors is the same for two separate markets, it would be reasonable to assume that the two markets display a high degree of co-movement.

This sub-section derives a set of research hypotheses which jointly explore whether the level of influence of global as well as local factors on transition economy equity returns changes as a result of the EU accession.

In this study, the rate of return for equity is defined as total return which implies combining the direct dividend with the indirect capital gains or losses associated with changes in asset prices over a given time horizon. While the dividend component of total return is largely a decision related to the individual company, the changes in asset prices are, according to APT (Ross, 1976), related to external economic factors.

Asset pricing in emerging markets has been analysed in the context of both microeconomic and macroeconomic factors. Company-specific microeconomic factors such as dividend yields, book-to-market and earnings-to-price ratios, have received attention with regard to return predictability in the context of both developed markets (Fama and French, 1992; Ferson and Harvey, 1991a) and emerging markets (Aydogan and Gursoy, 2001; Bekaert et al., 1997; Claessens et al., 1998; Harvey, 1995b; Lyn and Zychowicz, 2004). There is empirical evidence that book-to-market and dividend yield measures are significantly related to market returns and 12-month forward looking returns respectively in 13 Eastern European emerging markets (Lyn and Zychowicz, 2004).

These findings are relevant for practitioners since they suggest that future returns can be predicted not only at the individual stock level but also on an aggregate level as a means of supporting market timing decisions. The predictive nature of microeconomic factors is also relevant for academic research as it suggests that given that an event has an impact on the predicting factor, it is likely to also affect the market return. In this context it is relevant to observe that the level of predictability has been found to be higher among emerging markets compared to that in developed markets (Harvey, 1995b).

Macroeconomic factors have also attracted academic interest in terms of their relationship with asset returns. There is general consensus that macroeconomic variables such as industrial production, interest rates, inflation, real gross national product and the money supply can explain stock returns in developed markets (Chen, 1991; Chen et al., 1986; Fama, 1981, 1990; Ferson and Harvey, 1991a).

With regard to emerging markets, the amount of research related to predicting macroeconomic factors is less extensive. There are, however, a few comprehensive studies that analyse the role of global variables, including world-market equity return, foreign-currency index return, oil prices, world industrial production and world inflation rate, in explaining cross-sectional variations in the returns of 21 emerging markets (Harvey, 1995b, 1995a). The conclusion is that global factors are insufficient in explaining the returns of emerging stock markets. Local factors provide complementing insights as is concluded in a more recent study of 13 markets in which GDP, inflation, the money supply, interest rates, world industrial production and world inflation explain the fluctuations of emerging market returns, although to different degrees across the markets (Fifield et al., 2002).

As described earlier in this chapter, EU membership implies significant centralisation and harmonisation of political, economic and financial influences and factors. The first research hypothesis explores whether any overall changes in the level of correlation can be identified as a result of the EU accession. However, with an analysis of the overall correlation between two markets, little can be concluded about the reasons for any potential change. Therefore, the second research hypothesis builds on existing academic research as well as the expectations that equity markets will be influenced by a different mix of local versus global factors in trying to determine how this mix has changed as a result of EU accession.

When observing the influence of global versus local risk factors on equity markets, existing research suggests that local rather than global risk factors influence the required rate of return in segmented emerging markets (Bilson et al., 2000). This view is supported by other research findings where it is found that the cost of equity capital in segmented markets is related to the local volatility of the particular market while the cost of capital in integrated markets on the other hand is related to the covariance with world market returns (Bekaert and Harvey, 2000).

Based on the expected effects on market integration as a result of the EU accession, the following hypotheses regarding the influence of global as well as local macroeconomic factors are formulated:

H0_2.1: EU accession implies no change in the level of influence of global macroeconomic factors on the equity market returns of European transition economies
HA_2.1: EU accession does imply a change in the level of influence of global macroeconomic factors on the equity market returns of European transition economies
H0_2.2: EU accession implies no change in the level of influence of local macroeconomic factors on the equity market returns of European transition economies
HA_2.2: EU accession does imply a change in the level of influence of local macroeconomic factors on the equity market returns of European transition economies

3.2 EU Accession and Equity Market Performance

An interesting and important research area associated with the EU enlargement is whether accession has any impact on the performance of equity markets in the new member states. Performance in the form of rate of return has been a key subject in emerging market research as well as market integration research (Barry et al., 1997; Barry et al., 1998; Bekaert et al., 1997; Claessens et al., 1995; De Santis and Imrohoroglu, 1997). As discussed in Chap. 2, it has been concluded that market integration leads to lower levels of required rate of return after an initial appreciation of asset prices in immediate association with the integration phase.

In this context it is relevant to analyse whether the potential increase in the level of integration associated with EU accession results in further asset appreciation and the corresponding increases in returns, or whether the integration effects are already reflected in the required returns and thus not affecting the equity rate of return. Related and equally important, the research question of whether the risk levels of the transition economy equity markets are affected by the EU accession should be explored.

The following sub-sections explore the research hypotheses related to the impact of EU accession on equity market risk and return in European transition economies.

3.2.1 Impact of EU Accession on Equity Market Volatility

Understanding market volatility in emerging economies is important as it is tightly linked to the issue of cost of capital and influences investment decisions related to asset allocations. The effects of EU accession on equity market volatility not only affect policy makers but also foreign as well as local investors. If accession is associated with changes in the level of market integration, it is possible that a change also occurs in the level of equity market volatility.

Emerging markets have been shown to possess different return characteristics in comparison with those in developed markets. As discussed in Sect. 2.1, early research on the performance characteristics of emerging equity markets suggests that emerging equity markets, in comparison with developed markets, are associated with higher volatility which is compensated with higher return levels (Claessens et al., 1995; Gottschalk, 2005; Harvey, 1995a). These findings are in line with financial theory (Lintner, 1965; Sharpe, 1964) suggesting that investors require compensation for taking on systematic, or non-diversifiable, risk.

However, empirical research using a composite emerging market index based on data from S&P/IFC's Emerging Markets Data Base over the period December 1975 to June 1995 show that while returns for emerging market in certain periods outperformed that of US stocks, this was not the case for the period as a whole (Barry et al., 1998). In fact for the 20-year period, the IFC emerging market index provided 1.15% arithmetic average return while the S&P 500 and the NASDAQ resulted in 1.20% and 1.21% respectively. Volatility, however, was found to be higher in the emerging market composite than for that of the S&P 500 and NASDAQ indices over the equivalent time horizon.

The long-term validity of the superior returns of emerging markets have been questioned in light of significant return declines in periods of crises (Bilson et al., 2000). On the other hand, the higher volatility of emerging markets has consistently been proven in empirical studies. However, as emerging markets become increasingly integrated with world markets and assets are increasingly priced in a way that does not differentiate emerging assets from developed assets, the volatility of emerging equity returns would be assumed to transition toward volatility levels of developed equity markets.

As mentioned, if it can be assumed that EU accession involves a higher level of integration, market integration theory argues that improved diversification opportunities for both local and foreign investors will affect the equity market volatility in a way that reduces volatility. Similarly, financial theory (Lintner, 1965; Sharpe, 1964) suggests that investors require compensation for taking on systematic risk. If return levels are shown to be affected by the EU accession as is explored in the previous section, it should, at least in part, be combined with a related change in risks associated with the equity market investments.

Volatility in equity market returns is partly the result of perceived risks in a market. Risk associated with a financial investment in a particular country can be measured by a series of political, economic and financial risk components as suggested by the International Country Risk Guide (ICRG). Political risk components include factors such as stability of government, corruption, socioeconomic conditions and the level of tension and conflict in the country. Economic components jointly provide an indication of the country's economic strength and weakness whereas the financial risk components evaluate the country's ability to meet its financial obligations including the stability of the currency. A more complete list of risk components for the three index fields is illustrated in Table 3.1.

Academic research based on time-series data suggests that there is not only a high level of correlation between the three indices but also that there is a predictive power for future equity returns, particularly for the financial risk measures (Erb et al., 1996).

Country risk also constitutes a critical dimension in determining country sovereign credit ratings. A sovereign credit rating refers to the overall ability of a country to provide a secure investment environment. It reflects many of the factors listed in Table 3.1 and is provided on a daily basis by several credit rating institutes including S&P, Moody's and Fitch. S&P applies a 22-step rating scale ranging from D for Default to AAA, the highest grade.

The sovereign credit ratings are typically divided into short-term ratings, which refer to credit worthiness within the next 365 days, and long-term ratings which reflect a longer perspective. Furthermore, the ratings are divided into local and foreign currencies based on the currency of repayment. The local and foreign currency

Table 3.1 Country risk components as suggested by International Country Risk Guide

Risk Components		
Political	Economic	Financial
Government Stability	GDP per Capita	Foreign Debt as % of GDP
Corruption	Real GDP Growth	Foreign Debt Service as % of Exports of Goods & Services
Investment Profile	Annual Inflation Rate	Current Account as % of Exports of Goods & Services
Internal Conflict	Budget Balance as % of GDP	Net International Liquidity as Months of Import Cover
External Conflict	Current Account as % of GDP	Exchange Rate Stability
Socioeconomic Conditions		
Military in Politics		
Religious Tensions		
Law and Order		
Ethnic Tensions		
Democratic Accountability		
Bureaucracy Quality		

Source: International Country Risk Guide, 2006

sovereign credit ratings tend to be different since the estimated ability of a government to repay obligations in local currencies might be different from the equivalent ability in a foreign currency (Standard & Poor's, 2006). Research suggests that there is a close relationship between S&P and Moody's sovereign credit ratings and the ICRG risk components (Erb et al., 1996).

In addition to the credit ratings, each country receives one of three long-term outlook indications. The outlook reflects recent or upcoming events that potentially will affect the grading. For example, the prospects of a delayed entry into the European Monetary Union (EMU), resulted in S&P's degrading of Estonia's long-term outlook from Positive to Stable in July 2006 (Dally, 2006).

With regard to the eight economies targeted within the scope of this study, Fig. 3.1 illustrates that while the average long-term local currency sovereign credit rating has remained relatively stable since 1997, the foreign currency rating has improved steadily. As of January 2005 the local currency and foreign currency ratings are largely harmonised, suggesting a reduction in risk for investors based in foreign currency.

Another factor reducing the overall risk of equity assets in emerging markets is that the EU membership application process has triggered an improvement in property rights, corporate governance regulations combined with an implementation of stricter legal enforcement. While these dimensions might not yet be as strict or as strictly enforced as within the developed EU countries, the changes imply less risk for both foreign and local investors. As discussed in Sect. 3.1, a series of measures related to corporate governance have been implemented around the time of the acceptance of EU accession.

Market integration theory suggests that overall risk exposure to the investor is reduced as a result of integration since it broadens investment opportunities and allows for the individual investor to diversify the portfolio (Bekaert and Harvey, 2003; Stulz, 1999). As such, this would not necessarily imply a lower level of volatility for the equity markets in the individual emerging market but rather the level of volatility of a well-diversified portfolio containing emerging equity assets.

However, if accession to the EU positively influences the granular risk components of country risk or liquidity risk, the risk of the individual asset class should

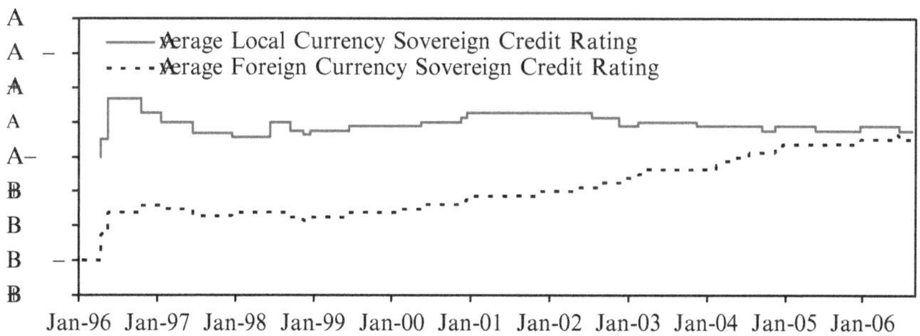

Fig. 3.1 Average long-term sovereign credit ratings for the eight European transition economies, January 1996–July 2006
Source: Standard & Poor's, 2006

in fact decline. Given that the EU accession is associated with political and economic reform, it is likely that drivers of risk have been reduced and should subsequently imply a lower level of volatility in equity returns.

As discussed in Chap. 2, existing empirical research on the impact of market liberalisation and market integration on volatility of return is ambivalent (Bekaert and Harvey, 1997; Bekaert and Harvey, 2003; Kim and Singal, 2000). However, if EU accession involves changes in the level of integration and changes in the country risk components, it is feasible to assume that equity market volatility would change.

Based on the theoretical logic that EU accession and the associated reforms jointly imply a more stable investment environment for domestic as well as foreign investors, the hypothesis is that volatility of return is affected by EU accession in a way that involves lower levels of volatility. The formulation of the null and alternative hypotheses to be tested is

H0_3: Level of volatility in equity markets of European transition economies remain unchanged as a result of the EU accession

HA_3: Level of volatility in equity markets of European transition economies change as a result of the EU accession

3.2.2 *Impact of EU Accession on Equity Market Returns*

Market volatility is an important part of equity performance but it is not a sufficient measure in isolation. An important complement is the market return level and an interesting and associated question is how the EU accession affects equity market returns. If the third research hypothesis, described above, can be rejected, it is possible that changes appear also in the level of return.

Financial theory (Gordon, 1982) suggests that asset prices are determined by the present value of the projected cash flows to shareholder where projected cash flows can be estimated by all future dividends. The value of these dividends must, however, also reflect the cost of capital and the projected growth rate of the reoccurring dividend payment. The link between these three parameters is presented in the dividend discount model (Gordon, 1982) which is illustrated in Eq. 3.1.

Eq. 3.1: Dividend discount valuation model

$$P_0 = \frac{D_1}{\mathrm{k} - \mathrm{g}}$$

where,

P_0 = Share price at time 0

D_1 = Dividend at time 1

k = Required rate of return based on the risk associated with the asset measured by β, the risk free rate of return (RFR) and the market risk premium (E(r) – RFR) according to CAPM, k = RFR + β (E(r)-RFR) (Sharpe, 1964)

g = Expected annual dividend growth rate

Based on this theoretical model, any event that affects the aggregate dividends, the expected growth rates of the aggregate dividends or the aggregate cost of capital, should influence asset prices and thus also the return levels. Given that EU accession and the associated economic and political reforms leading up to the accession result in increased political and economic stability, a reduction in the required return would be consistent with financial theory (Gordon, 1982). It would also be consistent with market integration theory which predicts lower required rates of return based on increased potential for diversification (Stulz, 1999).

Both theoretical models and empirical tests suggest that market integration leads to a reduction in required rate of return. The reduction in required rate of return is caused by a significant increase in asset prices shortly prior to and during a successful liberalisation phase. If the accession to the EU implies an extension of market integration benefits, it is possible that a similar increase in asset prices could be identified temporarily only to be followed by a period of lower rates of returns at a future time period.

In addition, EU accession could provide a platform for faster economic growth due to increased inflows of FDI as well as easier access to export markets within the EU. More specifically, EU membership facilitates access to major European markets for manufacturers that previously targeted primarily the domestic market. Independent of whether the production of the increased volumes sold within the newly accessed EU is handled domestically, and thereby increasing the value of exports, or produced in other markets, with only the profits being repatriated to the domestic market, revenue and cash flows are likely to be positively affected.

Growth in the real economy is a potential driver for higher expected dividend growth leading to an increase in return levels. This is supported by empirical research focusing on Asian emerging markets (Greenwood, 1993). As can be derived from Table 3.2, real GDP growth rates have increased in association with the EU accession in May 2004 for all economies covered within the scope of this study with the exception of Lithuania which demonstrated a distinct peak in GDP growth in the year 2003.

As illustrated in Eq. 3.1, both lower required rates of return and higher growth rates of dividends suggest increased firm value, holding all else constant. With higher GDP growth rates vis-à-vis those in developed European markets, it is possible that the dividends also grow at a higher rate.

An important question then arises around the duration of the real economic growth rates. Clearly, superior rates are not expected to last in the long term. However, given significant FDI combined with the opportunities associated with access to the export markets of the EU, superior growth rates can be expected to remain in the medium term. Independent of the length of the superior growth rates, an impact on the equity market returns could appear.

Based on a combination of market integration theory and finance theory, it is expected that the rate of return increases during the EU accession process given that reforms result in improved economic conditions in terms of stability and growth opportunities. The research question relates to whether the EU accession has an

Table 3.2 Actual and expected annual real GDP growth rates

	1996	1997	1998	1999	2000	2001	2002	2003	2004	2005	2006E	2007E
Czech Republic	4.2%	–0.7%	–1.1%	1.2%	3.9%	2.6%	1.5%	3.2%	4.7%	6.0%	5.3%	4.7%
Estonia	4.4%	11.1%	4.4%	0.3%	7.9%	6.5%	7.2%	6.7%	7.8%	9.8%	8.9%	7.9%
Latvia	3.8%	8.3%	4.7%	4.7%	6.9%	8.0%	6.5%	7.2%	8.5%	10.2%	8.5%	7.6%
Lithuania	4.7%	7.0%	7.3%	–1.7%	3.9%	6.4%	6.8%	10.5%	7.0%	7.5%	6.5%	6.2%
Hungary	1.3%	4.6%	4.9%	4.2%	6.0%	4.3%	3.8%	3.4%	5.2%	4.1%	4.6%	4.2%
Poland	6.2%	7.1%	5.0%	4.5%	4.2%	1.1%	1.4%	3.8%	5.3%	3.2%	4.5%	4.6%
Slovenia	3.7%	4.8%	3.9%	5.4%	4.1%	2.7%	3.5%	2.7%	4.2%	3.9%	4.3%	4.1%
Slovak Republic	6.1%	4.6%	4.2%	1.5%	2.8%	3.2%	4.1%	4.2%	5.4%	6.1%	6.1%	6.5%
Simple Average[a]	4.3%	5.9%	4.2%	2.5%	5.0%	4.4%	4.4%	5.2%	6.0%	6.4%	6.1%	5.7%
Overall EU (15 countries)	1.7%	2.6%	2.9%	3.0%	3.9%	1.9%	1.1%	1.1%	2.3%	1.5%	2.2%	2.0%
Overall EU (25 countries)	1.8%	2.7%	2.9%	3.0%	3.9%	1.9%	1.2%	1.2%	2.4%	1.6%	2.3%	2.2%

[a]Simple average is calculated by taking the arithmetic mean of the eight economies ignoring any size weighting

Source: Eurostat, 2006

impact on the level of aggregate equity market returns or not. The associated research hypotheses are defined as

HO_4: Equity market return levels remain unchanged as a result of EU accession
HA_4: Equity market return levels change as a result of EU accession

3.3 Concluding Remarks on Research Questions and Hypotheses

The research hypotheses defined in the previous sections jointly explore the understanding of the effects of EU accession on transition economy equity markets. None of the questions have so far been explored from an academic perspective.

Figure 3.2 provides an overview of the context of the research hypotheses addressed within the scope of this study. As can be derived from the figure, the EU accession is assumed to take place in markets that have already experienced market liberalisation. This assumption will be explored and clarified in the following chapters. In traditional emerging markets, the road to liberalisation involves reforms that allow foreign investors increasingly smooth access to domestic capital markets. In this study, the focus is on transition economies where a series of reforms relating to EU accession have been implemented and enforced prior to the actual EU accession.

The conclusions of these research hypotheses are useful not only from the perspective of individual investors but also for institutional investors incorporating equity assets from current and potential EU members in their portfolios and for policy makers responsible for applying financial regulations during the accession periods. The hypotheses can be evaluated in several ways and the next chapter contains an introduction to the research methodology applied to test the individual research hypotheses.

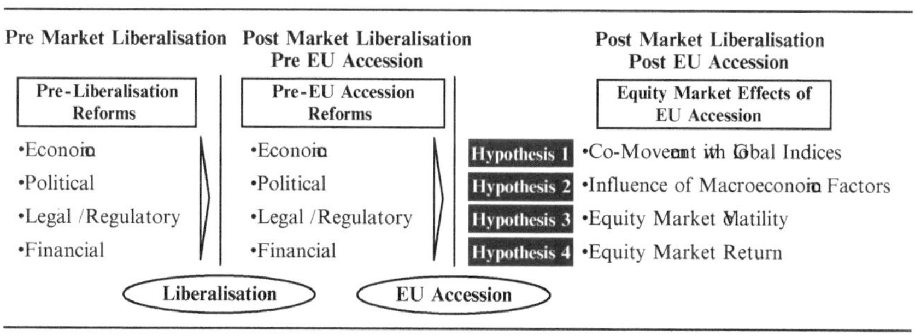

Fig. 3.2 Overview of research area

Chapter 4
Methodology

With the research hypotheses defined and formulated in the previous chapter, the focus is shifted to describing the research methodology applied to explore and test the respective research hypotheses. In several cases, multiple approaches are applied to provide improved insights and understanding of the empirical findings.

Each research hypothesis requires a unique approach to test whether it can be rejected or not. Nevertheless, one important dimension which reoccurs across several research approaches is the date at which point effects are expected to occur. As will be discussed in the subsequent parts of this chapter, an understanding of this date is required for the analyses of all research questions. The EU accession process is discussed extensively in sub-section 5.1.3. However, in order to facilitate the discussion of the research approach it is helpful to indicate, already at this stage, that the effects of EU accession on the financial markets are expected to occur at the announcement of the accession decision rather than at the accession date itself. Further details on this assumption are provided in sub-section 5.1.3.3.

The structure of this chapter follows that of Chap. 3 in the sense that each of the four research hypotheses is discussed in a separate section. Section 4.1 introduces the methodology applied for the initial two research hypotheses, both of which relate to the impact of EU accession on the level of integration. Section 4.2 contains the details of the methodology applied to test the EU accession effects on market performance, including impact on equity market volatility and return levels.

4.1 Impact of EU Accession on Level of Integration

Measuring the level of integration is a complicated task due to the dynamic nature of the integration process. Within this study, the research question on how the level of integration is affected by EU accession is divided into two research hypotheses, each requiring a particular test approach.

The first hypothesis involves testing whether the level of co-movement between return levels of local equity markets and those of global and European equity indices is significantly different in the period before versus in the period after the EU accession. The second hypothesis explores the level of influence by

T. Southall, *European Financial Markets*,

global and local macroeconomic factors on the equity market returns in European transition economies to determine any significant changes as a result of the EU accession. Each of the test approaches will be described in detail in the following sub-sections.

4.1.1 Co-movement of Equity Market Returns

Testing whether there is a statistically significant change in the level of co-movement between equity markets in the European transition economies and reference indices incorporating global or European markets as a result of the EU accession is done through three complementary methods. Although distinctly different, the methods are related and are based on the same data.

Before exploring the details of the three methods it is appropriate to mention a few words regarding two dimensions which appear in each method; the definition of an operational parameter representing co-movement and the identification of relevant global and European indices against which the local indices are compared.

With regard to the co-movement parameter there are a number of alternatives available depending on the definition applied (Baur, 2003). One measure for co-movement which has been used in previous academic research incorporating co-movement is the Pearson correlation coefficient (Barberis et al., 2005). The Pearson correlation coefficient is defined as the covariance of the two variables divided by product of the two standard deviations (DeFusco et al., 2004).

Regarding the relevant reference indices, the aim is to apply indices which represent the global and European equity markets. For the global equity market, one extensively used reference indices is the MSCI World Index. The MSCI World Index is a total return index composed of over 1,400 stocks listed on exchanges in 23 countries across Europe, North America, Australasia and the Far East (MSCI, 2006).

The decision to complement the MSCI World Index with European indices is based on the fact that the expected political and economic integration of the focus markets might be different with regard to the incumbent EU member states as opposed to overall global markets. This makes it relevant to also apply indices that focus exclusively on the EU markets. One of the most comprehensive indices available for the European region is the FTSEurofirst 300 Index which incorporates the 300 largest companies ranked by market capitalisation in the EU. Given the concentration of large companies in the FTSEurofirst 300 Index, an additional EU index is included. This additional index should include constituents of a smaller character. The FTSE EuroMid Eurozone Index is selected as it comprises mid-sized companies listed in markets where the local currency is EUR. Further details are provided on both the MSCI World Index and the European indices in Chap. 5.

The subsequent three sub-sections describe the details of the three test approaches applied to evaluate whether the initial null hypothesis can be rejected.

4.1.1.1 Significant Difference in Correlation Before and After EU Accession

The null hypothesis is formulated in such a way that if the hypothesis can be rejected at a certain significance level, it is possible to conclude that the correlation is different before the accession announcement compared to after. The aim of the first and primary test method implies testing the significance of the difference in correlation coefficients derived from the two non-overlapping periods before and after the announcement of the EU accession for each of the local indices and the world or EU indices.

One method to test the null hypothesis that the correlation coefficient between two variables in one population is the same as that in a different population is provided by Fisher (1921). The method implies transforming the two correlation coefficients according to Fisher's z-transformation. The definition of the transformed correlation coefficient is presented in Eq. 4.1.

Eq. 4.1: Derivation of the transformed correlation coefficient related to Fisher's z-transformation

$$r' = \frac{1}{2}\ln\frac{|1+r|}{|1-r|}$$

where,

r' = the transformed correlation coefficient
ln = the natural logarithm
r = the Pearson correlation coefficient

The test statistic is subsequently calculated according to the transformation formula (Fisher, 1921) described in Eq. 4.2.

Eq. 4.2: Derivation of the z-value related to Fisher's z-transformation

$$z = \frac{r'_1 - r'_2}{\sqrt{\frac{1}{n_1 - 3} + \frac{1}{n_2 - 3}}}$$

where,

Z = Fisher's test statistic which follows the normal distribution
r_i' = the transformed correlation coefficient in population i as defined in Eq. 4.1
n_i = the sample size for the correlation coefficient in population i

The final step in testing the hypothesis is to compare the z-value of the test statistic with z-value of the standard normal distribution at the 5% significance level to determine whether the null hypothesis can be rejected or not. If the z-value of the test statistic is either below –1.96 or above 1.96, the null hypothesis of identical correlation coefficients can be rejected.

4.1.1.2 Correlation Coefficient Significantly Different from Zero

A complementary approach that can contribute to the understanding of shifts in the level of co-movement is to verify whether the correlation coefficients are significantly different from zero both prior to and after the accession announcement. This test can be achieved through the use of a traditional t-test applied to a reformulated null hypothesis. This reformulated null hypothesis is subsequently tested for the data series prior to the announcement and compared with tests applying the data series subsequent to the announcement.

The relevant null hypothesis for this test states that the correlation coefficient equals zero. In order to reject this hypothesis at the 5% significance level, the t-statistic needs to be either inferior to –1.96 or superior to 1.96. The definition of the t-statistic is presented in Eq. 4.3.

Eq. 4.3: Definition of t-statistic

$$t = \frac{r\sqrt{n-2}}{\sqrt{1-r^2}}$$

where,

r = the Pearson correlation coefficient

n = the sample size

If the null hypothesis can be rejected for one time period but not the other, there is empirical evidence that rejects the original null hypothesis H0_1.

One benefit associated with approaches involving a test of significant differences in correlation coefficients before and after the accession and a test evaluating the absence of zero correlations before and after accession, is that the results are relatively easy to interpret. However, these approaches to testing the null hypothesis of unchanged co-movement also imply certain limitations. One such limitation is that while the above described analyses provide useful insights in the average levels of correlation before and after the EU accession announcement date, they do not offer any insights in the dynamic developments of the correlation coefficients over time.

4.1.1.3 Time-Varying Trends in Correlation Coefficients

In order to expand the test of the null hypothesis with regard to the time-varying developments of the correlation coefficients, an additional analysis is suggested as a complement to the two described above. This additional analysis involves the calculation and graphical illustration of subsequent, shorter-term correlation coefficients and an evaluation of shifts over time. More specifically, the analysis involves a correlation coefficient between the respective local market index and each of the global and European equity indices based on 26-week periods calculated on a rolling weekly basis. A mean correlation coefficient is subsequently calculated for the eight local markets and the respective global and European index.

This additional analysis provides an understanding of the dynamic trend surrounding the static results of the initial two analyses. Although it does not provide a statistical tool to reject the initial null hypothesis in itself, together with the other two analyses it does provide a sufficient basis to comprehensively test the null hypothesis.

4.1.2 Influence of Global and Local Macroeconomic Factors

The tests described in the previous sub-section provide empirical evidence of any potential changes in the level of co-movement with global and European indices as a result of EU accession. However, the previous analyses provide limited indications with regard to the reasons for these changes. The following sub-sections describe the methods associated with measuring changes in the level of influence of global and local macroeconomic factors on the equity markets in the Central European transition economies.

By complementing the previous analysis with empirical tests related to whether the influence of global and local macroeconomic factors on the local transition economy equity market returns changes in connection with the EU accession announcement, a further understanding of the effects of the event with regard to level of market integration can be established.

The test of the hypotheses relating to the changes in the dependence of global and local macroeconomic factors requires a series of steps. First, the relevant global and local macroeconomic factors need to be identified and defined. Second, the equity market index data from the transition economies need to be adjusted to ensure that the data are corresponding to that of the macroeconomic factors. Finally, the statistical approaches related to testing the influence of global as well as local macroeconomic factors must be defined. The data on local market return will be explored in detail in Chap. 5. The subsequent sub-sections include descriptions of the derivation of relevant macroeconomic factors as well as the statistical test method for the null hypotheses related to influence of macroeconomic factors.

4.1.2.1 Definition of Relevant Global and Local Macroeconomic Factors

There is both theoretical and empirical evidence suggesting that asset prices are affected by macroeconomic variables (Bodurtha et al., 1989; Chen, 1991; Chen et al., 1986; Fama, 1990, 1981; Ferson and Harvey, 1991b; Roll and Ross, 1980). This sub-section introduces the derivation of the relevant global and local factors.

Global Macroeconomic Factors

Asset prices are likely to be affected by a wide range of factors outside a country's borders. The dividend discount model (Gordon, 1982) proposes that any economic factor that directly or indirectly influences the value of future dividend cash flows, such as the discount rate and the expected growth rate of the dividend cash flows, will influence the value of an asset. Real economic factors such as industrial production are likely to affect the level of growth in dividend cash flows. In parallel, financial factors such as interest rates, inflation and money supply are likely to influence the cost of capital and the associated discount rate.

Numerous other factors can be linked to the components of the asset pricing model in a similar way. However, empirical research related to how economic factors affect asset prices requires limitations in the number of factors included in an analysis. Previous research has tested the relationships between US equity returns and a range of macroeconomic variables such as industrial production, gold and oil prices, real GNP, GDP, unanticipated inflation as well as changes in anticipated inflation, interest rates, term premium, junk bond premium and money supply (Chen, 1991; Chen et al., 1986; Fama, 1990, 1981; Ferson and Harvey, 1991b; Roll and Ross, 1980). The findings are that many macroeconomic variables can be used to predict the performance of equity markets. Analyses of data from other developed markets including Japan, Germany, the UK, France, Canada and Australia, have provided similar conclusions regarding the selected factors (Bodurtha et al., 1989; Cheung and Ng, 1998; Ferson and Harvey, 1993).

Empirical studies of the relationship between asset prices and macroeconomic factors based on emerging market data are more limited. Global factors evaluated in the perspective of emerging equity market returns include world market equity returns, the return on a foreign currency index, oil prices, world industrial production and world inflation (Harvey, 1995b, 1995a). In addition, Fifield et al. (2002) use a set of additional variables in the study of 13 emerging stock markets. These factors include US short-term interest rates, average balance of money, balance of trade and GDP.

The choice of global macroeconomic factors for this study is based on a combination of previous empirical studies (Bodurtha et al., 1989; Fifield et al., 2002) and data availability. In line with Fifield et al. (2002) the number of global economic factors is reduced to six factors, all of which have proven to possess significant relationships with equity returns. The six global factors include the world oil price, the world industrial production, the world equity market return, the world inflation, the world commodity prices and the US interest rate.

The aim of the analysis is to evaluate how changes in the macroeconomic variables can explain the changes in the local equity market returns. The variables derived from macroeconomic factors are consequently defined so that the monthly change is emphasized. Table 4.1 illustrates the exact definition and the

Table 4.1 Definition and source of global macroeconomic factors

Global factor	Definition	Source
Commodity price	Monthly per cent change in IMF All Commodity Index	IMF
Oil price	Monthly per cent change in IMF Spot Crude Petroleum Index - an equally weighted average of UK Brent, Dubai, West Texas Intermediate in USD per barrel indexed to 100 in 1995	IMF
Industry production	Monthly per cent change in OECD Production of Total Industry Index	OECD
Equity return	Monthly per cent change in MSCI World Index	MSCI
Inflation	Monthly per cent change in OECD All Member Consumer Price Index	OECD
US interest rate	US three-month money market interest rate	Eurostat

source for each of the global macroeconomic variables. As can be seen in the table, five of the six variables are defined as monthly per cent changes in an index. The US interest rates, however, is defined as the prevailing 3-month interest rate which partially indicates the alternative cost of investing in the equity market for an international investor.

Local Macroeconomic Factors

The relevance of local factors in this analysis is based on the theoretical and empirical conclusions that the return of equity markets in segmented markets cannot be explained exclusively by global factors (Harvey, 1995a, 1995b).

Six local macroeconomic factors, which have been demonstrated to possess statistically significant explanatory power over equity returns in previous research by Chen et al. (1986), Fifield et al. (2002) and Harvey (1995b), are included in the analysis. The six factors include local short-term interest rates, inflation, industrial production, money supply, balance of trade as well as foreign exchange rates. Fifield et al. (2002) apply data on GDP instead of industrial production in their analysis of 13 emerging markets. However, for the eight transition economies included in this study, GDP data is only available on a quarterly basis which would not allow for enough granularity in the analysis. Table 4.2 provides detailed definitions and sources relating to the local macroeconomic variables.

Just as for the selected global macroeconomic factors, the aim of the local factors is to measure change from one month to the next for most of the variables. Therefore, the variables related to inflation, industrial production, money supply and exchange rates have been defined to measure the monthly change. The interest

Table 4.2 Definition and source of local macroeconomic factors

Local Factor	Definition	Source
Interest rates	Short-term, unregulated local interest rates - The Czech Republic, Estonia, Latvia and Poland: local three month money market rate from Eurostat; Hungary and the Slovak Republic: local deposit rates and Lithuania and Slovenia: local money market rates both sourced from IMF's International Financial Statistics	Eurostat and IMF
Inflation	Monthly per cent change in Consumer Price Index	IMF
Industrial production	Monthly per cent change in unadjusted Industrial Production Index	Eurostat and IMF
Money supply	Monthly per cent change in Money Supply as defined by IMF for all markets except for Hungary where data for money in circulation is applied - Money Supply data in billions of local currency	IMF and Hungary Statistics Office
Trade balance	The net of exports and imports in millions denominated in local currency	IMF and Hungary National Bank
Exchange rate	Monthly per cent change in inter-bank rates of USD per local currency unit	oanda.com

rate variable, however, is defined as the prevailing short-term, unregulated interest rate in the respective local market and the trade balance variable is defined as the net of exports and imports denominated in local currency.

4.1.2.2 Statistical Test of Change in Influence of Global and Local Factors

The aim is to test whether any significant change in the level of influence can be determined in the period prior to the announcement compared to that after the announcement for the two categories of macroeconomic variables, global and local. While the analyses of the global and local macroeconomic factors need to be conducted separately, the approach applied is similar and will be defined and explained below.

Once the relevant factors have been identified, different approaches are possible. All approaches would involve separate analyses of the global and local factors. Furthermore, the approaches would also all involve conducting separate regression analyses using data before and after the EU accession announcement and measuring changes in the explanatory power of model over the two time periods.

One approach that has been applied in earlier empirical studies involves defining a standardised regression model for the emerging markets which comprises a wide range of global or local variables respectively in a reduced form (Fifield et al., 2002). The reduction of the variables is achieved through a principal component analysis which ensures that the ordinary least square assumption of no multicollinearity among the explanatory variables is met.

There are two challenges with this approach with regard to this study. First, given that eight different markets are studied, it is possible that a regression model that is significant for one market is less suited for other markets. This implies a risk that variables are insignificant in many markets which in turn results in distorting noises inhibiting the derivation of conclusions. Given that the aim is not to test a specific model as such, but rather to statistically test whether the level of influence of certain types of macroeconomic factors changes as a result of EU accession, the aim is to find the most appropriate model for each emerging market based on the global as well as the local macroeconomic factors.

Second, while principal component analyses include benefits such as simplification of regression models and elimination of multicollinearity, the drawback is that they are more difficult to interpret with regard to individual results. This is due to the fact that the explanatory variables contain variance from several macroeconomic factors independent of whether they are significant or not.

An alternative approach is therefore more appropriate in this particular case. This alternative approach involves conducting regression analyses using the macroeconomic factors directly, without data reduction. The approach implies identifying the regression model with the largest explanatory power based on significant variables for each of the two time periods. The approach involves identifying the models with the highest explanatory power measured by the adjusted R^2, calculated based on the formula described in Eq. 4.4.

Eq. 4.4: Definition of adjusted R^2

$$R_a^2 = 1 - \left[\left(\frac{n-1}{n-k-1}\right) * \left(1 - R^2\right)\right]$$

where,

R_a^2 – the adjusted R^2
n = the number of observations
k = the number of independent variables
R^2 = the unadjusted R^2

As is clear from Eq. 4.4, the adjusted R^2 takes into consideration the difference in number of explanatory variables incorporated in the regression models. It also takes into consideration the number of observations. Both of these adjustments are important in this case as it is likely that the models applied and compared across the time periods differ both with regard to the number of independent variables and the number of observations.

The initial step in identifying the most effective regression models for each time period in each of the eight markets involves conducting single regressions with each macroeconomic factor as independent variable. The regression models are defined in Eq. 4.5.

Eq. 4.5: Single regression model for initial test of macroeconomic factors

$$R_{it} = \alpha + \beta MEF_{nt} + \varepsilon_{it}$$

where,

R_{it} = the index returns for market i in time period t
α = the intercept of the model
β = the parameter of the model
MEF_{nt} = the value of the nth macroeconomic factor in time period t
ε_{it} = the random error term

The subsequent step involves an iterative process evaluating each possible combination of macroeconomic factors separately to identify the model based on significant explanatory factors with the highest explanatory power. With regard to the global macroeconomic factors, the optimal model could contain between a single independent variable up to all six global factors as independent variables. The actual optimal model is one form of derivation of the model described in Eq. 4.6.

Eq. 4.6: Regression model based on global macroeconomic factors

$$R_{it} = \alpha_i + \beta_1 OILPRIC_t + \beta_2 INDPRD_t + \beta_3 WLDRET_t + \beta_4 WLDCPI_t + \beta_5 USINT_t + \beta_6 COMMPR_t + \varepsilon_{it}$$

where,

R_{it} = the index returns for market i in time period t
$OILPRIC_t$ = the variable representing the oil price index in time period t
$INDPRD_t$ = the variable representing the industrial production in time period t
$WLDRET_t$ = the variable representing the world index return in time period t

$WLDCPI_t$ = the variable representing the world consumer price index in time period t
$USINT_t$ = the variable representing the US interest rates in time period t
$COMMPR_t$ = the variable representing the commodity price index in time period t
α_i = the intercept of the model for market i
β_n = the parameter of the model for global macroeconomic factor n
ε_{it} = a random error term

Similarly, with regard to the local macroeconomic factors, the optimal model will consist of between one and six local factors as independent variables. The optimal model consists of parts, or all, of the model depicted in Eq. 4.7

Eq. 4.7: Regression model based on local macroeconomic factors

$$R_{it} = \alpha_i + \beta_1 INT_{it} + \beta_2 INPR_{it} + \beta_3 INFL_{it} + \beta_4 MOSU_{it} + \beta_5 TRBA_{it} + \beta_6 EXCH_{it} + \varepsilon_{it}$$

where,

R_{it} = the index returns for market i in time period t
INT_{it} = the variable representing interest rates in market i in time period t
$INPR_{it}$ = the variable representing the industrial production in market i in time period t
$INFL_{it}$ = the variable representing the inflation in market i in time period t
$MOSU_{it}$ = the variable representing the money supply in market i in time period t
$TRBA_{it}$ = the variable representing the trade balance in market i in time period t
$EXCH_{it}$ = the variable representing the exchange rate between the currency in market i and the USD in time period t
α_i = the intercept of the model for market i
β_n = the parameter of the model for local macroeconomic factor n
ε_{it} = the random error term

The iterative process of determining the optimal regression model involves two categories of tests. The first category involves confirming that the key underlying assumptions of the ordinary least square regression approach are met. This implies testing for the presence of, and potentially correcting for, serial correlation, heteroskedasticity and, when applicable, multicollinearity. The presence of serial correlation is explored using the Durbin-Watson test while the presence of heteroskedasticity is evaluated with the Breusch-Pagan test. If the assumptions regarding serial correlation and heteroskedasticity are not met, robust standard errors are applied to determine the correct significance levels for each of the independent variables. Issues related to multicollinearity are tested using the maximum value of the condition index. A certain level of multicollinearity is present in any multiple regression analysis and the aim is merely to ensure that there are no serious disturbances caused by multicollinearity. As a rule of thumb, multicollinearity disturbances of a severe nature can be assumed to exist if the maximum condition index takes a value exceeding 30 whereas moderate to strong multicollinearity exists when the maximum value is between 10 and 30 (Gujarati, 1995). If serious disturbances are detected, the number of explanatory variables is reduced.

The second category of tests involves ensuring that both the individual independent variables and the model as a whole are statistically significant. This is achieved with a t-test for the individual independent variables and with an F-test for the overall model. The F-test assesses how well the independent variables, as a group, explain the variation in the dependent variable. This implies that the test evaluates whether at least one of the independent variables explains a significant portion of the variation of the dependent variable. In order to avoid disturbances, only significant models based exclusively on significant independent variables are considered.

Once the assumptions and the statistical significance have been evaluated, the potential change in the explanatory power of the regression models across the two time periods is reviewed using the adjusted R^2. If it can be shown that the explanatory power of the regression models derived from post announcement data of the global macroeconomic variables is different from that derived in the period prior to the announcement, there is evidence to reject the null hypothesis of no change in influence of global macroeconomic factors on the local market returns as a result of the EU accession announcement in that particular market. In addition, if several of the markets demonstrate similar results, it is possible to generalise the findings more broadly.

Similarly, an analysis of the explanatory power of the local macroeconomic variables can provide evidence to reject the null hypothesis of no change in the level of influence of local factors on the local market as a result of the EU accession announcement. In this case, the expectation from market integration theory (Bekaert and Harvey, 2003) would be to see a reduced level of influence from local factors in the period subsequent to the accession announcement.

4.2 Impact of EU Accession on Performance

With empirical methods used to test the impact on the level of market integration explored, the focus is now shifted to empirical tests determining whether there is any impact on the performance of equity market returns as a result of accession to the EU. The research question is divided into two related hypotheses with the initial one relating to the level of volatility and the second one relating the returns.

Each of the two research hypothesis is explored using several complementary test approaches. The following sections provide the details of each of the test approaches.

4.2.1 Impact of EU Accession on Equity Market Volatility

As mentioned in Sect. 3.2.1, the third null hypothesis is formulated in a way that assumes no changes in volatility among Central and Eastern European transition economies as a result of EU accession. The alternative research hypothesis subsequently states that either a higher or lower level of return volatility prevails after the EU accession announcement.

In academic research related to equity market performance, a commonly used measure of volatility is variance and standard deviation (Barry et al., 1998; Bekaert and Harvey, 1997). The subsequent sub-sections describe two approaches jointly used to test the hypotheses.

4.2.1.1 Time-Varying Trends in Standard Deviation

The initial method is similar to the approach applied for the first research hypothesis in the sense that a particular time when changes are expected to occur is identified and that time series data on market returns covering periods prior and subsequent to this date are collected.

For each market, the return level is calculated on a weekly basis and used to calculate a 26-week rolling average standard deviation. The rolling average is then graphically plotted for each market. The graphical illustration demonstrates when changes in the volatility occur. While this initial approach does not provide a means to statistically reject the null hypothesis, it does offer an opportunity to put the statistical test into a broader context.

4.2.1.2 Statistical Test of Change in Level of Volatility

The second method of testing the null hypothesis relating to the volatility of the equity markets applies the same sample data as that used in calculations of the rolling standard deviation averages. Furthermore, it involves similarities with the approach applied to test changes in the level of co-movement in the sense that it requires the weekly return data to be divided into a pre-announcement period and post-announcement period for each of the eight markets. The variance is subsequently calculated for the respective samples and compared across the two time periods in order to determine whether any significant change can be determined.

A frequently used method to determine the statistical difference between variances of two populations when independent random samples are available from the both populations is the F-test (DeFusco et al., 2004). The approach is best suited for sample data which are largely random and independent. The original null and alternative hypotheses are reformulated to better fit the approach:

$$H_0 : \sigma^2_{\text{Before}} = \sigma^2_{\text{After}}$$

$$H_A : \sigma^2_{\text{Before}} \neq \sigma^2_{\text{After}}$$

The null hypothesis can be tested by evaluating the quote $\sigma^2_{Before} / \sigma^2_{After}$. In the case the quote is statistically found not to equal one, there is evidence to reject the null hypothesis. Given the mathematical attributes of the quote, the value will never go below zero and the F-distribution is therefore an appropriate distribution choice in this test since it is an asymmetrical distribution limited to values above zero.

The relevant F-statistic to test the null hypothesis against can be formulated according to (4.8) (DeFusco et al., 2004).

Eq. 4.8: Definition of the F-statistic

$$F = \frac{s_1^2}{s_2^2}$$

where,

s^2_1 = the square of the standard deviation of the sample with the higher volatility
s^2_2 = the square of the standard deviation of the sample with the lower volatility

The test is conducted with $n_1 - 1$ degrees of freedom for the numerator and $n_2 - 1$ degrees of freedom for the denominator (DeFusco et al., 2004). Where n_1 is the number of observations in the sample with the higher volatility and n_2 is the number of observations in the sample with the lower volatility.

4.2.2 Impact of EU Accession on Equity Market Return

In terms of testing whether there is any impact on the level of equity market return as a result of accession to the EU, three complementary methods are applied. The initial method does not constitute a statistical test approach but rather a graphical illustration which supports the subsequent two tests.

In the first two approaches, return is measured as total return to shareholders incorporating both dividends and changes in terms of closing prices of the index constituents. The third approach applies the same definition of returns but adds the important dimension of measuring the performance in the perspective of volatility. In line with existing empirical research (Bekaert and Harvey, 2003; Bekaert et al., 2005; Fifield et al., 2002), transaction or management fees are not taken into consideration.

The following sections provide the details of the three test approaches.

4.2.2.1 Time Varying Trends in Index Closing Price

The initial analytical approach is defined so that the time-varying trends can be evaluated. The method implies an analysis of a graphical illustration of the index over a period which incorporates time horizons both before and after the date when a change is expected to occur. The illustration of the equity index data is based on closing prices of weekly data and covers as long a period as possible to provide perspectives on both the medium and the long term.

As with the graphical illustration of the standard deviation applied in the test of the impact on volatility, the illustration of equity index closing prices for the local markets will not generate any statistical evidence on whether the hypothesis can be rejected or not. Instead, it provides contextual information which helps to interpret the evidence.

4.2.2.2 Statistical Test of Change in Level of Equity Market Return

The second approach has similarities to the test applied for the research hypothesis on market volatility. The date at which point effects are expected to appear is identified. Samples containing weekly equity market returns for each of the eight transition economies are subsequently collected both before and after the identified date. The mean return levels are calculated based on closing prices in local currencies as well as in USD to provide the perspectives of a local as well as a foreign investor. The next step in the approach implies statistically testing whether the mean returns for the pre-event period are significantly different from those in the post-event period.

Given an assumption of roughly normally distributed populations, a relevant and commonly used approach to test whether any identified difference in mean between the two samples is statistically significant or the result of chance is a t-test with a t-statistic defined as in Eq. 4.9 (DeFusco et al., 2004).

Eq. 4.9: t-Statistic to determine statistically significant difference in means

$$t = \frac{(\overline{X}_1 - \overline{X}_2) - (\mu_1 - \mu_2)}{\left(\frac{s_1^2}{n_1} + \frac{s_2^2}{n_2} \right)^{1/2}}$$

where,

t = the test statistic for t-test assuming unequal and unknown variances
$\overline{X}_1$ = the sample mean for post-event period
$\overline{X}_2$ = the sample mean for pre-event period
μ_1 = the population mean for post-event period
μ_2 = the population mean for pre-event period
s_1 = the sample standard deviation for post-event period
s_2 = the sample standard deviation for pre-event period
n_1 = the post-event period sample size
n_2 = the pre-event period sample size

The number of modified degrees of freedom associated with the t-statistic is calculated according to Eq. 4.10.

Eq. 4.10: Number of modified degrees of freedom associated with the t-statistic

$$df = \frac{\left(\frac{s_1^2}{n_1} + \frac{s_2^2}{n_2} \right)^2}{\frac{(s_1^2 / n_1)^2}{n_1 - 1} + \frac{(s_2^2 / n_2)^2}{n_2 - 1}}$$

where,

df = the number of degrees of freedom
s_1 = the sample standard deviation for post-event period
s_2 = the sample standard deviation for pre-event period

n_1 = the post-event period sample size
n_2 = the pre-event period sample size

The above t-test is robust to moderate departures from normality except for outliers and strong skewness (DeFusco et al., 2004). The central limit theorem suggests that when the underlying variables are random, independent and follow an identical distribution, the distribution of the t-statistic of (4.9) tends to be standard normal when n becomes large (Newbold, 1991). Generally, a sample size of 30 is perceived as large (DeFusco et al., 2004). As will be discussed in the subsequent chapter, the sample sizes in this study range from 49 to 363 and are therefore large enough to facilitate the application of the central limit theorem as long as randomness can be ascertained.

The absence of randomness in the data can be of concern when analysing samples based on time series data. However, return data from stocks are usually dynamic and demonstrate vast movements which should reduce the risk of non-randomness (Fama, 1965). Normality and randomness in the samples are tested for in Chap. 5. However, even if both of these dimensions are confirmed and the normal distribution would be applicable, the population variance is unknown and the more conservative distribution to apply is the t-distribution which approaches the normal distribution when the number of degrees of freedom increases.

4.2.2.3 Change in Risk-Adjusted Equity Market Return Levels

The above described approach covers weekly return levels both in local currency and in USD which implies that exchange rate effects can be isolated. However, an analysis of return levels is only partly complete if the return is not put into the context of the risk that is associated with achieving the return. As was concluded in the analysis of the previous research hypothesis, the volatility in the equity market indices of the transition economies could change across the two time periods. This implies that the required returns adjusted for the changes in the risk levels might be lower, as is suggest in the CAPM (Lintner, 1965; Sharpe, 1964).

The third empirical approach to analyse the changes in the return levels as a result of the EU accession therefore involves evaluating the change in the risk-adjusted return levels. While there are many different measures for risk-adjusted returns, a commonly applied measure for risk-adjusted returns in both academic research and in practice is the Sharpe ratio (Sharpe, 1966, 1994). The Sharpe ratio is defined as the excess return generated by the portfolio divided by the standard deviation of the portfolio. The more detailed definition of the Sharpe ratio according to Sharpe (1994) is presented in Eq. 4.11.

Eq. 4.11: Definition of historic Sharpe ratio

$$S_h \equiv \frac{\overline{D}}{\sigma_D}$$

where,

S_h = the historic Sharpe ratio

$$\bar{D} \equiv \frac{1}{T}\sum_{t=1}^{T} D_t$$

$$D_t \equiv R_{Ft} - R_{Bt}$$

R_{Ft} = the return on the fund in time period t
R_{Bt} = the return on the reference fund in time period t

$$\sigma_D \equiv \sqrt{\frac{\sum_{t=1}^{T}(D_t - \bar{D})^2}{T-1}}$$

In this study, the term fund refers to the equity market indices of the eight transition economies. The reference is set to the average deposit rates in each of the markets for the given time period. The time periods refer to each weekly period for which data are available. The average differential return between the weekly index returns and the associated deposit rates is calculated for the period before and after the announcement of the EU accession details. The weekly return data applied for the respective market index and deposit rates applied as reference returns for each market are discussed in more detail in Chap. 5.

4.3 Concluding Remarks on Methodology

As discussed in the previous sections, each research hypothesis is explored with several complementary methods. Not all methods provide statistically significant evidence whether the null hypotheses can be rejected or not. However, at least one empirical test is statistically robust for each of the hypotheses.

Each of the approaches is empirical in nature and the data requirements have been discussed along with the introduction of the respective approach. Although the approaches vary across research hypotheses, some of the data samples can be used to explore several research hypotheses. The next chapter provides an introduction to the qualitative information and quantitative data applied in the research methods introduced earlier in this chapter.

Chapter 5
Review of Empirical Data

Prior to presenting the details and findings of the analyses, it is useful to introduce the empirical data. The analyses of this study require several types of empirical data to address the identified research hypotheses.

First, information of a more qualitative nature relating to the launch of equity trading in the eight targeted financial markets is relevant for building the foundation of the integration analysis associated with the first two research hypotheses. While market liberalisation does not constitute a separate topic within the scope of this study, it is nevertheless relevant to establish whether it has occurred prior to the EU accession. If liberalisation occurred prior to the EU accession and additional effects of the accession on the level of integration are found, this study offers valuable contributions to the understanding of the market integration process.

Second, key steps in the Eastern European EU enlargement process are explored to determine at what point in time any potential effects are likely to occur. This involves detailing the process from the date of application to the actual accession date including descriptions of what each step in the application process implies.

Third, quantitative return data are required for each of the studied equity markets as well as for a set of global and European reference indices. This involves determining appropriate market indices, the frequency of the data as well as the relevant currency for each of the applicable research questions.

Finally, quantitative data on a selected number of local and global macroeconomic factors related to explaining the performance of equity markets are required to enable the detailed analysis of how different factors affect the performance of equity markets prior to versus after the EU accession.

This chapter includes a description and a review of both the qualitative and the quantitative data and associated sources applied within the scope of this study.

5.1 Review of Qualitative Information and Data

This section describes the more qualitative data required for the analyses of the research hypotheses. The review of the qualitative information is structured into three sub-sections covering the liberalisation of Eastern European financial markets, the initiation of equity trading in these markets and finally the process of EU accession.

5.1.1 *Liberalisation of Eastern European Financial Markets*

As discussed in Chap. 2, an important dimension of the emerging market integration process is market liberalisation. Understanding the liberalisation process of financial markets in Central and Eastern European transition economies can help clarify later stages in the market integration process which are largely unexplored in academic research.

The definition of liberalisation applied in this study is in line with that of several other studies relating to market integration (Bekaert and Harvey, 2001, 2000) and refers the fact that local financial markets are accessible to foreign investors while, simultaneously, domestic investors have access to foreign markets.

In several emerging markets, official liberalisation dates are determined based on a combination of factors such as the introduction of the first ADRs, the introduction of the first country fund, estimates of increases in net US capital flows as well as an analysis of structural break tests of a host of economic and financial time series (Bekaert et al., 2002). Using a combination of these factors, official liberalisation dates have been estimated for 31 emerging markets (Bekaert et al., 2003). Only three out of the 31 emerging markets with estimated liberalisation dates are located within in a geography covering a broad definition of Europe.

Despite the broad scope of the existing liberalisation research conducted by Bekaert and Harvey (1995, 2000), market liberalisation in the Central and Eastern European transition economies have not been examined explicitly. However, the fact that none of the African, Asian, South American or European markets had an official liberalisation date later than April 1997, there is strong reason to believe that the eight most advanced Eastern and Central European transition economies included in this study would have experienced liberalisation before the EU accession in May 2004.

In fact, in these advanced transition economies there has been a strong interest in attracting foreign real and financial investment capital ever since the end of the communist era. The eagerness to attract foreign capital to local equity assets is illustrated by the fact that Western companies were invited to help establish local financial exchanges soon after the end of the Soviet era and that many assets were privatised by targeting international buyers. One such example is the privatisation of Lietuvos Telekomas, the Lithuanian incumbent telecommunications company, which occurred through an international tender in June 1998 during which a consortium containing Telia of Sweden and Sonera of Finland won the tender and became majority owners (EBRD, 2000).

Financial markets in the eight transition economies covered within the scope of this study were largely open to foreign investors from the beginning and the fundamental issue is therefore rather to understand when equity trading exchanges were launched in the first place.

5.1.2 *Initiation of Equity Trading in European Transition Economies*

During the Soviet era, the centralisation of private ownership to the state made the existence of financial exchanges not only illegal but also irrelevant. Given the status of the targeted eight transition economies as satellite states to the Soviet Union, none of them had financial trading in place while the Soviet Union functioned. With the disassembly of the Soviet Union beginning in 1989, most of the Central European and Baltic satellite states embarked on processes to establish, or in many cases re-establish, financial market places and the associated financial regulatory institutions. This sub-section includes a presentation of the post-Soviet launch dates of financial market places in each of the eight economies.

In Poland, the first financial exchange was established in 1817 and it continued to evolve and grow until 1938 when the exchange was closed as a result of war. After the war the exchange remained closed due to the political environment and trading was not re-launched until April 1991 when the first orders were placed on the Warsaw Stock Exchange (WSE). The official opening of the WSE took place in July 1991 along with the establishment of the Polish Securities Commission (Warsaw Stock Exchange, 2006).

Just as in Poland, capital markets in Hungary and the Czech Republic were launched in the 19th century and played a role in European financial markets until the 1930s when trading was discontinued. More recently, the Budapest Stock Exchange (BSE) was inaugurated in June 1990 at which point the first transactions also took place (Budapest Stock Exchange, 2006). The Prague Stock Exchange (PSE) was officially established in November 1992, but it would not be until April 1993 that the first trades would occur (Prague Stock Exchange, 2006).

In Slovenia, the Ljubljana Stock Exchange (LJSE) was officially established in December 1989 although the first trading did not occur until March 1990. Also the LJSE had a previous history of trading stretching from 1924 to 1942 after which it was forbidden by a political decree (Ljubljana Stock Exchange, 2006).

Trading in the Slovak Republic began in April 1993 on the Bratislava Stock Exchange (BSSE) although the actual foundation took place in March 1991 (Bratislava Stock Exchange, 2006).

In the Baltic States, the financial exchanges took somewhat longer to establish. Trading on the Vilnius, Riga and Tallinn Stock Exchanges was not initiated until September 1993, July 1995 and May 1996 respectively (OMX Group, 2006).

Table 5.1 illustrates a summary of the official exchange launch and trading initiation dates in each of the eight countries.

Table 5.1 Dates for initiation of financial markets and trading in Eastern European economies

Country	Exchange Name	Official Exchange Launch Date	Actual Trading Initiation
Czech Rep.	Prague Stock Exchange	Nov-92	Apr-93
Estonia	Tallinn Stock Exchange	Apr-95	May-96
Hungary	Budapest Stock Exchange	Jun-90	Jun-90
Latvia	Riga Stock Exchange	Dec-93	Jul-95
Lithuania	Vilnius Stock Exchange	Sep-93	Sep-93
Poland	Warsaw Stock Exchange	Jul-91	Apr-91
Slovak Rep.	Bratislava Stock Exchange	Mar-91	Apr-93
Slovenia	Ljubljana Stock Exchange	Dec-89	Mar-90

Source: Reports from respective local exchanges, 2006

5.1.3 EU Accession Process of Eastern European Economies

The following section explores relevant qualitative data on the history of the EU enlargement and the accession process for the Central and Eastern European states that joined the EU in May 2004. The data constitute an important part of addressing all of the research questions.

5.1.3.1 Enlargement of the European Union

The first form of the EU was officially initiated with the Treaty of Rome on 25 March 1957 when six European states decided to pool resources to preserve and strengthen peace and liberty in the region (European Commission, 2006). Since its inception the EU has expanded from six to 27 members in 2007. The original members of what is now known as the EU include Belgium, France, Italy, Luxemburg, the Netherlands and West Germany. The first enlargement took place in 1973 when Denmark, Ireland and the UK joined followed by additions of Greece in 1981, Spain and Portugal in 1986 and Austria, Finland and Sweden in 1995.

Building on the Maastricht Treaty of 1992, the 1993 European Council summit in Copenhagen involved a commitment to an enlargement of the EU towards Central and Eastern Europe (Heijdra et al., 2002). Subsequent to the applications that followed in the 3 years after the Copenhagen summit, formal negotiations were initiated in two waves. Participants in the first negotiation wave, named the Luxembourg Group after the location of the summit of 1997, included the Czech Republic, Estonia, Hungary, Poland and Slovenia while the participants in the second wave, called the Helsinki Group after the summit of 1999, involved Bulgaria, Latvia, Lithuania, Romania and the Slovak Republic (European Commission, 2006).

The enlargement of 2004 included 10 states and was in many respects the most extensive expansion in the history of the EU. Not only was it the expansion with the most new member states joining simultaneously, it also involved an addition of 75 million individuals, raising the EU population by 25%to 455 million (Trichet, 2004).

The 2004 enlargement has made the EU the world's most prominent unified economic market, accounting for a quarter of world's trade and global income (Trichet, 2004). Table 5.2 provides further details of the EU member states as of January 2007.

While the enlargement of 2004 was unique in its scope, the Eastern enlargement process will continue over the coming years. For example, Bulgaria and Romania joined the EU in January 2007. The negotiations were concluded in December 2004 and a Treaty of Accession signed in April 2005 upon which the treaty was ratified in each member state (European Commission, 2005).

As of October 2006, there are also two candidate countries, Croatia and Turkey, which are still in negotiation with the EU. Actual accession is dependent on the completion of negotiations as well as on the fulfilment of the accession criteria. Furthermore, there are several potential candidate states in the Western Balkans including Albania, Bosnia and Herzegovina, Macedonia, Serbia and Montenegro. While there are negotiations on Stabilisation and Association Agreements with Serbia and

Table 5.2 Overview of the EU member states as of 2007

Country	Population (Millions)	GDP (EUR bn)	GDP per capita (EUR)	EU Member Since	EURO Since
Austria	8.17	237	29,013	1995	1999
Belgium	10.42	288	27,648	1957	1999
Bulgaria	7.4	21.8	2,947	2007	
Cyprus	0.74	13	16,932	2004	
Czech Republic	10.21	87	8,500	2004	
Denmark	5.40	196	36,352	1973	
Estonia	1.36	9	6,647	2004	
Finland	5.23	150	28,629	1995	1999
France	62.18	1,648	26,510	1957	1999
Germany	82.50	2,216	26,856	1957	1999
Greece	11.06	167	15,115	1981	2001
Hungary	10.11	81	8,024	2004	
Ireland	4.06	149	36,591	1973	1999
Italy	58.25	1,351	23,199	1957	1999
Latvia	2.31	11	4,823	2004	
Lithuania	3.44	18	5,256	2004	
Luxembourg	0.45	26	57,022	1957	1999
Malta	0.40	4	10,675	2004	
Netherlands	16.27	489	30,033	1957	1999
Poland	38.17	204	5,337	2004	
Portugal	10.50	142	13,552	1986	1999
Romania	22.30	61	2,753	2007	
Slovak Republic	5.38	33	6,156	2004	
Slovenia	2.00	26	13,075	2004	
Spain	42.69	837	19,614	1986	1999
Sweden	8.99	282	31,369	1995	
United Kingdom	59.84	1,717	28,685	1973	

Source: CIA World Fact Book, 2006; European Commission, 2006

Montenegro, most of these states are far from meeting any the political or economic criteria associated with EU accession. Table 5.3 provides a list of European transition economies which are exploring possibilities to access the EU in the future.

5.1.3.2 EU Accession Criteria

As indicated in the above sub-section, accession to the EU is dependent on meeting a set of specific conditions. At a general level, Article 49 of the Treaty on European Union states that any European state is allowed to apply for EU membership as long as it respects the principles of liberty, democracy, human rights, fundamental freedom and the rule of law (European Council, 2002). However, a set of more specific criteria of accession were defined by the European Council in Copenhagen in 1993 and reinforced at the Council in Madrid in 1995. The accession criteria cover four areas spanning political, economic, financial and judicial dimensions.

More explicitly the Copenhagen membership criteria, as presented in the Conclusions of the Presidency at the European Council (European Council, 1993) require that a candidate country has achieved

- "stability of institutions guaranteeing democracy, the rule of law, human rights and respect for and protection of minorities";
- "the existence of a functioning market economy as well as the capacity to cope with competitive pressure and market forces within the EU"; and
- "the ability to take on the obligations of membership including adherence to the aims of political, economic and monetary union."

Table 5.3 Overview of European non-EU emerging and transition economies as of January 2007

Country	Population (Millions)	GDP (EUR bn)	GDP per Capita (EUR)	EU Membership Status
Croatia	4.5	29.5	6,564	Candidate
Macedonia	2.1	4.5	2,183	Candidate
Turkey	70.4	280.8	3,987	Candidate
Albania	3.6	7.3	2,041	Potential Candidate
Bosnia and Herzegovina	4.5	7.2	1,595	Potential Candidate
Montenegro	0.6	0.9	1,505	Potential Candidate
Serbia	9.4	16.2	1,725	Potential Candidate
Armenia	3.0	4.1	1,381	Currently Not Considered
Belarus	10.3	22.5	2,190	Currently Not Considered
Georgia	4.7	5.4	1,159	Currently Not Considered
Moldova	4.5	2.0	457	Currently Not Considered
Ukraine	46.7	63.4	1,358	Currently Not Considered

Sources: CIA World Fact Book, 2006; European Commission, 2006

The Madrid Council added the requirement that candidate countries must achieve the conditions for integration by adjusting its administrative structures, transposing the European Community legislation into the national legislation and implementing appropriate administrative and judicial structures (European Council, 1995).

Finally, accession requirements also include that the EU must be able to absorb new members. The EU has thereby reserved the right to determine the accession time independent of when candidate countries meet the criteria.

Given that the Central and Eastern European countries were emerging from planned rather than free market economies, the accession criteria have served two main purposes. First, they have ensured rapid reforms which have positively influenced economic and political stability in the candidate economies. Second, they have limited the negative impact on the incumbent EU member states as a result of the addition of members with largely different levels of development.

5.1.3.3 Relevant Dates of EU Accession of Eastern European Economies

When determining the accession date relevant for the purpose of this study, it is important to take into consideration when effects are likely to appear. As discussed in the previous sub-sections, the EU accession process for the Central and Eastern European economies has been long-lasting and filled with uncertainties regarding the conditions and exact timing of the accession.

In this perspective, the official application date, which occurs at an early stage when the terms and timing of the accession are unclear, does not constitute an appropriate date around which to measure the accession effects. The actual accession date is also a less appropriate point in time for the purpose of this study since the decision and details of the membership were clear at an earlier stage. Given the assumption of efficient financial markets, any changes caused by new information should be reflected in the market on the announcement date plus any potential delays to measure the effects.

Consequently, the most appropriate point in time to study is when the conditions and the exact date of accession were announced. The official decision to accept the ten new European nations to the EU was taken by the European Council on 14 April 2003 after the affirmative vote of the EU Parliament on 9 April 2003. However, the effective decision had already been taken months prior to this at the last day of the Copenhagen European Council of 12–13 December 2002 when negotiations between the EU and the ten accession countries came to an end. It is therefore appropriate to use 13 December 2002 as the official announcement date in this study since this is the point at which it was announced at what date and under what terms the accession would occur.

Table 5.4 Overview of accession process for May 2004 EU members

Country	Submission of Accession Application	Negotiations Launched	Recommendation to Conclude Negotiations by European Commission	Negotiations Closed	Affirmative Vote by European Parliament	Positive Decision by European Council	Official EU Accession Aate
Czech Rep.	Jan-96	31-Mar-98					
Estonia	Nov-95	31-Mar-98					
Hungary	Mar-94	31-Mar-98					
Latvia	Oct-95	15-Feb-00					
Lithuania	Dec-95	15-Feb-00					
Poland	Apr-94	31-Mar-98	9-Oct-02	13-Dec-02	9-Apr-04	14-Apr-04	1-May-04
Slovak Rep.	Jun-95	15-Feb-00					
Slovenia	Jun-96	31-Mar-98					
Cyprus	3-Jul-90	31-Mar-98					
Malta	16-Jul-90	15-Feb-00					

Source: DG Enlargement Information Unit of the European Union

Table 5.4 provides a summary of the EU application and accession process for the eight EU member states included in this study.

5.2 Review of Quantitative Data Samples

In addition to the more qualitative information presented in Sect. 5.1, the analysis of this study involves several sets of quantitative data samples. This section includes a description of the samples as well as a review of the considerations applied in the process of defining and selecting these data samples. The section is divided into four sub-sections covering market return data for equity markets in European transition economies, market return data for World and European equity indices, data on global and local macroeconomic factors and risk-free deposit rates for the calculation of the risk-adjusted return measure.

5.2.1 Market Return Data for European Transition Economies

Each of the research questions relates either directly or indirectly to effects associated with equity market returns in eight Central European and Baltic economies. Consequently, market return data for these markets constitute the core for testing the hypotheses within the scope of this study. The importance of the equity market data for the results of this study has implied that selection of the data has been subject to significant considerations with regard to sources and structure. This subsection introduces the selection considerations and describes the data sample.

5.2.1.1 Local Equity Markets

Before discussing the selected sources for market return data, it is relevant to introduce some key information about the local equity markets. As discussed in sub-section 5.1.2, the financial markets of the eight transition economies are rather recently established. This short-term legacy in combination with limited size of markets for most of the eight economies has resulted in financial exchanges with narrow scope in comparison with Western European equity exchanges. With the Warsaw Stock Exchange as the only exception, no market has more than 50 companies listed on the official markets. Estonia, Latvia and the Slovak Republic have 15 or less listed companies. This should be compared with 835 domestic companies listed on the Frankfurt Stock Exchange (Deutsche Boerse, 2006). Looking at the London Stock Exchange, close to 1,300 companies are listed on the Main Market UK (London Stock Exchange, 2006).

Also in terms of market capitalisation, the equity exchanges in the selected European transition economies are significantly smaller. Poland stands out as having the most substantial market capitalisation of the equity exchanges in the eight 2004 accession economies. The market capitalisation of the Polish equity market was EUR80bn at the end of 2005. This can be compared with the EUR2,716bn market capitalisation of the listed companies on the Main Market UK of the London Stock Exchange (London Stock Exchange, 2006). Table 5.5 illustrates the number of listed companies and the associated market capitalisation of the eight transition economies in focus of this study.

Given the limited scope of these markets, there is a risk that a market is dominated by a single company or small group of companies. This potential dominance implies that the distribution by industry is important to map as different industries have different performance characteristics. However, prior to entering into an analysis of industry sector dominance, it is appropriate to determine the sample of equity securities from each market which will be included in the market index.

Table 5.5 Number of listed companies and total market capitalisation of the equity markets in eight 2004 EU accession economies as of end of year 2005

Market	Listed equity Securities	Total Market Capitalisation (EUR bn)
Poland	255	80.0
Hungary	44	27.6
Lithuania	43	6.9
Czech Republic	39	45.9
Slovenia	25	4.9
Estonia	15	3.0
Slovak Republic	13	2.1
Latvia	12	1.7

Notes: Listed equity securities in Poland refers to domestic companies only. Listed securities for Slovenia refers to equity shares listed on the official market. List for the three Baltic states includes the Baltic Main Market and the Baltic I-list

Sources: Reports of Local Stock Exchanges for December 2005 and Local Exchange Web Sites

The subsequent sub-section discusses alternative sources and explores the arguments for each of the market index sources in the context of this study.

5.2.1.2 Selection of Equity Market Indices

Market return is commonly analysed by looking at a collection of companies joined together in the form of an index that represents a large portion of the listed companies in a particular market (Walter, 1993). Given that return to an investor involves both capital gains over time as well as periodical dividend payments, the most appropriate type of index is a total return index. From an investor's perspective, the returns should actually be measured net of costs. However, in order to simplify the analyses, costs associated to transactions, fund management and administration are ignored in this study. This is largely aligned with previous emerging market analyses (Bekaert and Harvey, 2000; Bekaert et al., 2002; Fifield et al., 2002; Harvey, 1995b).

A commonly used source of index return data in empirical emerging market research is the Emerging Markets Database (EMDB) which was launched in 1975 and maintained by the IFC until 2000 at which point the database was acquired by S&P. S&P has since continued to manage the indices according to the same standards. The EMDB contains three different indices which are all calculated in the same standardised way.

First, the IFC Global Index contains a subset of the listed companies representing no less than 75% of the total market capitalisation. The index is provided both as a price index and a total return index with the latter being the most commonly used index in analysing returns in emerging markets.

Second, any country included in the Global Index is also included in the Investable Index which includes a smaller number of constituents that are both legally and practically available to foreign portfolio investors. This index is also available in the form of either price or total return denomination.

Third, small emerging markets, in which equity trading volumes remain limited, are not covered by the Global Index or the Investable Index. Instead, they are included in the index called Frontier Market Index which is also available on the basis of price or total return.

All EMDB indices are calculated both in local currency and in USD and the Global and Investable indices are calculated on a daily basis while the Frontier Market Index is maintained on a monthly basis only. Details on the availability of index data from the EMBD are presented in Table 5.6.

Another frequently used provider of standardised emerging market indices is Morgan Stanley Capital International (MSCI) which offers a series of emerging market indices. In this context it is worthwhile noting that the EMDB and the MSCI indices have proven to be highly correlated (Bekaert et al., 1998). However, out of the eight Central European economies accessing the EU in 2004, MSCI only provides data on the Czech Republic, Hungary and Poland making it less applicable for this study.

Table 5.6 Overview of available index data

Market	Index Name	S&P/IFC EMDB Index Available From	Frequency	Index Name	Local Exchange Index Available From	Frequency
Czech Republic[a]	Global/ Investable	30-Jun-95	Daily	PX/PX50[b]	06 Apr-94	Daily
Estonia	Frontier	31-Dec-97	Monthly	OMX Tallinn GI	07-Jun-96	Daily
Hungary[a]	Global/ Investable	30-Jun-95	Daily	BUX	02-Jan-91	Daily
Latvia	Frontier	31-Dec-97	Monthly	OMX Riga GI	07-Jan-00	Daily
Lithuania	Frontier	31-Dec-95	Monthly	OMX Vilnius GI	07-Jan-00	Daily
Poland[a]	Global/ Investable	30-Jun-95	Daily	WIG	16-Apr-91	Daily
Slovak Republic	Frontier	31-Oct-04	Monthly	SAX	21-Sep-93	Daily
Slovenia	Frontier	31-Dec-95	Monthly	SBI	03-Jan-94	Daily

Notes: [a] Data for the Czech Republic, Hungary and Poland are available further back
[b] PX replaced PX50 as the official index in March 2006 but is based on PX50 for historical values
Source: Bloomberg

An alternative source of market data is the official total return indices for each local market. Local official total return indices tend to provide data more frequently and include a larger number of constituents. Furthermore, longer time series are in certain cases also available. Jointly, these facts must be weighted against the potential lack of standardisation available when using a single source when determining how to achieve a relevant and reliable analysis of the hypotheses.

The benefit of using a set of standardised emerging market indices is that each market index is calculated based on the same technique which can serve to enhance the accuracy of the results. However, there are also disadvantages in this particular case. First, availability is limited in the sense that both frequency and scope of historical data for some of the markets are limited. Second, the number of constituents is less in some of the standardised indices, as is illustrated in Table 5.7.

The standardisation of the index calculation methodology is useful when comparing the returns of one emerging market with that of another. However, within the scope of this study several research hypotheses aim to identify effects within the individual markets rather than across the markets. This opens up for the option of using local total return market indices to test the hypotheses as long as the local indices are calculated in a standardised way over time.

By applying local official total return indices for the markets where only monthly data is available from EMDB, the frequency of the time series data can be increased to a weekly level for all markets and the number of constituents can be increased in all but one market. Over longer time series, monthly frequency of

Table 5.7 Local exchange details and index constituents by market

Official Local Index		EMDB	EMDB	EMDB Frontier
Index Name	Number of Constituents	GlobalNumber of Constituents	InvestableNumber of Constituents	indexNumber of Constituents
PX/PX-50	14	6	6	–
OMX Tallinn GI	15	–	–	7
BUX	12	13	9	–
OMX Riga GI	12	–	–	8
OMX Vilnius GI	43	–	–	14
WIG	123	37	33	–
SAX	5	–	–	5
SBI	15	–	–	11

Notes: Number of constituents refers to end of year 2005. Listed equity securities in Poland refers to domestic companies only. Listed equity securities in Slovenia refers to equity shares listed on the official market. Listed equity securities for the three Baltic states includes the Baltic Main Market and the Baltic I-list

Sources: Reports of Local Stock Exchanges for December 2005 and Local Exchange Web Sites

index data tends to be used in order to limit data disturbances. However, in this case where the time horizon is less than 10 years for some of the markets, a weekly frequency is appropriate in order to ensure further granularity in the analysis.

Given the common practice in empirical research of using standardised EMDB data rather than local indices, it is relevant to conduct an analysis to test the correlation between the index categories. Table 5.8 includes an analysis of the correlation between monthly local currency returns derived from the EMDB standardised total return indices on the one hand, and the local total return indices on the other hand. Furthermore, each of the correlation values is tested and confirmed to be significantly different from zero.

While the correlation matrix in Table 5.8 provides cross-correlations for all variables, the focus is exclusively on the correlations between each EMDB index and the corresponding local market index.

As can be concluded from the correlation analysis, the EMDB indices and the local indices are highly correlated in each market. The strongest correlation levels are found in Hungary, Poland and the Czech Republic each showing a correlation coefficient of 0.97. Each of these markets involved a sample of over 125 monthly data points.

For the other markets, the correlation coefficient ranges from 0.80 for the Slovak Republic to 0.94 for Latvia. While not quite at the levels of the first three markets, these are nevertheless very strong positive correlations.

A t-test is applied to confirm that all the above discussed correlation values are significantly different from zero at the 1% significance level. Based on these analyses it can be concluded that local exchange index data are highly correlated to the EMDB index data and that local indices can be used within the scope of the study with limited risk of distorting the conclusions.

The indices selected for this study are therefore based on the EMDB indices for the Czech Republic, Hungary and Poland and on local market indices for Estonia, Latvia, Lithuania, the Slovak Republic and Slovenia.

Table 5.8 Correlation matrix of monthly returns in local currency

	IDGTPLTL	WIG	IDGTHUTL	BUX	IDGTCZTL	PX	IDFTLITL	VILSE	IDFTLATL	RIGSE	IDFTESTL	TALSE	IDFTSRTL	SVSM	IDFTSLTL	SKSM
IDGTPLTL	1															
WIG	**0.97**	1														
IDGTHUTL	0.68	0.67	1													
BUX	0.69	0.67	**0.96**	1												
IDGTCZTL	0.56	0.54	0.62	0.62	1											
PX	0.56	0.54	0.62	0.61	**0.97**	1										
IDFTLITL	0.35	0.36	0.38	0.43	0.28	0.27	1									
VILSE	0.30	0.27	0.27	0.30	0.39	0.35	**0.86**	1								
IDFTLATL	0.22	0.28	0.24	0.30	0.21	0.19	0.38	0.11	1							
RIGSE	0.08	0.08	0.04	0.11	0.08	0.05	0.26	0.22	**0.94**	1						
IDFTESTL	0.13	0.09	0.24	0.23	0.25	0.21	0.46	0.44	0.16	0.04	1					
TALSE	0.25	0.23	0.33	0.34	0.30	0.30	0.47	0.41	0.24	0.16	**0.91**	1				
IDFTSRTL	0.14	0.12	0.28	0.30	0.11	0.10	0.54	0.05	0.11	0.03	0.10	0.23	1			
SVSM	0.07	0.08	0.27	0.27	0.06	0.04	0.43	0.01	0.12	0.03	0.06	0.21	**0.90**	1		
IDFTSLTL	0.18	0.11	0.29	0.25	0.29	0.42	0.33	0.21	0.16	0.06	0.63	0.57	−0.26	−0.16	1	
SKSM	0.16	0.20	0.16	0.19	0.24	0.19	0.08	0.10	0.17	0.09	0.28	0.19	−0.02	−0.04	**0.80**	1

Notes: All bolded values are significantly different from 0 at the 1% signficance level
IDGTPLTL = S&P/IFC EMDB Global Total Return Index Poland
WIG = Local Total Return Index Poland
IDGTHUTL = S&P/IFC EMDB Global Total Return Index Hungary
BUX = Local Total Return Index Hungary
IDGTCZTL = S&P/IFC EMDB Global Total Return Index Czech Republic
PX = Local Total Return Index Czech Republic
IDFTLITL = S&P/IFC EMDB Frontier Total Return Index Lithuania
VILSE = Local Total Return Index Lithuania
IDFTLATL = S&P/IFC EMDB Frontier Total Return Index Latvia
RIGSE = Local Total Return Index Latvia
IDFTESTL = S&P/IFC EMDB Frontier Total Return Index Estonia
TALSE = Local Total Return Index Estonia
IDFTSRTL = S&P/IFC EMDB Frontier Total Return Index Slovenia
SVSM = Local Total Return Index Slovenia
IDFTSLTL = S&P/IFC EMDB Frontier Total Return Index Slovak Republic
SKSM = Local Total Return Index Slovak Republic
Source: Bloomberg

5.2.1.3 Concentration and Industry Distribution of Local Equity Market Indices

Prior to conducting analyses around equity index performance, it is relevant to explore the key characteristics of each of the markets. As is illustrated in Table 5.9, the equity indices analysed within the scope of this study are quite concentrated. The single largest company accounts for between 12% and 35% of the total market capitalisation depending on the market. When looking at the market capitalisation of the top five companies, the share ranges from 52% to 100%. The high level of

Table 5.9 Influence of largest five companies in market as of year end 2005

Share of Market Capitalisation	Poland	Lithuania	Slovenia	Czech Republic	Estonia	Latvia	Hungary	Slovak Republic
Share of Largest Company	12.2%	28.1%	16.5%	25.7%	35.0%	32.9%	29.4%	32.0%
Share of Largest Three Companies	33.9%	45.1%	45.8%	62.3%	67.8%	79.4%	75.2%	90.6%
Share of Largest Five Companies	52.0%	58.0%	62.7%	81.7%	81.9%	87.9%	93.9%	100.0%

Notes: Data for all markets refer to the official local market index
Sources: Annual Reports and Web Sites for Respective Local Exchange, 2006

concentration is largely a result of the small number of listed companies present in each market. For example, the number of companies listed on the official market in the Slovak Republic is no more than five as of end of year 2005.

Also in terms of industry concentration, emerging markets with more limited scope tend to be dominated to a certain extent by a single or a small number of industries. Dominance of a few industries could influence the level and character of the index performance. As depicted in Table 5.10, the industry distribution in the eight equity indices within this study are distributed across a number of industries although two or three industries tend to play a more significant role in most markets. Only two indices are dominated by a single industry; the Latvian index is highly influenced by the oil and gas sector and the Slovak index is dominated by the transportation sector.

An important observation from Table 5.10 is that while certain industries are highly influential in more than one market, if observing the indices jointly as a whole, a larger number of industry sectors are represented. This suggests that when including all markets in the analysis, the direct influence of particular industry sectors is reduced.

5.2.1.4 Selected Time Horizon

When analysing market return data, it is important to identify an appropriate time horizon for the analysis. Too long a time horizon results in the inclusion of obsolete data components whereas too short a time horizon implies missing relevant trends. A particular issue in much of the emerging market research is the limited availability of long-term time series. This is particularly the case for the transition economies in Central Europe which did not have any established capital markets or listed companies until well into the 1990s.

The markets incorporated within the scope of this study have experienced both positive and negative cycles over the last 15 years indicating that there are enough time-series data to analyse these markets.

Barry et al. (1998) highlight the occasional criticism of using historical data when analysing emerging markets. The criticism is based on the suggestion that

Table 5.10 Distribution of equity indices by industry sector as of year end 2005

Industry Sector	Poland	Lithuania	Slovenia	Czech Republic	Estonia	Latvia	Hungary	Slovak Republic
Banking	34.4%	7.7%		32.7%			29.4%	
Oil and Gas	20.2%	37.4%	11.0%	4.8%		57.1%	31.2%	27.6%
ICT and Media	18.4%	9.3%	2.2%	23.3%	36.7%		15.5%	
Transport	10.9%	4.0%	15.5%		22.6%	22.3%		63.0%
Mining	4.7%			1.6%		3.0%		
Textile and Furniture	2.9%	1.8%					0.0%	
Food, Beverages and Tobacco	2.1%	5.9%	11.5%	3.9%	4.2%	2.9%	0.4%	
Chemicals	1.7%	4.0%	1.8%				4.5%	
Financial Investments	1.3%	2.4%		1.1%			0.2%	
Pharmaceuticals	0.8%	0.6%	13.3%	4.8%	0.2%	4.1%	12.8%	2.1%
Construction	0.4%	1.0%		0.7%	14.6%		0.2%	
Utilities		21.8%		27.1%	9.0%		4.4%	
Industrial Production		0.2%	17.9%		5.2%	7.4%	0.4%	7.3%
Retail Trade		1.5%	16.4%		7.6%		0.4%	
Manufacturing Electric Goods		1.8%	8.0%			3.1%		
Other	2.4%	0.6%	2.30%				0.7%	

Notes: Data for Poland refer to the 37 largest companies of the WIG index representing 87% of the entire WIG index and is comparable with the 37 companies available in the S&P/IFC EMDB Global Index. Data for all other markets refer to the official local market index. Other category includes Pulp and paper, Tourism and Insurance

Sources: Annual Reports and Web Sites for Respective Local Exchange, 2006

radical reforms make historical emerging market data irrelevant for the future outlook. Barry et al. (1998) oppose this criticism by stating that it is not uncommon that emerging markets implement wide-spread reforms one year only to replace them shortly after their enactment by reforms in the opposite direction.

In the case of the Central European transition economies covered in this study, there are, however, arguments that recent reforms are unlikely to be reverted in the medium term. The EU membership and the associated pressure and support by the EU imply that the recent reforms are likely to remain in the longer term. The effect of these more enduring reforms is that historical data applied within this study might not constitute an appropriate basis for long-term projections. However, this fact does not constitute an issue for this study given the formulation and aim of the hypotheses.

With regard to the selected time horizon, the availability of data for some of the markets in this study implies certain limitations. The number of listed companies in the equity markets of the eight transition economies is limited. For some of the markets, the number of listed companies is less than 20 even at the end of 2004. A limited scope of companies potentially results in a biased sample in terms of industries or company sizes. In addition, the trading volumes and frequency were limited in the initial years of the exchanges' existence. These arguments support the decision to initiate the analysis no earlier than 1996.

5.2.1.5 Description of Local Market Return Data Sample

With the relevant data sources and time horizons described and defined, it is appropriate to provide further description of the local market return sample collected from these sources. This sub-section includes an introduction to the basic descriptive statistics of the sample as well as some of the issues inherent in the analysis of emerging market data samples.

When analysing return data in an international setting involving comparisons based on a single currency, it is important to ensure that currency effects are taken into consideration. Actual market return in the single currency is derived by multiplying the return in local currency with the return effects associated with exchange rate fluctuations. As this study comprises analyses based on both the local currency returns and returns in a single currency, this descriptive sub-section will present the return data based on local currencies and the currency effects separately. Furthermore, in order to facilitate the overview of the market returns, the data are described and presented across two time horizons for each of the eight markets, one prior to the EU accession announcement and another after the announcement.

As depicted in Table 5.11, the number of weekly observations is larger in the time period prior to the announcement for all countries except for Lithuania and Latvia where index time series data were not available before January 2000.

As mentioned earlier in this sub-section, when comparing return levels in a single currency, the total return is the result of the return derived from local currencies and the exchange rate fluctuations. Three currencies are applied to construct single currency comparisons. The first is the USD, which is applied in several analyses to harmonise the units compared, such as in the case of the first research question when local market returns are compared with returns of a world index denominated in USD.

In testing the first research hypothesis, European indices denominated in Euro (EUR) are also applied. In order to establish a single currency unit for the comparative analysis, the exchange rates for the local currencies and the EUR are used. However, the exchange rates for the EUR are only available as of 15 December 1998. Consequently, for the time series data that stretch further back than December 1998, the exchange rates of the EUR are estimated by a third currency, the German Mark (DEM). The DEM is selected based on its important role in Europe in general and its historical dominance with regard to trade with Eastern and Central parts of Europe in particular.

Table 5.12 lists the related returns associated with fluctuations in exchange rates between the local currencies and the USD. When comparing the data in Tables 5.11 and 5.12, it is clear that the means and standard deviations of the returns derived from exchange rates are less than the equivalent values found for the local currency market returns.

Variables measuring the return levels based on a single currency, the USD, are presented in Table 5.13. Compared with the local currency performance two points are worth mentioning. First, when taking the exchange rate fluctuations into account,

Table 5.11 Descriptive statistics of market return data in local currencies

Variable	Market	Time period	Start date	N	Mean	Std dev	Min	Max	Skew-ness	Excess Kurtosis
PLPRANLC	Poland	Pre Ann.	1-Jan-96	363	0.3%	4.4%	−19.3%	15.6%	0.023	1.535
PLPOANLC	Poland	Post Ann.	13-Dec-02	184	0.5%	2.7%	−7.1%	6.8%	−0.272	0.234
HUPRANLC	Hungary	Pre Ann.	1-Jan-96	363	0.6%	4.8%	−27.6%	17.7%	−0.455	3.932
HUPOANLC	Hungary	Post Ann.	13-Dec-02	184	0.6%	3.1%	−10.4%	7.5%	−0.678	1.352
CZPOANLC	Czech Rep.	Pre Ann.	1-Jan-96	358	0.1%	3.0%	−10.6%	11.7%	−0.123	0.945
CZPRANLC	Czech Rep.	Post Ann.	13-Dec-02	144	0.9%	2.7%	−10.5%	8.2%	−0.632	1.976
LTPRANLC	Lithuania	Pre Ann.	7-Jan-00	152	−0.1%	2.0%	−6.8%	5.8%	0.085	1.067
LTPOANLC	Lithuania	Post Ann.	13-Dec-02	184	0.9%	2.6%	−7.7%	10.3%	0.190	1.682
LVPRANLC	Latvia	Pre Ann.	7-Jan-00	153	0.5%	5.0%	−25.0%	27.4%	0.885	12.785
LVPOANLC	Latvia	Post Ann.	13-Dec-02	184	0.6%	2.3%	−12.0%	9.0%	−0.438	5.322
ESPRANLC	Estonia	Pre Ann.	7-Jun-96	338	0.4%	5.7%	−22.5%	36.3%	0.390	7.508
ESPOANLC	Estonia	Post Ann.	13-Dec-02	184	0.6%	2.2%	−6.8%	9.2%	0.440	3.247
SVPRANLC	Slovenia	Pre Ann.	1-Jan-96	360	0.3%	3.5%	−17.0%	22.2%	0.448	10.035
SVPOANLC	Slovenia	Post Ann.	13-Dec-02	180	0.3%	1.4%	−3.2%	8.2%	1.231	5.033
SKPRANLC	Slovak Rep.	Pre Ann.	5-Jan-96	343	0.0%	3.4%	−9.3%	20.7%	0.388	4.482
SKPOANLC	Slovak Rep.	Post Ann.	13-Dec-02	164	0.6%	2.7%	−6.6%	11.8%	0.632	1.961

Notes: Market data on Poland, Hungary and the Czech Reublic refer to IFC/S&P EMDB Global indices. Market data on the remaining markets refer to local total return indices. Ann. refers to 13 December 2002 when the accession negotiations ended and the timing and terms of the EU accession were announced

Source: Index data are sourced from Bloomberg

Table 5.12 Descriptive statistics of exchange rate driven return data

Variable	Local Currency	Time period	Start date	N	Mean	Std dev	Range	Min	Max	Skewness	Excess Kurtosis
USPLPRAN	Polish Zloty	Pre Ann.	1-Jan-96	363	–0.11%	1.34%	12.26%	–7.86%	4.40%	–0.8447	5.0952
USPLPOAN	Polish Zloty	Post Ann.	13-Dec-02	184	0.11%	1.70%	8.76%	–4.58%	4.18%	–0.1669	–0.1733
USHUPRAN	Hungarian Forint	Pre Ann.	1-Jan-96	363	–0.14%	1.26%	9.04%	–3.67%	5.36%	0.5874	1.7618
USHUPOAN	Hungarian Forint	Post Ann.	13-Dec-02	184	0.04%	1.75%	9.38%	–5.77%	3.60%	–0.4045	0.1902
USCZPRAN	Czech Koruna	Pre Ann.	1-Jan-96	363	–0.03%	1.64%	14.88%	–4.64%	10.25%	0.9129	5.0246
USCZPOAN	Czech Koruna	Post Ann.	13-Dec-02	184	0.18%	1.58%	8.94%	–4.45%	4.49%	–0.1806	0.0269
USLTPRAN	Lithuanian Litas	Pre Ann.	7-Jan-00	154	0.11%	0.75%	6.33%	–2.15%	4.19%	1.3419	7.0269
USLTPOAN	Lithuanian Litas	Post Ann.	13-Dec-02	184	0.13%	1.33%	6.25%	–3.42%	2.83%	–0.2457	–0.4563
USLVPRAN	Latvian Lats	Pre Ann.	7-Jan-00	154	–0.01%	0.58%	3.03%	–1.61%	1.42%	0.1416	–0.1237
USLVPOAN	Latvian Lats	Post Ann.	13-Dec-02	184	0.05%	0.96%	5.73%	–3.27%	2.46%	–0.3664	0.6155
USESPRAN	Estonian Kroon	Pre Ann.	7-Jun-96	345	–0.07%	1.36%	12.03%	–6.73%	5.30%	0.0376	1.7962
USESPOAN	Estonian Kroon	Post Ann.	13-Dec-02	184	0.13%	1.33%	6.25%	–3.42%	2.83%	–0.2455	–0.4564
USSVPRAN	Slovenian Tolar	Pre Ann.	1-Jan-96	363	–0.14%	1.30%	8.84%	–4.43%	4.41%	0.2852	0.5087
USSVPOAN	Slovenian Tolar	Post Ann.	13-Dec-02	184	0.10%	1.32%	7.33%	–3.76%	3.56%	–0.2698	–0.2447
USSKPRAN	Slovak Koruna	Pre Ann.	5-Jan-96	362	–0.08%	1.31%	12.45%	–4.86%	7.59%	0.4963	3.3431
USSKPOAN	Slovak Koruna	Post Ann.	13-Dec-02	184	0.18%	1.56%	8.55%	–4.96%	3.60%	–0.2683	–0.3280

Notes: Ann. refers to 13 December 2002 when the accession negotiations ended and the timing and terms were announced.

Sources: Exchange rates are sourced from www.oanda.com

Table 5.13 Descriptive statistics of market return data in USD

Variable	Market	Time period	Start date	N	Mean	Std dev	Min	Max	Skew-ness	Excess Kurtosis
PLPRANLC	Poland	Pre-Ann.	1-Jan-96	363	0.2%	4.9%	–20.3%	15.2%	–0.124	1.330
PLPOANLC	Poland	Post-Ann.	13-Dec-02	184	0.6%	3.5%	–9.5%	10.6%	–0.310	0.372
HUPRANLC	Hungary	Pre-Ann.	1-Jan-96	363	0.4%	4.9%	–28.4%	17.5%	–0.476	4.012
HUPOANLC	Hungary	Post-Ann.	13-Dec-02	184	0.6%	3.8%	–11.6%	9.9%	–0.726	1.321
CZPOANLC	Czech-Rep.	Pre-Ann.	1-Jan-96	363	0.1%	3.4%	–10.3%	14.4%	0.011	0.762
CZPRANLC	Czech-Rep.	Post-Ann.	13-Dec-02	184	0.9%	3.2%	–11.8%	10.5%	–0.638	1.906
LTPRANLC	Lithuania	Pre-Ann.	7-Jan-00	153	0.0%	2.1%	–6.8%	5.8%	0.096	0.924
LTPOANLC	Lithuania	Post-Ann.	13-Dec-02	184	1.0%	2.7%	–8.8%	10.9%	–0.050	1.320
LVPRANLC	Latvia	Pre-Ann.	7-Jan-00	153	0.5%	5.1%	–25.6%	27.2%	0.857	12.300
LVPOANLC	Latvia	Post-Ann.	13-Dec-02	184	0.6%	2.4%	–13.2%	8.2%	–0.349	5.668
ESPRANLC	Estonia	Pre-Ann.	7-Jun-96	340	0.3%	5.8%	–22.9%	37.2%	0.376	7.741
ESPOANLC	Estonia	Post-Ann.	13-Dec-02	184	0.7%	2.4%	–6.3%	8.9%	0.368	1.202
SVPRANLC	Slovenia	Pre-Ann.	1-Jan-96	361	0.1%	3.8%	–18.4%	21.8%	0.152	7.472
SVPOANLC	Slovenia	Post-Ann.	13-Dec-02	180	0.3%	1.9%	–4.6%	9.6%	0.577	2.510
SKPRANLC	Slovak-Rep.	Pre-Ann.	5-Jan-96	344	–0.1%	3.6%	–10.6%	18.5%	0.438	2.163
SKPOANLC	Slovak-Rep.	Post-Ann.	13-Dec-02	166	0.7%	3.2%	–9.4%	13.5%	0.562	2.299

Notes: Market data on Poland, Hungary and the Czech Reublic refer to IFC/S&P EMDB Global indices. Market data on the remaining markets refer to local total return indices. Ann. refers to 13 December 2002 when the accession negotiations ended and the timing and terms of the EU accession were announced.

Source: Index data are sourced from Bloomberg

return levels are consistently higher for the period after the announcement in each of the markets. Second, the volatility, measured by the standard deviation, is higher for the USD-denominated time series vis-à-vis the local currency time series.

In the following sub-sections, a series of tests to better understand the data are conducted. Given that the returns based on local currencies appear in most of the analyses either directly or indirectly and that these returns represent the major portion of the overall return, the tests conducted in the subsequent sub-sections are based on return data in local currencies.

Test of Randomness

The market efficiency hypothesis in its semi-strong form asserts that asset prices incorporate all currently available public information and that future prices cannot be predicted (Fama, 1965). This would suggest that equity returns are randomly distributed. However, there is also empirical evidence suggesting that equity returns are not randomly distributed (Lo and MacKinlay, 1988).

As the randomness of the distribution has an impact on how the sample can be analysed, it is appropriate to conduct a test of randomness. The Wald-Wolfowitz test, a non-parametric test that explicitly evaluates the hypothesis of a time series being random, is applied. Given that the alternative is two-sided, the hypothesis of randomness is rejected at the 5% significance level if the Z-value of the test is either below −1.96 or above 1.96. As can be derived from Table 5.14, for 13 of the 16 time series the hypothesis of randomness cannot be rejected at the 5% level. Only for the pre-announcement time series for the Czech Republic and for both pre- and post-announcement time series for Estonia, can the hypotheses of randomness be rejected. Descriptions of the variable names appearing in Table 5.14 can be found in Table 5.11 and in Appendix 6D.

The assumption of a random sample is required for the central limit theorem to be applicable. The central limit theorem suggests that when the underlying variables are random, independent and follow an identical distribution, the distribution of the t-statistic tends to be standard normal when n becomes large (Newbold, 1991). Generally, a sample size of 30 is perceived as large (DeFusco et al., 2004). The above described results confirm that these samples are dominantly random which suggests that the central limit theorem can be applied. However, rather than relying on the central limit theorem, it would also be possible to directly test whether the return samples actually follow the normal distribution.

Test of Normality

Understanding the distribution of the sample is relevant as it influences the choice of approach in analysing the sample data. One factor indicating that a distribution is not normal is the presence of higher moments, such as skewness and excess kurtosis.

When observing the last two columns in Table 5.11, it becomes clear that some of the time series samples show a certain level of skewness and excess kurtosis compared

Table 5.14 Runs test of randomness of market returns in local currencies

	PLPRANLC	PLPOANLC	HUPRANLC	HUPOANLC	CZPRANLC	CZPOANLC	LTPRANLC	LTPOANLC
Test Value	0.001	0.006	0.004	0.008	0.003	0.012	0.003	0.007
Cases < Test Value	181	92	181	92	179	72	76	92
Cases > = Test Value	182	92	182	92	179	72	76	92
Total Cases	363	184	363	184	358	144	152	184
Number of Runs	182	96	187	90	143	82	72	90
Z	−0.052	0.444	0.473	−0.444	**−3.917**	1.505	−0.814	−0.444
Asymp. Sig. (2-tailed)	0.958	0.657	0.636	0.657	0.000	0.132	0.416	0.657
a	Median							

	LVPRANLC	LVPOANLC	ESPRANLC	ESPOANLC	SVPRANLC	SVPOANLC	SKPRANLC	SKPOANLC
Test Value	0.002	0.006	0.002	0.004	0.001	0.001	0.000	0.004
Cases < Test Value	76	92	169	92	180	90	171	82
Cases > = Test Value	77	92	169	92	180	90	172	82
Total Cases	153	184	338	184	360	180	343	164
Number of Runs	84	87	142	77	163	80	169	75
Z	1.055	−0.887	**−3.051**	**−2.366**	−1.900	−1.644	−0.378	−1.253
Asymp. Sig. (2-tailed)	0.291	0.375	0.002	0.018	0.057	0.100	0.705	0.210
a	Median							

to a normally distributed sample. As discussed by Bekaert et al. (1998) emerging market data are not necessarily fully described by mean and variance alone.

The column on skewness in Table 5.11 shows a mix of positive and negative skewness. In a sample of over 100 taken from a normal distribution, a sample skewness coefficient above 0.5 or below –0.5 would be considered unusually large (DeFusco et al., 2004). In Table 5.11, six of the 16 time series are considered to have unusually large skewness in this sample. Furthermore, when comparing the time horizons, there is a trend of declining or increasingly negative skewness which, from the perspective of the investor, is likely to be perceived as something negative since positive skewness would imply higher probability of positive returns.

In terms of excess kurtosis depicted in Table 5.11 three observations are noteworthy. First, excess kurtosis seemingly constitutes a larger issue than skewness in this sample given that an excess kurtosis of over 1.00 in either direction is considered unusually large (DeFusco et al., 2004). Such an unusually large level is found for all but three time series in this sample. Second, the excess kurtosis is positive for all markets and time series. This suggests a leptokurtic distribution corresponding to a concentration of observations very close to the mean as well as in the tails. This tendency is particularly clear when looking at the distribution of Slovenian returns illustrated in Fig. 5.1. Third, just as observed by Bekaert et al. (1998), the

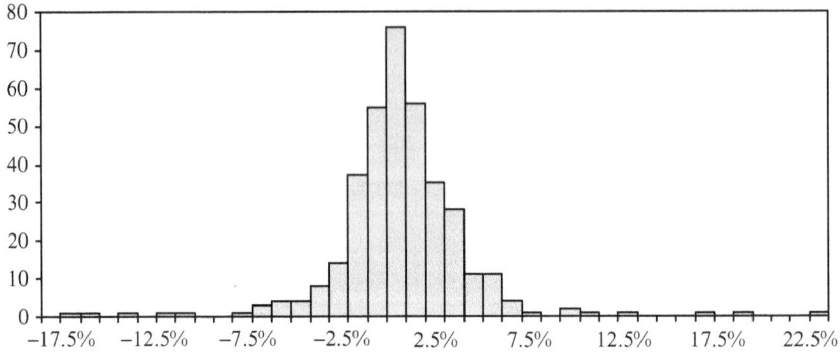

Fig. 5.1 Histogram of Slovenian weekly market returns prior to accession announcement based on local currencies
Source: Return data are sourced from Bloomberg

excess kurtosis levels tend to change over time in all of the markets. This time-varying return distribution is to be expected for markets that transition from segmentation to integration (Bekaert and Harvey, 1995). In this sample, the excess kurtosis for all but two time series declines, sometimes significantly, when comparing data before the announcement with data after the announcement.

The important question that arises is whether the presence of excess kurtosis and a certain level of skewness impact the applicability of models based on the normal distribution. In their study of 19 emerging markets, Bekaert et al. (1998) apply the Kolmogorov–Smirnov test of normality and find that the hypothesis of normality is rejected in more than half of the cases.

The hypothesis of normality is rejected at the 5% significance level when the Kolmogorov–Smirnov Z value is below −1.96 or above 1.96. When applying the Kolmogorov–Smirnov test to the sample of local currency returns, the hypothesis of normal distribution is rejected in only three out of 16 time series, as is illustrated in Table 5.15. The time series that are rejected at the 5% level include the pre-accession time series of Latvia, Estonia and Slovenia. At the 1% level, the hypothesis of normal distribution cannot be rejected in any of the time series.

The conclusion is that despite the presence of certain levels of skewness and excess kurtosis, the data samples within this study can be assumed to have a normal distribution. This facilitates the application of specific statistical tests which are applied in the analysis of the research hypotheses.

5.2.1.6 Effects of Survivorship Biases in Equity Indices

In the analysis of equity index samples, survivorship biases could influence the accuracy of data over time. Survivorship bias refers to the fact that an index is inaccurately boosted by the fact that poorly performing companies go out of business and are consequently removed from the index while the well performing companies

Table 5.15 Kolmogorov-Smirnov test of normality of weekly market returns based on local currencies

		PLPRANLC	PLPOANLC	HUPRANLC	HUPOANLC	CZPRANLC	CZPOANLC	LTPRANLC	LTPOANLC
N		363	184	363	184	358	144	152	184
Normal Parameters	Mean	0.3%	0.5%	0.6%	0.6%	0.1%	0.9%	−0.1%	0.9%
	Std. Dev.	4.4%	2.7%	4.8%	3.1%	3.0%	2.7%	2.0%	2.6%
Most Extreme Differences	Absolute	7.7%	5.0%	7.7%	5.4%	4.1%	8.2%	5.5%	5.5%
	Positive	7.7%	3.5%	4.8%	3.3%	3.6%	4.8%	5.5%	4.8%
	Negative	−4.9%	−5.0%	−7.7%	−5.4%	−4.1%	−8.2%	−4.3%	−5.5%
Kolmogorov-Smirnov Z		1.468	0.679	1.468	0.731	0.768	0.983	0.678	0.746
Asymp. Sig. (2-tailed)		0.027	0.745	0.027	0.658	0.597	0.289	0.747	0.635
		LVPRANLC	**LVPOANLC**	**ESPRANLC**	**ESPOANLC**	**SVPRANLC**	**SVPOANLC**	**SKPRANLC**	**SKPOANLC**
N		153	184	338	184	360	180	343	164
Normal Parameters	Mean	0.5%	0.6%	0.4%	0.6%	0.3%	0.3%	0.0%	0.6%
	Std. Dev.	5.0%	2.3%	5.7%	2.2%	3.5%	1.4%	3.4%	2.7%
Most Extreme Differences	Absolute	20.0%	8.2%	11.1%	9.4%	11.6%	6.1%	6.7%	7.3%
	Positive	20.0%	8.2%	11.1%	9.1%	10.9%	6.1%	6.7%	7.3%
	Negative	−17.6%	−7.1%	−10.8%	−9.4%	−11.6%	−4.6%	−6.0%	−4.7%
Kolmogorov-Smirnov Z		**2.473**	1.113	**2.032**	1.278	**2.200**	0.816	1.235	0.935
Asymp. Sig. (2-tailed)		0.000	0.168	0.001	0.076	0.000	0.519	0.095	0.346

remain. A bias can also occur when a company changes in terms of size and moves from, for example, a mid-cap index to a large-cap index.

The indices applied within the scope of this study incorporate a large portion of the market capitalisation in each respective market. The EMDB Global indices cover at least 75% of the total market capitalisation and the local indices cover an even larger share. As there are no explicit size categories involved in the indices used within this study, the effects of changing company sizes are limited. Furthermore, the extensive scope of the indices in terms of market capitalisation implies that also poorly performing companies are largely included, at least until they go out of business or are removed from trading. Consequently, survivorship bias is not eliminated but its impact is not worse than for indices in the developed market against which the emerging indices are compared in some of the analyses. Given that the performance characteristics of the emerging market indices are compared with other indices or the same indices at different time horizons, disturbing effects on many of the analyses are expected to be limited.

5.2.1.7 Bias Effects of Inflation

Another potential source of bias when analysing certain quantitative data is inflation. The index return data presented and analysed in this study are indirectly derived from closing prices on the local financial exchanges. As such they are denominated in nominal terms and are fully influenced by prevailing inflation rates. Inflation in emerging markets has historically been significant and could potentially distort the comparisons within and across markets, particularly when comparing with data from markets with low inflation levels.

The per cent changes in the harmonised consumer price index (CPI) (Eurostat, 2006) depicted in Table 5.16 provide a proxy for the prevailing inflation rates which are likely to affect return levels. Three observations are noteworthy.

First, annual change in CPI in the eight markets that accessed the EU in 2004 is less than that in other transition economies. Comparing with Romania and Turkey, the per cent change in CPI of the 2004 EU members is significantly lower with the exception of the first 6 months of 2006.

Second, annual change in CPI for the 2004 EU members has decreased significantly over the last 10 years. The period from 1996 to 2000 demonstrated a higher level of change compared to the more recent years. Assuming that asset prices denominated in local currencies are affected by inflation, the difference in CPI changes implies that nominal return levels in the 1990s have been boosted more positively than those in more recent years.

Table 5.16 Annual per cent change in harmonised indices of consumer prices

	1996	1997	1998	1999	2000	2001	2002	2003	2004	2005	2006 1H
Czech Rep.	6.0%	9.4%	5.8%	2.5%	4.0%	3.9%	0.1%	1.0%	2.5%	1.9%	0.9%
Estonia	9.6%	10.9%	5.2%	3.7%	5.0%	4.2%	2.7%	1.2%	4.8%	3.6%	2.3%
Hungary	14.7%	18.6%	10.1%	11.4%	10.0%	6.8%	4.9%	5.6%	5.5%	3.3%	3.1%
Latvia	9.0%	6.4%	2.7%	3.0%	1.7%	3.2%	1.5%	3.5%	7.4%	7.1%	2.8%
Lithuania	12.2%	8.5%	3.1%	0.4%	1.6%	2.1%	−0.9%	−1.3%	2.8%	3.0%	1.6%
Poland	14.5%	13.2%	8.6%	9.8%	8.4%	3.5%	0.8%	1.6%	4.4%	0.8%	1.2%
Slovenia	7.5%	8.8%	6.4%	8.1%	8.9%	7.1%	7.1%	4.7%	3.3%	2.4%	2.6%
Slovak Rep.	4.7%	6.1%	5.8%	14.1%	8.4%	6.7%	3.2%	9.4%	5.8%	3.9%	1.3%
EU 15	2.0%	1.6%	1.0%	1.6%	2.3%	1.9%	2.2%	1.8%	2.2%	2.1%	1.9%
Bulgaria	n.a.	n.a.	1.6%	7.0%	11.3%	4.8%	3.8%	5.6%	4.0%	6.5%	2.1%
Romania	55.0%	151.6%	40.6%	54.8%	40.7%	30.3%	17.8%	14.1%	9.3%	8.7%	1.7%
Turkey	67.2%	98.8%	66.5%	64.9%	37.2%	74.6%	30.2%	17.4%	9.8%	7.1%	4.1%

Notes: n.a. refers to not available. Values for 1996 refer to end of January to end of year whereas for all other years except 2006, values refer to full 12 months

Source: Eurostat, 2006

Third, while the inflation levels are large in the early years when observed on an annual basis, the average impact on the weekly data largely applied within this study is derived by dividing the annual data with 52 weeks.

In line with previous emerging market research (Bekaert and Harvey, 2000), the analysis in this study will be kept at the nominal level. Just as no direct measure is taken against impact of survivorship bias, no measure is taken against inflation effect. Given that these effects are providing positive effects in different time horizons, it is reasonable to assume the overall effect on the analysis is reduced although not eliminated.

5.2.2 Return Data on Global and European Indices

In determining whether the EU accession has had an impact on the level of co-movement between emerging markets and global as well as pan-European markets, return data for relevant global and European indices are required. The reference indices have already been defined in Chap. 4 and the aim in this sub-section is to provide an overview of the data samples.

An initial overview is provided in Fig. 5.2 where the indexed weekly closing values are presented. The values are indexed to 100 either at the beginning of 1996 or when the index was initiated if data were not available in 1996. As is illustrated in Fig. 5.2, the closing prices went through a trend of increasing prices between early 1996 and mid-2000 with the exception of a dramatic decline in the autumn of 1998. In the period between 2001 and early 2003, all three indices decline steadily only to start regaining again in the subsequent months.

A more exact description of the data samples is provided in Table 5.17. An interesting observation when comparing with the return data from the eight transition economies is that the mean and variance in the transition market indices are all superior to those of the indices in the developed markets represented in Table 5.17.

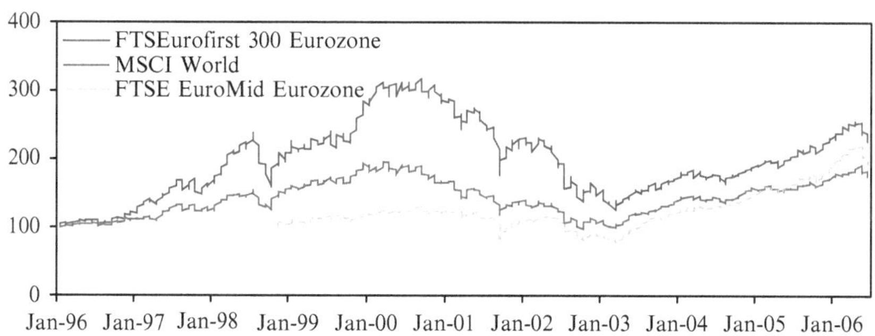

Fig. 5.2 Closing values of MSCI World and selected FTSE indices
Notes: The MSCI and FTSEurofirst 300 indices are set to 100 at the beginning of January 1996
The FTSE EuroMid index is set to 100 on 13 November 1998
Sources: Bloomberg (2006)

Table 5.17 Descriptive statistics of returns of global and European indices and local markets

Variable	Index	Start date	N	Mean	Std Dev	Min	Max	Skew-ness	Excess Kurtosis
MSCIALL	MSCI World	1-Jan-96	547	0.12%	2.04%	-9.48%	8.16%	-0.1946	1.7855
FT3ECALL	FTSEurofirst 300	5-Jan-96	536	0.17%	2.59%	-9.27%	13.80%	-0.0277	2.0248
MOEBALL	FTSE EuroMid Eurozone	20-Nov-98	374	0.15%	2.04%	-11.36%	9.34%	-0.6911	4.8715
PLLCALL	Poland	1-Jan-96	547	0.34%	3.94%	-19.27%	15.58%	-0.0326	2.0546
HULCALL	Hungary	1-Jan-96	547	0.56%	4.26%	-27.56%	17.74%	-0.5025	4.4640
CZLCALL	Czech Rep.	1-Jan-96	547	0.29%	2.98%	-11.42%	11.72%	-0.3403	1.2216
LTLCALL	Lithuania	7-Jan-00	337	0.42%	2.37%	-7.65%	10.27%	0.2946	1.7136
LVLCALL	Latvia	7-Jan-00	337	0.56%	3.79%	-24.99%	27.37%	0.8636	19.4886
ESLCALL	Estonia	7-Jun-96	524	0.46%	4.76%	-22.48%	36.29%	0.4115	11.0341
SVLCALL	Slovenia	1-Jan-96	541	0.26%	2.99%	-17.04%	22.17%	0.5348	13.9022
SKLCALL	Slovak Rep.	5-Jan-96	510	0.20%	3.19%	-9.26%	20.74%	0.7988	4.1588

Source: Index data are sourced from Bloomberg

This is in line with financial theory (Sharpe, 1964) suggesting premium returns for higher levels of volatility.

A runs test is conducted to test whether the samples from the MSCI and FTSE are randomly distributed. Based on the runs test, the hypothesis of random distribution cannot be rejected at the 5% significance level for the MSCI or the FTSEurofirst 300 indices. However, the hypothesis is rejected at the 5% level for the FTSE EuroMid Eurozone Index. Table 5.18 provides further details of the runs test.

Also, a Kolmogorov–Smirnov test of normality is conducted to confirm that the sample distribution can be assumed to be normal. Based on the results in Table 5.19, there are suggestions that all samples could be assumed to be normally distributed.

Based on the tests of randomness and normality, no barriers hindering the use of the return data relating to the global and European reference indices are found. The focus is therefore shifted to the data relating to the global and local macroeconomic factors applied in the test of the second research hypothesis.

5.2.3 Data on Global and Local Macroeconomic Factors

The identification and definition of relevant macroeconomic factors were conducted in Sect. 4.1.2.1. This section provides an overview of the empirical details related to the samples for the respective factors. Data for most of the global and local factors are available on a monthly basis as the most granular frequency level. This implies that the local market return data samples need to be revisited although this time on a monthly basis which matches the availability of the macroeconomic data.

Table 5.18 Runs test of randomness of global and European index returns

	MSCIALL	FT3ECALL	MOEBALL
Test Value	0.0025	0.0031	0.0037
Cases < Test Value	273	262	187
Cases > = Test Value	274	263	187
Total Cases	547	525	374
Number of Runs	264	259	169
Z	−0.8986	−0.3931	−1.9676
Asymp. Sig. (2-tailed)	0.3688	0.6943	0.0491
a	Median		

Notes: MSCIALL, FT3ECALL and MOEBALL refer to the MSCI World, FTSEurofirst 300, FTSE EuroMid Eurozone indices respectively

Table 5.19 Kolmogorov-Smirnov test of normality of global and European index returns

		MSCIALL	FT3ECALL	MOEBALL
N		547	525	374
Normal Parameters	Mean	0.12%	0.15%	0.15%
	Std. Dev.	2.04%	2.75%	2.04%
Most Extreme Differences	Absolute	4.44%	4.79%	6.28%
	Positive	3.79%	4.22%	6.02%
	Negative	−4.44%	−4.79%	−6.28%
Kolmogorov-Smirnov Z		1.039	1.098	1.214
Asymp. Sig. (2-tailed)		0.230	0.179	0.105

Notes: MSCIALL, FT3ECALL and MOEBALL refer to the MSCI World, FTSEurofirst 300, FTSE EuroMid Eurozone indices respectively

5.2.3.1 Global Macroeconomic Factors

Six global macroeconomic factors were identified as relevant for this analysis in sub-section 4.1.2.1. The six global factors include the world oil price, the world industrial production, the world equity market return, the world inflation, the world commodity prices and the US interest rate.

Each global factor is estimated using an index or a particular parameter. The commodity prices are estimated based on an index containing all commodity categories available from IMF. The oil price is derived from IMF's Spot Crude Petroleum Index based on an equal weighting of the prices of three different petroleum categories in USD per barrel (IMF, 2006a). The industry production refers to the index of production of total industry for all OECD members (OECD, 2006). The equity return is estimated by the return of the MSCI World Index. The inflation is derived from the average consumer price index of all of the members of the OECD. Finally, the US interest rate, which acts as a proxy for the world interest rate, refers to the 3-month money market interest rates.

Table 5.20 Overview of descriptive statistics of the global macroeconomic factors

Variable	Global Factor	N	Mean	Std dev	Min	Max	Skewness	Excess Kurtosis
COMMPR	Commodity Price Change	125	0.84%	4.57%	−11.49%	10.57%	−0.240	−0.183
INDPRD	Change in Industry Production	125	0.20%	0.43%	−1.03%	1.28%	−0.396	0.047
OILPRIC	Oil Price Change	125	1.40%	8.06%	−21.80%	22.39%	−0.167	−0.002
USINT	US Interest Rate	125	4.11%	1.90%	1.11%	6.79%	−0.392	−1.434
WLDCPI	Inflation Rate	124	0.27%	0.20%	−0.37%	0.76%	−0.130	−0.111
WLDRET	Equity Return Rate	125	0.56%	4.13%	−13.45%	8.91%	−0.616	0.624

The starting and ending months of the data samples are January 1996 and May 2006 respectively. Table 5.20 provides an overview of the descriptive statistics of the selected global macroeconomic factors.

As can be detected in Table 5.20, there have been large swings in some of the variables within this time horizon. Monthly per cent changes in the oil price index declined over 21% 1 month and rose over 22% another month. Significant monthly per cent changes are also found in the commodity price index and the world equity returns. These changes reflect the rapid movements in raw material prices, particularly that of metal and oil products. As is expected, the monthly per cent changes in the global industry production index and the global consumer price index as well as the changes in the US interest rates are more limited.

5.2.3.2 Local Macroeconomic Factors

In addition to the global factors, six local macroeconomic factors were identified in sub-section 4.1.2.1. The local factors include short-term interest rates, inflation, industrial production, money supply, balance of trade as well as the exchange rate to the USD. The local macroeconomic data are collected from various sources due to reasons related to data availability but no more than two sources are used per factor. The definitions of the factors are largely derived from specifications applied within the main source, the International Financial Statistics database (IMF, 2006b). Despite the application of two sources for many of the local factors, the definitions are largely homogenous. Only in one instance do the definitions applied for a local factor differ somewhat. This instance relates to interest rates where the limitations of data have implied the use of three different short-term unregulated interest rates. Given that the main point is the movement of the interest rates rather than the actual value for any one month, the trends will be identified with limited disturbances using the three different interest rate definitions. Table 5.21 provides an overview of the descriptive statistics of the local economic factors.

Table 5.21 Overview of descriptive statistics of the local macroeconomic factors

Variable	Factor	Market	N	Mean	Std Dev	Min	Max	Skewness	Excess Kurtosis
CZINT	Interest rate	Czech Rep	125	6.80%	5.18%	1.75%	25.99%	1.097	0.526
CZINFL	Inflation	Czech Rep	125	0.35%	0.67%	−0.78%	4.02%	2.621	10.144
CZINPR	Industrial prod.	Czech Rep	124	0.71%	8.43%	−17.24%	18.04%	−0.241	−0.391
CZMOSU	Money supply	Czech Rep	125	0.90%	3.15%	−10.49%	24.37%	2.626	25.499
CZTRBA	Trade balance	Czech Rep	125	−10,026	8,491	−30,696	12,306	0.292	0.013
CZEXCH	Exchange rate	Czech Rep	124	0.23%	3.38%	−6.51%	9.87%	0.290	−0.254
ESINT	Interest rate	Estonia	125	5.97%	3.82%	2.32%	18.71%	1.551	2.318
ESINFL	Inflation	Estonia	125	0.46%	0.61%	−0.49%	3.45%	2.200	7.932
ESINPR	Industrial prod.	Estonia	100	0.56%	0.82%	−1.72%	2.43%	−1.024	1.182
ESMOSU	Money supply	Estonia	125	1.56%	2.73%	−7.56%	11.36%	0.052	1.879
ESTRBA	Trade balance	Estonia	124	−1,853	698	−5,366	−700	−1.175	3.998
ESEXCH	Exchange rate	Estonia	124	−0.01%	2.82%	−6.31%	9.83%	0.444	0.396
HUINT	Interest rate	Hungary	125	11.33%	4.81%	3.89%	23.47%	0.677	−0.578
HUINFL	Inflation	Hungary	125	0.75%	0.79%	−0.39%	4.39%	1.619	4.328
HUINPR	Industrial prod.	Hungary	124	0.98%	8.90%	−17.25%	26.19%	0.430	−0.053
HUMOSU	Money supply	Hungary	100	1.20%	3.52%	−9.50%	11.37%	−0.586	2.521
HUTRBA	Trade balance	Hungary	125	−245	129	−831	37	−1.096	2.761
HUEXCH	Exchange rate	Hungary	124	−0.25%	2.86%	−8.97%	9.97%	0.473	1.008
LAINT	Interest rate	Latvia	109	5.48%	2.07%	2.71%	12.81%	1.226	1.589
LAINFL	Inflation	Latvia	125	0.42%	0.61%	−1.11%	3.52%	0.957	4.957
LAINPR	Industrial prod.	Latvia	124	0.27%	1.14%	−8.96%	2.42%	−4.443	34.350
LAMOSU	Money supply	Latvia	125	1.50%	2.44%	−5.39%	8.40%	−0.274	0.923
LATRBA	Trade balance	Latvia	123	−89	45	−228	−28	−1.041	0.580
LAEXCH	Exchange rate	Latvia	124	0.03%	1.48%	−3.93%	3.26%	0.017	−0.065
LIINT	Interest rate	Lithuania	125	5.54%	5.81%	0.64%	25.00%	2.160	4.230
LIINFL	Inflation	Lithuania	125	0.26%	0.65%	−0.80%	3.15%	1.728	5.195
LIINPR	Industrial prod.	Lithuania	112	1.24%	9.73%	−22.73%	36.67%	0.460	0.863
LIMOSU	Money supply	Lithuania	125	1.33%	3.61%	−9.11%	11.68%	−0.251	1.405
LITRBA	Trade balance	Lithuania	125	−649	235	−1,483	−74	−0.659	1.305

(continued)

Table 5.21 (continued)

Variable	Factor	Market	N	Mean	Std Dev	Min	Max	Skewness	Excess Kurtosis
LIEXCH	Exchange rate	Lithuania	124	0.33%	1.73%	–4.46%	6.29%	1.026	2.857
PLINT	Interest rate	Poland	125	13.73%	7.07%	4.12%	25.74%	0.059	–1.496
PLINFL	Inflation	Poland	125	0.54%	0.70%	–0.59%	3.39%	1.316	2.984
PLINPR	Industrial prod.	Poland	125	0.76%	6.63%	–19.89%	20.91%	0.291	0.459
PLMOSU	Money supply	Poland	120	1.35%	3.53%	–10.05%	15.54%	–0.035	2.859
PLTRBA	Trade balance	Poland	123	–89	45	–228	–28	–1.041	0.580
PLEXCH	Exchange rate	Poland	124	–0.10%	3.04%	–8.05%	8.77%	–0.036	0.413
SNINT	Interest rate	Slovenia	125	6.91%	3.10%	3.31%	18.73%	1.630	3.223
SNINFL	Inflation	Slovenia	125	0.53%	0.49%	–0.64%	1.66%	–0.007	0.100
SNINPR	Industrial prod.	Slovenia	125	1.04%	11.51%	–21.28%	32.68%	0.542	0.380
SNMOSU	Money supply	Slovenia	123	1.67%	4.75%	–10.71%	29.68%	1.595	9.369
SNTRBA	Trade balance	Slovenia	125	–19,287	12,592	–73,415	5,379	–1.071	2.496
SNEXCH	Exchange rate	Slovenia	124	–0.23%	2.81%	–6.53%	9.19%	0.264	–0.019
SKINT	Interest rate	Slovak Rep	125	8.45%	4.58%	2.25%	18.57%	0.517	–0.935
SKINFL	Inflation	Slovak Rep	125	0.56%	0.94%	–0.37%	5.69%	3.425	13.770
SKINPR	Industrial prod.	Slovak Rep	125	0.60%	6.32%	–11.55%	17.15%	0.177	–0.550
SKMOSU	Money supply	Slovak Rep	125	1.07%	4.94%	–11.58%	37.79%	3.098	24.145
SKTRBA	Trade balance	Slovak Rep	125	–5,472	16,773	–31,717	102,354	5.657	33.557
SKEXCH	Exchange rate	Slovak Rep	124	0.06%	2.76%	–5.49%	8.13%	0.489	0.021

5.2.3.3 Corresponding Market Return Data

As indicated in the previous sub-sections, the availability of macroeconomic factors is largely limited to a monthly frequency. Consequently, the market return data need to be adapted to a corresponding frequency for this analysis. This sub-section provides a brief introduction to the local monthly market return data applied in the analysis which was previously introduced in weekly form.

As was introduced in Table 5.6, the local market data can be sourced from primarily two sources, the EMDB Index or a local exchange index, which have different levels of availability. The choice of complementing the EMDB data with local exchange index data was primarily based on the lack of daily or weekly frequencies for the markets in the EMDB Frontier Index. However, given that this particular analysis must be conducted on a monthly basis, the opportunity to apply the EMDB index more extensively appears. The monthly local market return data is therefore based primarily on the EMDB Global and Frontier Indices but is complemented by local exchange index data for the Slovak Republic, where EMDB contains very limited data, and for a few monthly sequences in the beginning and the end of the time series for Estonia, Latvia and Lithuania. Table 5.22 introduces an overview of the monthly local market return data presented in per cent terms calculated from closing prices in local currencies and USD.

Table 5.22 Overview of descriptive statistics of monthly local market return data

Variable	Market	Currency	N	Mean	Std Dev	Range	Min	Max	Skew-ness	Excess Kurtosis
PLRTUS	Poland	USD	125	1.54%	9.92%	71.5%	−37.7%	33.7%	−0.21	1.79
PLRTLC	Poland	Local	125	1.60%	8.88%	70.5%	−32.3%	38.2%	0.18	2.84
HURTUS	Hungary	USD	125	2.36%	10.16%	78.0%	−38.1%	39.9%	−0.12	2.64
HURTLC	Hungary	Local	125	2.65%	9.91%	81.2%	−35.8%	45.4%	0.25	3.88
CZRTUS	Czech Rep.	USD	125	1.57%	7.97%	50.1%	−24.8%	25.4%	−0.26	0.92
CZRTLC	Czech Rep.	Local	125	1.35%	7.05%	39.7%	−22.7%	17.0%	−0.43	0.73
LIRTUS	Lithuania	USD	125	1.65%	8.20%	72.6%	−16.5%	56.1%	2.36	14.82
LIRTLC	Lithuania	Local	125	1.32%	8.02%	72.6%	−16.5%	56.1%	2.57	16.70
LARTUS	Latvia	USD	101	1.21%	10.38%	94.9%	−39.5%	55.4%	0.47	9.03
LARTLC	Latvia	Local	101	1.12%	10.36%	93.4%	−39.1%	54.3%	0.44	8.53
ESRTUS	Estonia	USD	119	2.16%	11.44%	77.8%	−37.6%	40.2%	−0.60	3.13
ESRTLC	Estonia	Local	119	2.19%	11.70%	74.5%	−36.2%	38.2%	−0.49	2.78
SNRTUS	Slovenia	USD	125	1.69%	8.03%	57.0%	−13.7%	43.3%	1.46	5.31
SNRTLC	Slovenia	Local	125	1.99%	8.25%	64.9%	−13.9%	50.9%	2.40	11.10
SKRTUS	Slovak Rep.	USD	125	1.07%	8.11%	54.9%	−17.4%	37.5%	0.86	3.12
SKRTLC	Slovak Rep.	Local	125	1.01%	7.32%	50.8%	−17.1%	33.7%	0.82	3.15

5.2.4 *Deposit Rates for Calculation of Risk-Adjusted Return Measure*

In the calculation of risk-adjusted returns, the local risk-free deposit rates are applied as the reference return in the calculation of the Sharpe Ratio (Sharpe, 1994). The deposit rates are sourced from the International Monetary Fund for all markets except the Slovak Republic where the data are not available and instead sourced directly from the Slovak central bank.

The data refer to average deposit rates which are stated on an annualised basis. In order to achieve return rates which are comparable with the weekly index returns applied in this research hypothesis, the weekly deposit rates are calculated based on weekly compounding. As can be interpreted from the graphical illustrations of the average deposit rates in Figs. 5.3–5.5, the deposit rates in each of the eight markets have declined significantly over the course of the last 10 years.

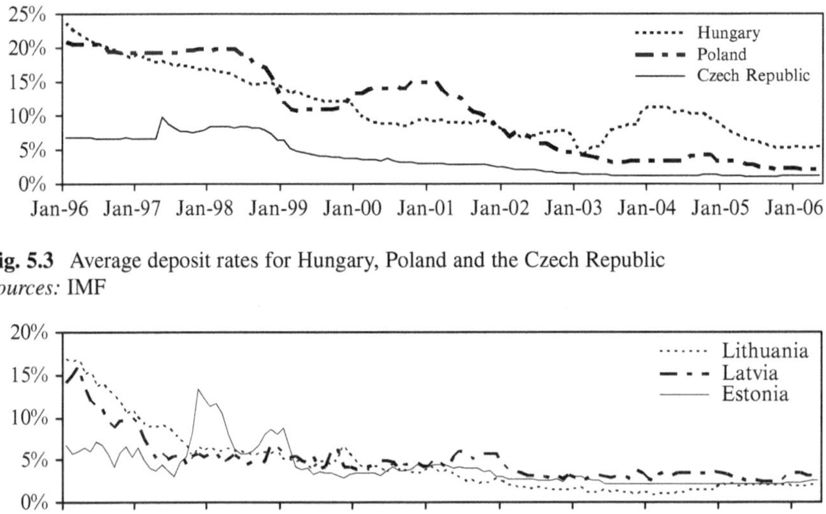

Fig. 5.3 Average deposit rates for Hungary, Poland and the Czech Republic
Sources: IMF

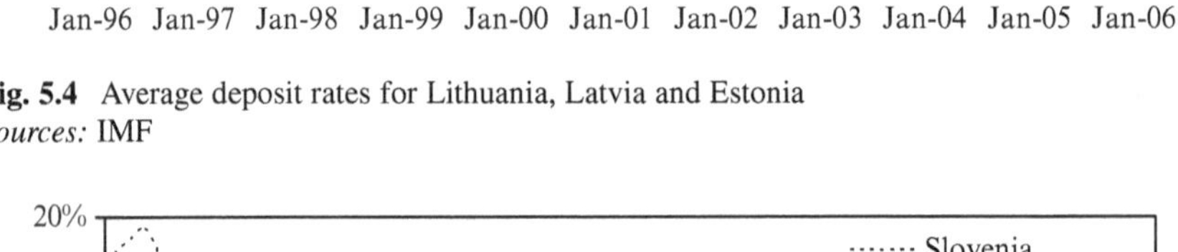

Fig. 5.4 Average deposit rates for Lithuania, Latvia and Estonia
Sources: IMF

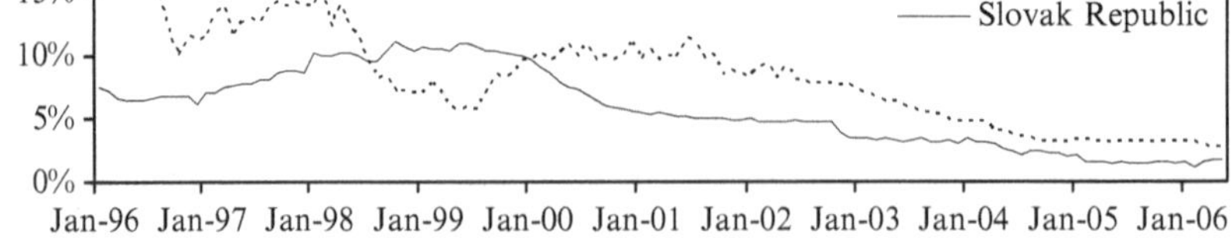

Fig. 5.5 Average deposit rates for Slovenia and the Slovak Republic
Sources: IMF and the National Bank of the Slovak Republic

5.3 Concluding Remarks on Empirical Data Review

This chapter has introduced data of both qualitative and quantitative nature which are used in the analyses of the hypotheses covered in this study.

With regard to the more qualitative type of information, it is noted that the EU accession process took up to 10 years for some of the nations in this study and that the most appropriate date for measuring changes in market integration and performance of stock market returns is the date when the details and exact timing of the EU accession is announced, namely in December 2002. Furthermore, the eight markets covered within the scope of this study experienced equity market liberalisation before the announcement of the EU accession in the sense that they were largely open to foreign investors at the very launch of trading. This implies that any findings relating to the research hypotheses can be classified as post-liberalisation event effects and will contribute insights to the understanding of the later phases of market integration.

In terms of the more quantitative data, this chapter included definitions and evaluations of both local and global market return data, global and European equity index data and data on macroeconomic factors influencing equity returns. In the selection of relevant indices, the aim is to include as many constituents as possible for the local market indices and the most representative global and European reference indices against which to measure the level of integration of the local equity market indices.

The empirical data constitute a key component in the analyses of this study as they allow for the appropriate testing of the research hypotheses. The subsequent chapter will illustrate how these data are applied in the empirical tests to provide answers to the specified research hypotheses.

Chapter 6
Findings and Discussion

With the research methods defined and the data samples explored, the focus now shifts to the presentation of the test results and the initial discussion of the statistical findings. Along with each empirical test presented in this chapter, key observations and findings will be presented and discussed. The overall conclusions and the interpretations of the findings in a broader context will be discussed in Chap. 7.

This chapter is structured according to the research questions. The chapter contains two main sections, each with two sub-sections. The first section discusses the findings from the tests of the two research questions on market integration whereas the second section explores the findings relating to the performance questions.

6.1 Findings on Impact of EU Accession on Equity Market Integration

The research hypotheses related to the effects of EU accession on the level of market integration are tested based on the methods described in Sect. 4.1. The following sub-sections provide the empirical results and observations of the tests.

6.1.1 Findings on Change in Co-movement Between Local and Global Indices

The hypothesis of no change in the level of co-movement between local market index returns and returns of global or European indices is tested with three methods, including two statistical tests and one graphical analysis of trends over time. The following sub-sections describe the results of the three complementary tests.

6.1.1.1 Test of Difference in Level of Correlation Before and After EU Accession

The initial step of the first statistical test involves calculating the Pearson correlation coefficients for each of the local market returns and the returns of the respective global and European indices for the periods before and after the EU accession announcement, which is set to mid-December 2002, as discussed in sub-section 5.1.3.3.

To reduce the distortion caused by different local inflation rates, the analyses of return level correlations are conducted in the currency of the reference index rather than in the local currencies. This implies USD for the MSCI World Index, a combination of the EUR and the DEM for the FTSEurofirst 300 Eurozone Index and EUR only for the FTSE EuroMid Eurozone Index. The decision to combine the EUR and the DEM in one of the FTSE index analyses is derived from the fact that exchange rates for the EUR are not available before December 1998 and that the DEM constitutes not only a key Euro zone currency but also the most important currency in terms of international trade for the new accession countries (Keuschnigg and Kohler, 2002).

Tables 6.1–6.3 contain the correlation coefficients and Fisher's z-values for the tests measuring the co-movement between the eight transition markets and the three reference indices. Table 6.1 relates to the correlation with the MSCI World Index, Table 6.2 to the FTSEurofirst 300 index and Table 6.3 to FTSE EuroMid Eurozone. When studying the results presented in the tables, four general observations are worth noting prior to exploring the results of the explicit hypothesis test.

First, all correlation coefficients except one are positive although the levels of correlation between the local and the global as well as European indices respectively vary substantially across the markets. This implies that returns tend to move in the same direction between the local market indices and the three reference indices.

Table 6.1 Correlation between local indices and the MSCI World Index pre- and post accession

Local Index / MSCI World	Poland	Hungary	Czech Rep.	Lithuania	Latvia	Estonia	Slovenia	Slovak Rep.
Currency basis for local returns: USD								
Correlation coefficient 1 (r1) Post Ann.	0.5286	0.4323	0.4336	0.1398	0.1714	0.2912	0.1213	0.1928
N (r1)	184	184	184	184	184	184	180	166
Correlation coefficient 2 (r2) Pre Ann.	0.4085	0.4401	0.2521	0.1210	0.0688	0.1044	0.0725	0.0442
N (r2)	363	363	363	153	153	340	361	344
Fisher's Z-value	1.6943	−0.1046	2.2680	0.1729	0.9437	2.1169	0.5366	1.5854

Notes: r1 refers to the correlation coefficient for the post-announcement period; r2 refers to the correlation coefficient for the pre-announcement period.

Table 6.2 Correlation between local indices and the FTSEurofirst 300 Eurozone Index pre- and post accession

Local Index/ FTSEuro first 300 Eurozone	Poland	Hungary	Czech Rep.	Lithuania	Latvia	Estonia	Slovenia	Slovak Rep.
Currency Basis for Local Returns: EUR/DEM								
Correlation coefficient 1 ($r1$) Post Ann.	0.4765	0.3295	0.3594	0.1401	0.1377	0.2500	−0.0368	0.0737
N ($r1$)	174	174	174	174	174	174	171	158
Correlation coefficient 2 ($r2$) Pre Ann.	0.4846	0.5147	0.3866	0.2710	0.0608	0.2314	0.1554	0.1125
N ($r2$)	351	351	351	146	147	327	349	336
Fisher's Z-value	−0.1126	−2.4283	−0.3388	−1.2087	0.6872	0.2080	−2.0584	−0.4025

Notes: r1 refers to the correlation coefficient for the post-announcement period. r2 refers to the correlation coefficient for the pre-announcement period.

Table 6.3 Correlation between local indices and the FTSE EuroMid Eurozone Index pre- and post-accession

Local index / FTSE EuroMid Eurozone	Poland	Hungary	Czech Rep.	Lithuania	Latvia	Estonia	Slovenia	Slovak Rep.
Currency basis for local returns: EUR								
Correlation coefficient 1 ($r1$) Post Ann.	0.5672	0.4331	0.4803	0.1831	0.1690	0.3241	0.0967	0.0861
N (r1)	174	174	174	174	174	174	171	158
Correlation coefficient 2 ($r2$) Pre Ann.	0.4501	0.4541	0.3494	0.2947	0.0764	0.4150	0.1982	0.1190
N (r2)	200	200	200	146	147	200	200	193
Fisher's Z-Value	1.5163	−0.2504	1.5165	−1.0456	0.8324	−1.0080	−0.9888	−0.3076

Notes: r1 refers to the correlation coefficient for the post-announcement period. r2 refers to the correlation coefficient for the pre-announcement period.

Second, the indices in the larger emerging economies, including Poland, Hungary and the Czech Republic, demonstrate a higher level of positive correlation with both the MSCI World Index and the FTSEurofirst 300 Index than those in the smaller emerging economies. This could suggest a higher level of integration between equity markets in the larger transition economies and the global and European reference indices.

Third, the correlation with the MSCI World Index is higher than that of the index representing the largest 300 companies in the Euro zone. Given that the time horizon covered for the transition economies within the scope of this study includes a period of political and economic integration with Western Europe and the Euro zone in particular, it would be expected to find a higher level of co-movement with an index that includes these markets rather than with the truly global MSCI World Index. However, as will be explored in detail in the next research hypothesis, global macroeconomic factors have become increasingly important as influencing factors for the return levels of the local equity markets in the transition economies covered within this study.

Fourth, when comparing the correlation levels in the period after the announcement, the index that shows the highest levels of co-movement in most of the transition economies is the FTSE EuroMid Eurozone, which has the highest correlation coefficient in five of the eight markets. This suggests that mid-sized rather than large companies in Europe better represent the trends in equity indices in the markets covered within this study.

The above observations are interesting in terms of establishing the context. However, the observations provide no insights into the accuracy of the actual research hypothesis. In terms of testing the null hypothesis of no statistically significant change in the level of co-movement between local market indices and global or European indices as a result of EU accession, Fisher's Z-values are defined and calculated as described in the previous sub-section. The Z-values are listed at the bottom of Tables 6.1–6.3.

In the case of the correlation with the MSCI World Index, the data in Table 6.1 illustrate that there is an increase in the correlation coefficient in all market indices except for the Hungarian index, where the correlation coefficient was 0.44 prior to the announcement and fell somewhat to 0.43 in the period after the announcement. For the other local markets, the correlation coefficient increases between 0.02 for Lithuania and 0.19 for Estonia. On average, the increase is 0.12 when excluding the small decline appearing in the Hungarian market index.

However, despite large positive changes in the correlation coefficients for several of the eight local market indices, only the changes in the Czech and Estonian correlation coefficients are significant at the 5% significance level according to Fisher's Z-values illustrated by the fact that the Z-values are superior to 1.96 in this two-sided test.

With regard to the correlation with European indices, the results are very different. First, for the FTSEurofirst 300 Index, data for which are depicted in Table 6.2, the changes in correlation coefficients are predominantly negative in the sense that all market indices except those in Latvia and Estonia demonstrate lower levels of correlation in the periods after the announcement compared to those prior to the announcement. As with the changes in the correlation coefficients related to the MSCI World Index, the reductions in coefficients are rarely significant at the 5% level. Only two markets, Hungary and Slovenia, contain results where the reduction in the coefficients is significant.

Also when studying the mid-cap Euro-zone index, depicted in Table 6.3, the frequency of declining correlation coefficients is high, with five market indices decreasing in the period after the official announcement and only three markets demonstrating an increased correlation coefficient after compared to before the accession announcement. The scope of the changes in the correlation coefficients for the FTSE EuroMid Eurozone Index is smaller than that found for the world index correlations. The largest individual change in correlation coefficient is seen in the Czech market index which changed 0.13 as opposed to the 0.19 point change for the MSCI World Index. Consequently, at a 5% significance level, none of the differences are significant, suggesting that the changes can be the result of chance.

Concluding Remarks on the Test of Difference in Level of Correlation Before and After EU Accession

Taking the findings from all three reference indices into consideration, the conclusion is that while the correlation tends to be the highest for the index incorporating mid-sized companies in the Euro-zone area, there is no significant positive change with regard to level of correlation with the local transition economy indices. This suggests that there is no support for rejecting the null hypothesis of no significant changes in the level of co-movement before and after the EU accession announcement.

A similar conclusion can be derived when studying the results from the correlation with the index containing the largest companies in the Euro-zone. While two markets demonstrate a significant negative change in level of co-movement, the findings from the remaining six markets are not significant at the 5% level. In no case are there indications of a significant increase in the level of co-movement in the period after the announcement.

Finally, observing the findings from the test of changes in level of correlation changes related to the MSCI World Index, there is only limited evidence of significant positive changes despite frequent large increases in the correlation coefficients. With only two markets demonstrating a significant positive change at the 5% significance level, limited evidence is available to reject the null hypothesis of no significant change in the level of co-movement.

The overall conclusion based on all three reference indices and this particular test methodology is consequently that no general evidence of a significant change, positive or negative, can be found as a result of the EU accession since limited evidence is found in both directions depending on which reference index that is applied.

6.1.1.2 Test of Correlation Coefficient Significantly Different from Zero

Given the somewhat ambivalent results of the previous test method, it is interesting to explore the results of the complementary test methodology of the null hypothesis that the correlation coefficient equals zero provides. It is possible that further insights in the hypothesis whether there is any impact on co-movements derived from the EU accession announcement can be derived.

Table 6.4 contains the results of the t-test of whether *r1*, the post-announcement correlation coefficient, and *r2*, the pre-announcement correlation coefficient, are significantly different from zero. If it can be shown that the correlation coefficient of one period but not the other is significantly different from zero, it could be interpreted as indications that correlation levels between local and global markets are different prior to compared with subsequent to the EU accession.

As discussed in the previous sub-section, Fisher's Z-test of significant change in correlation coefficient with regard to the MSCI World Index is supported for only two markets, the Czech Republic and Estonia. The data in Table 6.4 can be interpreted as confirmation that equity index returns in three markets, Latvia, Estonia and the Slovak Republic, demonstrate different correlation levels for the two periods. More specifically, while the hypothesis that the correlation coefficient prior to the announcement, *r2*, is different from zero cannot be rejected at the 5% level, the hypothesis using data after the announcement can be rejected.

With three out of eight markets providing significant test results which suggest rejecting the null hypothesis of no changes in the level of co-movement, there is still no convincing evidence.

When applying the FTSEurofirst 300 Eurozone Index as the reference index, conclusions are different, as is also expected based on the findings in the previous sub-section. The results in Table 6.4 suggest that the correlation coefficient is significantly

Table 6.4 t-Test of null hypothesis of correlation coefficients equalling zero

t-statistic	Poland	Hungary	Czech Rep.	Lithuania	Latvia	Estonia	Slovenia	Slovak Rep.
r1: Local index / MSCI World	8.4011	6.4685	6.4920	1.9044	2.3469	4.1062	1.6307	2.5157
r2: Local index / MSCI World	8.5038	9.3113	4.9505	1.4981	0.8474	1.9298	1.3771	0.8183
r1: Local index / FTSEurofirst 300 Eurozone	7.1089	4.5777	5.0504	1.8557	1.8231	3.3855	−0.4793	0.9231
r2: Local index / FTSEurofirst 300 Eurozone	10.3503	11.2148	7.8311	3.3791	0.7331	4.2887	2.9310	2.0691
r1: Local index / FTSE EuroMid Eurozone	9.0320	6.3012	7.1807	2.4430	2.2492	4.4935	1.2635	1.0794
r2: Local index / FTSE EuroMid Eurozone	7.0935	7.1716	5.2480	3.7007	0.9224	6.4179	2.8458	1.6570

Notes: r1 refers to the correlation coefficient for the post-announcement period. r2 refers to the correlation coefficient for the pre-announcement period.

different from zero before but not after the announcement for three markets. Markets in which this finding appears are Lithuania, Slovenia and the Slovak Republic. In the remaining five markets, data suggest that the correlation is significantly different from zero in either both or none of the time periods.

The data for the FTSE EuroMid Eurozone Index European indices, illustrated at the bottom of Table 6.4, suggest that the effects are more random. Data for all but two markets, Latvia and Slovenia, indicate that the null hypothesis of a correlation coefficient equalling zero is rejected in either both or none of the time periods. The markets in which the hypothesis is rejected in both periods include Poland, Hungary, the Czech Republic, Lithuania and Estonia. In the Slovak Republic, the test cannot support the rejection of a zero correlation hypothesis in any of the time periods.

Concluding Remarks on the Test of Correlation Coefficient Significantly Different from Zero

The results of the t-test of zero correlation coefficient is also somewhat ambivalent since the conclusions depend on which reference index that is used as comparison with the local markets. When using the MSCI World Index, there are some indications suggesting a non-zero correlation coefficient in the period subsequent to the announcement whereas the same indications are not as abundant for the pre-announcement period. When applying the FTSEurofirst 300 Eurozone Index, results suggest significant evidence of non-zero correlation in the period prior to the announcement. Finally, when applying the FTSE EuroMid Eurozone Index, it seems as if the periods before and after the EU accession announcement demonstrate the same level of co-movement in most markets.

In summary, it can be concluded that while there is some evidence of significantly increasing correlation levels in the period after the EU accession announcement, the evidence is not dominant and the overall conclusion from this test methodology is similar to that of the methodology in the previous sub-section in the sense that findings are dependent on which reference index that is applied. The overall finding is that the null hypothesis of no significant change as a result of EU accession cannot be rejected.

6.1.1.3 Analysis of Time-Varying Trends in Correlation Coefficients

The third approach to test the hypothesis of changes of correlation between local and global markets as a result of EU accession involves the calculation of a rolling 26-week correlation coefficient to facilitate an analysis of changes over time.

The correlation coefficients calculated for each local market and each of the three global and European reference indices. Details for the individual correlation coefficients are presented in Appendix 4. In the following sub-section an unweighted arithmetic mean of the correlation coefficients for the eight local markets and the respective reference index is presented in Figs. 6.1–6.3.

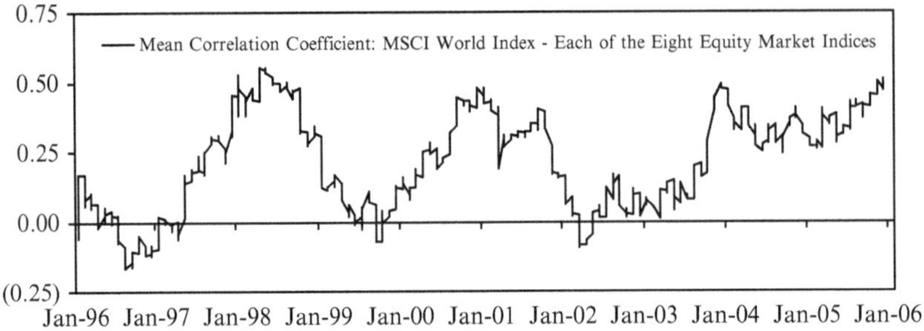

Fig. 6.1 Mean correlation coefficient between the MSCI World and the local equity market indices
Notes: Correlation coefficients are recalculated on a weekly basis based on a rolling 26-week time horizon
Sources: Correlation coefficients are calculated based on data from Bloomberg

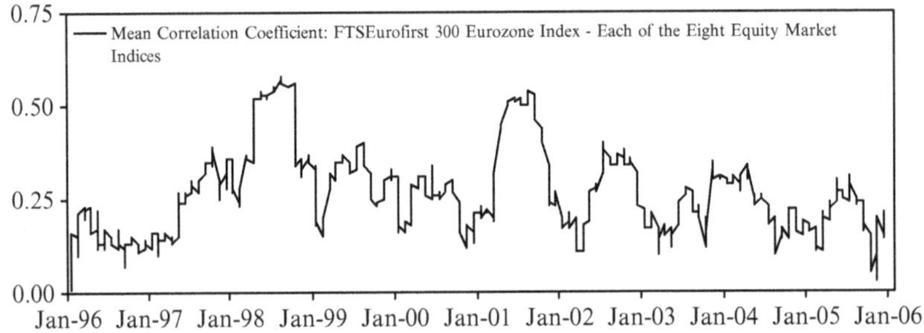

Fig. 6.2 Mean correlation coefficient between the FTSEurofirst 300 Eurozone and the local equity market indices
Notes: Correlation coefficients are recalculated on a weekly basis based on a rolling 26-week time horizon
Sources: Correlation coefficients are calculated based on data from Bloomberg

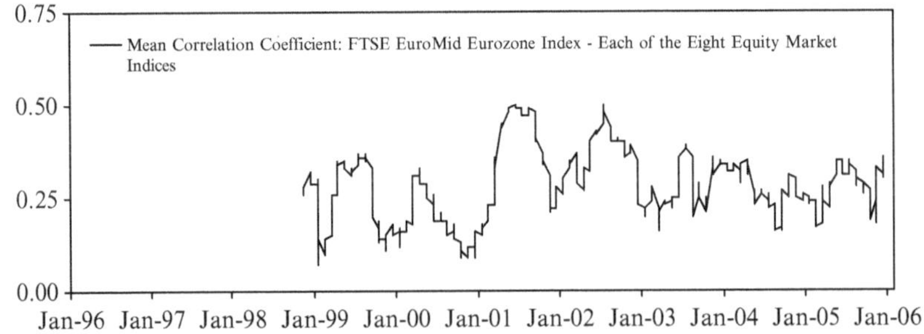

Fig. 6.3 Mean correlation coefficient between the FTSE EuroMid Eurozone and the local equity market indices
Notes: Correlation coefficients are recalculated on a weekly basis based on a rolling 26-week time horizon
Sources: Correlation coefficients are calculated based on data from Bloomberg

The historical dynamics of the correlation coefficient between local markets and the MSCI World Index illustrated in Table 6.1 suggest that the level of correlation moves in cycles spanning between 2 and 3 years. The swings from peak to trough have historically been substantial with ranges from negative correlations approaching –0.20 to positive correlations above or close to 0.50.

However, as of early 2002 the average rolling 26-week correlation coefficient has steadily increased towards the 0.50 level without declining below zero at any single point. Simultaneously, the cyclical character of the correlation level has decreased in strength although a cyclical trend is still detectable.

The illustration in Fig. 6.1 offers some interesting and relevant complementary insights regarding the level of co-movement which are not detected in the first two analyses. First, the overall trend of increasing levels of co-movement which was clearly detected with regard to the MSCI World Index and most of the local market indices can be confirmed. Although the highest individual level of mean co-movement does not occur in post-accession period, the longest cycle containing a correlation coefficient above 0.25 does occur after the announcement of the EU accession. When referring to the individual correlations related to the MSCI World Index illustrated in Appendix 4, it is clear that all markets, except Hungary and to a certain extent Poland, demonstrate a trend towards a higher and more stable level of correlation after the date of the EU accession announcement.

Second, while there was no overwhelming evidence to reject the null hypothesis of no significant change in the level of co-movement in the two previous test methods, the illustration in Fig. 6.1 provides complementary evidence which might help to explain the results from the first two methods.

There seems to be a period stretching from spring of 2002 to autumn of 2003 where the mean level of correlation measure by the correlation coefficient is particularly low. This naturally influences the mean values applied for the post-announcement period in the first two methods and reduces the potential of achieving significant results. If the analyses were to be conducted based on a different date for when to expect effects of EU accession, the tests do in fact suggest that the null hypothesis can be rejected at the 5% significance level in seven of the eight markets as is depicted in Table 6.5.

The major difference in Table 6.5, where 1 January 2004 is used as the break point for assumed effects of EU accession, compared to Table 6.1, which uses the EU accession announcement date of mid-December 2002 as the break point for any effects, is that the correlation coefficients for the second time period are significantly higher. Consequently, despite only limited changes in the correlation coefficients for the first time period, Fisher's Z-values suggest that the null hypothesis of no significant change in level of co-movement can be rejected for all markets except Lithuania. In many cases, the Z-values are substantially higher than 1.96, at which point the null hypothesis can be rejected.

Regarding the correlation between the local indices and the FTSEurofirst 300 Eurozone Index, displayed in Fig. 6.2, cyclical characteristics with decreasing volatility can be detected just as with the correlation between the local markets and the MSCI World Index. However, a key difference compared to the dynamics of the

Table 6.5 Correlation between local indices and the MSCI World Index pre- and post accession based on January 2004 as date for assumed effects of EU accession

Local Index / MSCI World	Poland	Hungary	Czech Rep.	Lithuania	Latvia	Estonia	Slovenia	Slovak Rep.
Currency basis for local returns: USD								
Correlation coefficient 1 ($r1$) after 1 Jan 2004	0.6254	0.5711	0.5539	0.1733	0.2773	0.3491	0.3086	0.3002
N (r1)	130	130	130	130	130	128	180	116
Correlation coefficient 2 ($r2$) before 1 Jan 2004	0.4039	0.4164	0.2502	0.1377	0.0589	0.1110	0.0558	0.0402
N (r2)	417	417	417	207	207	394	413	394
Fisher's Z-value	3.0110	2.0285	3.6314	0.3231	1.9982	2.4765	2.5748	2.5236

Notes: r1 refers to the correlation coefficient for the period after 1 January 2004. $r2$ refers to the correlation coefficient for the period before 1 January 2004.

MSCI Index clearly appears. The trend in the level of correlation between local markets and the index declines slowly from a historical high in mid-1998 although occasional peaks temporarily raise the co-movement. This finding is in line with the test results regarding the FTSEurofirst 300 Eurozone Index from the two previous tests which suggested that there is no empirical evidence for a positive change in the level of correlation as a result of the EU accession using this reference index.

Figure 6.3 graphically illustrates the mean correlation between the local market indices and the FTSE EuroMid Eurozone Index. The graphics suggest the presence of a cyclical pattern different from that found for the MSCI World Index in that the cycles tend to last less than a year. Another difference is that although the correlation coefficient during the last 3 years is higher than during the initial 3-year period, there is no indication of a rising level of correlation. Instead, the correlation level remains stable at around 0.25.

Another interesting finding apparent from Fig. 6.3 is that volatility in the cycles has decreased since the end of 2002. In certain periods before the end of 2002, the difference between peak and trough is up to 0.40 units whereas the period starting from 2003 tends to contain swings of around 0.20 units. This suggests that while the mean level of correlation might not have changed, the volatility of the correlation has become smaller.

Concluding Remarks on the Analysis of Time-Varying Trends in Correlation Coefficients

The analysis of time-varying trends in the correlation coefficients adds important and relevant complementary insights into the test of changes in the level of co-movement as a result of EU accession. While it confirms the findings from the initial two test methods for the correlation with the European reference indices, it suggests that the selected date at which point the effects of EU accession appears plays an important role in determining whether the null hypothesis can be rejected or not when the MSCI World Index is used as reference index.

Assuming that effects of EU accession on the level of correlation between the local markets and the MSCI World Index are delayed by approximately 1 year compared to the assumed date of the original analysis, there is clear evidence suggesting that the null hypothesis of no significant change in the level of co-movement can be rejected.

6.1.1.4 Summary of Test Results of Change in Level of Co-movement of Returns

In the preceding sub-sections, three complementary empirical tests of the hypothesis addressing the question whether EU accession has an impact on the level of correlation between local transition economy market returns and returns of world and European indices have been presented. The initial method tested for changes in the mean correlation coefficient using two time horizons, before and after the EU accession announcement. The second method included a test whether the correlation coefficient could be proven to be significantly different from zero during the same time horizons. The third approach involved graphically analysing the 26-week rolling correlation coefficient average for the entire time horizon.

Based on the originally selected time horizons, the overall findings are consistent across all three test methods. Each method provides only limited evidence suggesting that the null hypothesis of no significant change in level of correlation between local market returns and returns of global and European reference indices can be rejected. In fact, the conclusion is dependent, not only on which reference index that is applied, but also on which local transition economy that is studied and, in certain cases, what dates that are used to determine the time horizon.

Results from the analyses suggest that when measuring the change in level of correlation using the MSCI World Index, there is certain evidence to reject the null hypothesis H0_1 in favour of a positive impact based on results from four of the eight transition economy equity indices. Given that the hypothesis cannot be statistically rejected for the remaining four markets the result must be considered weak. However, when postponing the time of the assumed implications with about 12 months, the result is quite different. In this scenario, all but one market provide data which reject the null hypothesis, in many cases by large margins. With such overwhelming results it is easier to draw the conclusion that EU accession does have a positive impact on the level of co-movement between equity markets in transition economies and global equity markets, represented by the MSCI World Index.

With regard to the index based on the 300 largest companies in the Euro zone, the test results indicate limited evidence supporting the rejection of the H0_1 in favour of a negative impact on correlation levels after the announcement of the EU accession. The test results indicate that four markets have statistically significant lower levels of correlation in the period subsequent rather than prior to the announcement of the EU accession details.

Finally, when using the FTSE EuroMid Eurozone Index as reference index, data for the eight transition economies cannot reject the null hypothesis H1_0 that the correlation remains unchanged during EU accession.

In summary, empirical tests suggest that there is certain evidence of a statistically significant change in the level of correlation between equity markets in Central European transition economies and global as well as European equity indices as a result of the EU accession. However, the direction of the change is dependent on the reference index and on the local market selected. Further interpretations of these empirical test results will be discussed in Chap. 7.

6.1.2 Findings on Change in Level of Influence of Macroeconomic Factors

This sub-section explores the results of the tests related to the influence of global and local macroeconomic factors on local equity markets. The analyses of the global and local factors are separated in order to address each of the null hypotheses in detail. As discussed in Chap. 4, the test approach involves the development and comparison of two regression models for each market. The regression models contain exclusively significant explanatory variables. While the sub-section contains detailed descriptions of the results of each step in the process, not all iteration results will be illustrated.

6.1.2.1 Test of Change in Level of Influence of Global Macroeconomic Factors

The test of changes in the level of influence of global macroeconomic factors on the local equity markets is divided into two steps. As an initial step, a series of single factor regression analyses are presented in Tables 6.6 and 6.7. These single factor regressions will not in themselves provide sufficient evidence to derive conclusions regarding the hypotheses. They will, however, provide a useful overview of the data set across the two time periods which will help build an initial understanding of the hypotheses. As discussed in Chap. 4, the second and main step involves identifying regression models with the highest level of explanatory power and comparing them across the two time horizons.

Before entering into the results of the multiple regression analyses, certain observations from the single factor regression analyses are worth noting. First, the data in Table 6.6 suggest that there are only few occasions where the assumptions of no serial correlation and heteroskedasticity, measured by Durbin-Watson and Breusch-Pagan statistics respectively, are breached. In fact, the breach of the assumptions tends to be concentrated to a few selected markets, including Estonia, Lithuania and the Slovak

Table 6.6 Results of regression analyses and ordinary least square assumption tests of single global macroeconomic factors

Predictor	Dependent	B	t	Sig.	Before adj R square	DW	BP	N	B	t	Sig.	After adj R square	DW	BP	N
OILPRIC	CZRTLC	−0.03	−0.26	0.80	−1.15%	1.96	0.79	83	−0.01	−0.10	0.92	−2.47%	1.62	0.21	42
INDPRD	CZRTLC	1.10	0.56	0.58	−0.85%	1.95	0.16	83	−1.99	−0.98	0.33	−0.08%	1.65	0.10	42
WLDRET	CZRTLC	0.48	2.73	**0.01**	7.27%	2.07	**9.13**	83	0.87	3.34	**0.00**	19.89%	1.52	0.34	42
WLDCPI	CZRTLC	3.91	0.81	0.42	−0.42%	2.01	3.71	82	−2.37	−0.66	0.51	−1.40%	1.65	2.82	42
USINT	CZRTLC	−0.77	−1.42	0.16	1.21%	2.02	0.91	83	−0.60	−0.96	0.34	−0.19%	1.65	0.54	42
COMMPR	CZRTLC	0.01	0.04	0.97	−1.23%	1.97	1.69	83	−0.03	−0.15	0.88	−2.44%	1.62	0.01	42
OILPRIC	HURTLC	−0.17	−1.12	0.27	0.31%	1.88	0.71	83	0.03	0.23	0.82	−2.37%	1.89	0.01	42
INDPRD	HURTLC	0.15	0.05	0.96	−1.23%	1.86	0.87	83	−2.09	−0.91	0.37	−0.44%	1.93	0.34	42
WLDRET	HURTLC	1.26	5.33	**0.00**	25.09%	2.00	0.35	83	1.12	3.92	**0.00**	25.93%	1.63	0.45	42
WLDCPI	HURTLC	9.18	1.42	0.16	1.23%	2.06	1.20	82	−0.97	−0.24	0.82	−2.36%	1.91	0.99	42
USINT	HURTLC	0.13	0.15	0.88	−1.21%	1.86	1.92	83	−0.47	−0.66	0.51	−1.38%	1.92	2.73	42
COMMPR	HURTLC	−0.24	−0.82	0.41	−0.39%	1.86	1.13	83	0.03	0.16	0.87	−2.43%	1.90	0.18	42
OILPRIC	PLRTLC	−0.04	−0.28	0.78	−1.14%	1.93	0.35	83	0.04	0.30	0.77	−2.27%	2.24	0.34	42
INDPRD	PLRTLC	0.34	0.13	0.89	−1.21%	1.92	1.87	83	−2.72	−1.20	0.24	1.06%	2.18	0.53	42
WLDRET	PLRTLC	0.98	4.58	**0.00**	19.58%	1.86	0.41	83	1.34	5.25	**0.00**	39.36%	1.98	0.64	42
WLDCPI	PLRTLC	6.84	1.19	0.24	0.51%	2.14	1.87	82	−3.06	−0.76	0.45	−1.05%	2.32	1.71	42
USINT	PLRTLC	0.08	0.11	0.91	−1.22%	1.92	0.04	83	0.02	0.03	0.98	−2.50%	2.25	0.17	42
COMMPR	PLRTLC	−0.07	−0.29	0.78	−1.13%	1.92	0.71	83	0.04	0.20	0.84	−2.39%	2.25	0.08	42
OILPRIC	ESRTLC	−0.04	−0.23	0.82	−1.26%	**1.39**	0.00	77	0.14	0.83	0.41	−0.75%	1.58	1.44	42
INDPRD	ESRTLC	5.11	1.44	0.15	1.41%	**1.45**	0.74	77	−8.97	−3.55	**0.00**	22.11%	1.74	**5.16**	42
WLDRET	ESRTLC	0.09	0.28	0.78	−1.22%	**1.41**	0.15	77	0.45	1.10	0.28	0.51%	1.59	0.46	42
WLDCPI	ESRTLC	0.70	0.08	0.94	−1.33%	**1.40**	0.12	77	10.24	2.11	***0.04***	7.78%	**1.46**	**5.64**	42
USINT	ESRTLC	−0.48	−0.50	0.62	−1.00%	**1.40**	3.13	77	−1.57	−1.84	*0.07*	5.53%	1.69	2.13	42
COMMPR	ESRTLC	0.00	0.01	1.00	−1.33%	**1.39**	0.05	77	0.26	1.01	0.32	0.06%	1.56	1.99	42
OILPRIC	LIRTLC	0.06	0.47	0.64	−0.96%	1.73	0.05	83	−0.07	−0.55	0.59	−1.74%	**1.31**	0.27	42
INDPRD	LIRTLC	2.21	0.95	0.34	−0.11%	1.78	0.49	83	−1.45	−0.70	0.49	−1.26%	**1.34**	0.20	42
WLDRET	LIRTLC	0.34	1.60	0.11	1.87%	1.78	0.03	83	0.54	1.89	*0.07*	5.92%	**1.45**	1.38	42
WLDCPI	LIRTLC	5.20	0.92	0.36	−0.19%	1.76	1.85	82	0.69	0.19	0.85	−2.41%	**1.29**	0.02	42
USINT	LIRTLC	0.10	0.16	0.88	−1.20%	1.73	0.54	83	−1.39	−2.33	***0.02***	0.00%	1.47	0.00	42

(continued)

Table 6.6 (continued)

Predictor	Dependent	B	t	Sig.	Before adj R square	DW	BP	N	B	t	Sig.	After adj R square	DW	BP	N
COMMPR	LIRTLC	0.19	0.84	0.40	−0.36%	1.73	0.00	83	−0.11	−0.59	0.56	−1.61%	**1.31**	0.31	42
OILPRIC	LARTLC	−0.09	−0.47	0.64	−1.36%	1.84	1.34	59	0.03	0.26	0.80	−2.33%	1.74	0.87	42
INDPRD	LARTLC	−5.60	−1.60	0.12	2.60%	1.80	**5.84**	59	1.29	0.56	0.58	−1.70%	1.74	0.01	42
WLDRET	LARTLC	0.50	1.54	0.13	2.32%	1.78	0.96	59	0.46	1.43	0.16	2.47%	1.80	2.05	42
WLDCPI	LARTLC	−12.46	−1.38	0.17	1.53%	1.85	3.58	59	2.50	0.62	0.54	−1.53%	1.75	0.54	42
USINT	LARTLC	−0.34	−0.36	0.72	−1.52%	1.84	0.03	59	−0.79	−1.14	0.26	0.72%	1.84	0.00	42
COMMPR	LARTLC	−0.08	−0.24	0.81	−1.66%	1.84	2.45	59	0.04	0.17	0.87	−2.43%	1.76	0.48	42
OILPRIC	SNRTLC	0.10	0.78	0.44	−0.48%	1.98	0.21	83	−0.08	−0.89	0.38	−0.50%	1.72	2.12	42
INDPRD	SNRTLC	1.26	0.50	0.62	−0.92%	1.99	2.07	83	3.38	2.35	***0.02***	9.98%	2.06	0.59	42
WLDRET	SNRTLC	0.21	0.91	0.37	−0.22%	1.97	0.92	83	0.04	0.20	0.84	−2.39%	1.73	2.49	42
WLDCPI	SNRTLC	0.67	0.11	0.91	−1.24%	1.99	2.30	82	−1.80	−0.67	0.51	−1.37%	1.72	3.19	42
USINT	SNRTLC	−0.62	−0.89	0.38	−0.26%	2.02	0.46	83	−0.11	−0.23	0.82	−2.36%	1.70	0.13	42
COMMPR	SNRTLC	0.20	0.80	0.43	−0.45%	1.98	0.24	83	−0.06	−0.45	0.66	−1.99%	1.70	3.24	42
OILPRIC	SKRTLC	−0.05	−0.59	0.56	−0.80%	**1.61**	**6.52**	83	0.13	0.78	0.44	−0.97%	1.88	0.22	42
INDPRD	SKRTLC	−1.51	−0.84	0.41	−0.37%	**1.60**	0.04	83	−2.35	−0.81	0.42	−0.84%	1.87	1.54	42
WLDRET	SKRTLC	−0.09	−0.52	0.60	−0.89%	**1.60**	**7.15**	83	0.38	0.92	0.37	−0.40%	1.72	1.62	42
WLDCPI	SKRTLC	−5.05	−1.16	0.25	0.44%	**1.62**	0.10	82	6.47	1.28	0.21	1.56%	1.77	0.35	42
USINT	SKRTLC	−0.71	−1.44	0.15	1.28%	1.62	0.12	83	−0.89	−1.01	0.32	0.07%	1.86	0.00	42
COMMPR	SKRTLC	−0.08	−0.44	0.66	−0.99%	**1.59**	**6.73**	83	0.15	0.58	0.56	−1.64%	1.86	0.22	42

Notes: B refers to the slope coefficient of the regression analysis. t refers to the t-statistic. Sig. refers to the lowest level of significance. Adj. R Square refers to the value of the adjusted R square of the regression model. DW and BP refer to the Durbin-Watson and Breusch-Pagan test statistics and N represents the sample size.

In the case of the Sig. column, bolded values imply significance at the 1% level, bolded italic values suggest significance at the 5% level and italic values indicate significance at the 10% level. Bolded values in the DW column imply that there are possible issues with serial correlation whereas bolded values in the BP column suggest that the assumption of homoskedasticity can not be confirmed.

Table 6.7 Results of regression analyses of single global macroeconomic factors with robust standard errors

					Before adj							After adj			
Predictor	Dependent	B	t	Sig.	R square	DW	BP	N	B	t	Sig.	R square	DW	BP	N
OILPRIC	CZRTLC	−0.03	−0.26	0.80	−1.15%	1.96	0.79	83	−0.01	−0.10	0.92	−2.47%	1.62	0.21	42
INDPRD	CZRTLC	1.10	0.56	0.58	−0.85%	1.95	0.16	83	−1.99	−0.98	0.33	−0.08%	1.65	0.10	42
WLDRET	CZRTLC	0.48	2.37	***0.02***	7.27%	Robust std. err.		83	0.87	3.34	**0.00**	19.89%	1.52	0.34	42
WLDCPI	CZRTLC	3.91	0.81	0.42	−0.42%	2.01	3.71	82	−2.37	−0.66	0.51	−1.40%	1.65	2.82	42
USINT	CZRTLC	−0.77	−1.42	0.16	1.21%	2.02	0.91	83	−0.60	−0.96	0.34	−0.19%	1.65	0.54	42
COMMPR	CZRTLC	0.01	0.04	0.97	−1.23%	1.97	1.69	83	−0.03	−0.15	0.88	−2.44%	1.62	0.01	42
OILPRIC	HURTLC	−0.17	−1.12	0.27	0.31%	1.88	0.71	83	0.03	0.23	0.82	−2.37%	1.89	0.01	42
INDPRD	HURTLC	0.15	0.05	0.96	−1.23%	1.86	0.87	83	−2.09	−0.91	0.37	−0.44%	1.93	0.34	42
WLDRET	HURTLC	1.26	5.33	**0.00**	25.09%	2.00	0.35	83	1.12	3.92	**0.00**	25.93%	1.63	0.45	42
WLDCPI	HURTLC	9.18	1.42	0.16	1.23%	2.06	1.20	82	−0.97	−0.24	0.82	−2.36%	1.91	0.99	42
USINT	HURTLC	0.13	0.15	0.88	−1.21%	1.86	1.92	83	−0.47	−0.66	0.51	−1.38%	1.92	2.73	42
COMMPR	HURTLC	−0.24	−0.82	0.41	−0.39%	1.86	1.13	83	0.03	0.16	0.87	−2.43%	1.90	0.18	42
OILPRIC	PLRTLC	−0.04	−0.28	0.78	−1.14%	1.93	0.35	83	0.04	0.30	0.77	−2.27%	2.24	0.34	42
INDPRD	PLRTLC	0.34	0.13	0.89	−1.21%	1.92	1.87	83	−2.72	−1.20	0.24	1.06%	2.18	0.53	42
WLDRET	PLRTLC	0.98	4.58	**0.00**	19.58%	1.86	0.41	83	1.34	5.25	**0.00**	39.36%	1.98	0.64	42
WLDCPI	PLRTLC	6.84	1.19	0.24	0.51%	2.14	1.87	82	−3.06	−0.76	0.45	−1.05%	2.32	1.71	42
USINT	PLRTLC	0.08	0.11	0.91	−1.22%	1.92	0.04	83	0.02	0.03	0.98	−2.50%	2.25	0.17	42
COMMPR	PLRTLC	−0.07	−0.29	0.78	−1.13%	1.92	0.71	83	0.04	0.20	0.84	−2.39%	2.25	0.08	42
OILPRIC	ESRTLC	−0.04	−0.27	0.79	−1.26%	Robust std. err.		77	0.14	0.83	0.41	−0.75%	1.58	1.44	42
INDPRD	ESRTLC	5.11	1.85	*0.07*	1.41%	Robust std. err.		77	−8.97	−2.02	*0.05*	22.11%	Robust std. err.		42
WLDRET	ESRTLC	0.09	0.32	0.75	−1.22%	Robust std. err.		77	0.45	1.10	0.28	0.51%	1.59	0.46	42
WLDCPI	ESRTLC	0.70	0.11	0.92	−1.33%	Robust std. err.		77	10.24	1.16	0.25	7.78%	Robust std. err.	err.	42
USINT	ESRTLC	−0.48	−0.78	0.44	−1.00%	Robust std. err.		77	−1.57	−1.84	*0.07*	5.53%	1.69	2.13	42
COMMPR	ESRTLC	0.00	0.01	0.99	−1.33%	Robust std. err.		77	0.26	1.01	0.32	0.06%	1.56	1.99	42
OILPRIC	LIRTLC	0.06	0.47	0.64	−0.96%	1.73	0.05	83	−0.07	−0.71	0.48	−1.74%	Robust std. err.		42
INDPRD	LIRTLC	2.21	0.95	0.34	−0.11%	1.78	0.49	83	−1.45	−0.74	0.47	−1.26%	Robust std. err.		42
WLDRET	LIRTLC	0.34	1.60	0.11	1.87%	1.78	0.03	83	0.54	2.39	***0.02***	5.92%	Robust std. err.		42
WLDCPI	LIRTLC	5.20	0.92	0.36	−0.19%	1.76	1.85	82	0.69	0.17	0.87	−2.41%	Robust std. err.		42

(continued)

Table 6.7 (continued)

Predictor	Dependent	B	t	Sig.	Before adj R square	DW	BP	N	B	t	Sig.	After adj R square	DW	BP	N
USINT	LIRTLC	0.10	0.16	0.88	−1.20%	1.73	0.54	83	−1.39	−2.33	***0.02***	0.00%	1.47	0.00	42
COMMPR	LIRTLC	0.19	0.84	0.40	−0.36%	1.73	0.00	83	−0.11	−0.76	0.45	−1.61%	Robust std err.		42
OILPRIC	LARTLC	−0.09	−0.47	0.64	−1.36%	1.84	1.34	59	0.03	0.26	0.80	−2.33%	1.74	0.87	42
INDPRD	LARTLC	−5.60	−1.10	0.28	2.60%	Robust std. err.		59	1.29	0.56	0.58	−1.70%	1.74	0.01	42
WLDRET	LARTLC	0.50	1.54	0.13	2.32%	1.78	0.96	59	0.46	1.43	0.16	2.47%	1.80	2.05	42
WLDCPI	LARTLC	−12.46	−1.38	0.17	1.53%	1.85	3.58	59	2.50	0.62	0.54	−1.53%	1.75	0.54	42
USINT	LARTLC	−0.34	−0.36	0.72	−1.52%	1.84	0.03	59	−0.79	−1.14	0.26	0.72%	1.84	0.00	42
COMMPR	LARTLC	−0.08	−0.24	0.81	−1.66%	1.84	2.45	59	0.04	0.17	0.87	−2.43%	1.76	0.48	42
OILPRIC	SNRTLC	0.10	0.78	0.44	−0.48%	1.98	0.21	83	−0.08	−0.89	0.38	−0.50%	1.72	2.12	42
INDPRD	SNRTLC	1.26	0.50	0.62	−0.92%	1.99	2.07	83	3.38	2.35	***0.02***	9.98%	2.06	0.59	42
WLDRET	SNRTLC	0.21	0.91	0.37	−0.22%	1.97	0.92	83	0.04	0.20	0.84	−2.39%	1.73	2.49	42
WLDCPI	SNRTLC	0.67	0.11	0.91	−1.24%	1.99	2.30	82	−1.80	−0.67	0.51	−1.37%	1.72	3.19	42
USINT	SNRTLC	−0.62	−0.89	0.38	−0.26%	2.02	0.46	83	−0.11	−0.23	0.82	−2.36%	1.70	0.13	42
COMMPR	SNRTLC	0.20	0.80	0.43	−0.45%	1.98	0.24	83	−0.06	−0.45	0.66	−1.99%	1.70	3.24	42
OILPRIC	SKRTLC	−0.05	−0.58	0.56	−0.80%	Robust std. err.		83	0.13	0.78	0.44	−0.97%	1.88	0.22	42
INDPRD	SKRTLC	−1.51	−0.98	0.33	−0.37%	Robust std. err.		83	−2.35	−0.81	0.42	−0.84%	1.87	1.54	42
WLDRET	SKRTLC	−0.09	−0.55	0.58	−0.89%	Robust std. err.		83	0.38	0.92	0.37	−0.40%	1.72	1.62	42
WLDCPI	SKRTLC	−5.05	−1.15	0.26	0.44%	Robust std err.		82	6.47	1.28	0.21	1.56%	1.77	0.35	42
USINT	SKRTLC	−0.71	−1.44	0.15	1.28%	1.62	0.12	83	−0.89	−1.01	0.32	0.07%	1.86	0.00	42
COMMPR	SKRTLC	−0.08	−0.44	0.66	−0.99%	Robust std. err.		83	0.15	0.58	0.56	−1.64%	1.86	0.22	42

Notes: B refers to the slope coefficient of the regression analysis. t refers to the t-statistic. Sig. refers to the lowest level of significance. Adj. R Square refers to the value of the adjusted R square of the regression model. DW and BP refer to the Durbin-Watson and Breusch-Pagan test statistics and N represents the sample size. Bolded values indicate significance at the 1% level, bolded italic values suggest significance at the 5% level and italic values indicate significance at the 10% level.

Republic. Consequently, robust standard errors must be applied to appropriately determine significance levels of the explanatory variables for these markets. The results using the robust standard errors are presented in Table 6.7.

Second, when taking the robust significance tests from Table 6.7 into consideration, it is apparent from the column depicted Sig. that most of the single regression analyses are insignificant even at the 10% level. This suggests that many macroeconomic factors are irrelevant as predictors for the local equity market development when studied in isolation.

Third, a comparison across the two time horizons in Table 6.7 indicates that the post-announcement period contains a larger number of significant explanatory factors vis-à-vis the pre-announcement period. More specifically, in the pre-announcement period there are only four significant explanatory factors overall whereas the equivalent number for the post-announcement period is eight. While this does not provide sufficient evidence to derive conclusions on the null hypothesis, it does provide an indication that global factors might have a larger level of influence in the period after the announcement.

As discussed, the data in Table 6.7 do not offer any means of actually testing the null hypotheses. To test null hypothesis, it is required to study each individual market separately and compare the explanatory power, measured by the adjusted R^2, of the optimal combination of independent factors across the two time horizons. These analyses are illustrated in Tables 6.8–6.15.

Table 6.8 Models of global factors for the Czech Republic before and after announcement

Czech Republic	Before	B	t	Sig.	After	B	t	Sig.
Dependent	BCZRTLC				ACZRTLC			
Predictor 1	BWLDRET	0.521	2.637	**0.010**	AWLDRET	0.874	3.343	**0.002**
Predictor 2	BUSINT	–0.973	–1.859	*0.067*				
F-Statistic	4.080				11.179			
Sig. of F-Statistic	***0.021***				**0.002**			
Adjusted R Square	10.0%				19.9%			
Durbin-Watson Statistic	Robust std. err.				1.518			
Breusch-Pagan Statistic	Robust std. err.				0.338			
Condition Index, Max	6.703				n.a.			
N	83				42			

Notes: B refers to the slope coefficient of the regression analysis. t refers to the t-statistic. Sig. refers to the lowest level of significance and N represents the sample size. Bolded values indicate significance at the 1% level, bolded italic values suggest significance at the 5% level and italic values indicate significance at the 10% level.

Table 6.9 Models of global factors for Hungary before and after announcement

Hungary	Before	B	t	Sig.	After	B	t	Sig.
Dependent	BHURTLC				AHURTLC			
Predictor 1	BWLDRET	1.258	5.335	**0.000**	AWLDRET	1.119	3.918	**0.000**
F-Statistic	28.461				15.351			
Sig. of F-Statistic	**0.000**				**0.000**			
Adjusted R Square	25.1%				25.9%			
Durbin-Watson Statistic	1.996				1.629			
Breusch-Pagan Statistic	0.351				0.454			
Condition Index, Max	n.a.				n.a.			
N	83				42			

Notes: B refers to the slope coefficient of the regression analysis. t refers to the t-statistic. Sig. refers to the lowest level of significance and N represents the sample size. Bolded values indicate significance at the 1% level, bolded italic values suggest significance at the 5% level and italic values indicate significance at the 10% level.

Table 6.10 Models of global factors for Poland before and after announcement

Poland	Before	B	t	Sig	After	B	t	Sig.
Dependent	BPLRTLC				APLRTLC			
Predictor 1	BWLDRET	0.984	4.579	**0.000**	AWLDRET	1.531	5.968	**0.000**
Predictor 2					AOILPRIC	0.235	2.291	***0.027***
F-Statistic	20.966				17.893			
Sig. of F-Statistic	**0.000**				**0.000**			
Adjusted R Square	19.6%				45.2%			
Durbin-Watson Statistic	1.859				2.006			
Breusch-Pagan Statistic	0.411				1.089			
Condition Index, Max	n.a.				1.864			
N	83				42			

Notes: B refers to the slope coefficient of the regression analysis. t refers to the t-statistic. Sig. refers to the lowest level of significance and N represents the sample size. Bolded values indicate significance at the 1% level, bolded italic values suggest significance at the 5% level and italic values indicate significance at the 10% level.

Table 6.11 Models of global factors for Estonia before and after announcement

Estonia	Before	B	t	Sig.	After	B	t	Sig.
Dependent	BESRTLC				AESRTLC			
Predictor 1	BINDPRD	5.111	1.851	*0.068*	AINDPRD	−7.076	−2.332	***0.025***
Predictor 2					AWLDRET	0.56	2.2107	***0.033***
Predictor 3					AWLDCPI	11.085	1.755	*0.088*
Predictor 4					AUSINT	−1.574	−1.917	*0.063*
F-Statistic	3.420				3.65			
Sig. of F-Statistic	*0.068*				***0.013***			
Adjusted R Square	1.4%				34.9%			
Durbin-Watson Statistic	Robust std. err.				Robust std. err.			
Breusch-Pagan Statistic	Robust std. err.				Robust std. err.			
Condition Index, Max	n.a.				4.915			
N	77				42			

Notes: B refers to the slope coefficient of the regression analysis. t refers to the t-statistic. Sig. refers to the lowest level of significance and N represents the sample size. Bolded values indicate significance at the 1% level, bolded italic values suggest significance at the 5% level and italic values indicate significance at the 10% level.

Table 6.12 Models of global factors for Lithuania before and after announcement

Lithuania	Before	B	t	Sig.	After	B	t	Sig.
Dependent	BLIRTLC				ALIRTLC			
Predictor 1	No significant model				AWLDRET	0.516	1.892	*0.066*
Predictor 2					AUSINT	−1.345	−2.325	***0.025***
F-Statistic	n.a.				4.69			
Sig. of F-Statistic	n.a.				***0.015***			
Adjusted R Square	n.a.				15.3%			
Durbin-Watson Statistic	n.a.				1.634			
Breusch-Pagan Statistic	n.a.				1.583			
Condition Index, Max	n.a.				4.066			
N	n.a.				42			

Notes: B refers to the slope coefficient of the regression analysis. t refers to the t-statistic. Sig. refers to the lowest level of significance and N represents the sample size. Bolded values indicate significance at the 1% level, bolded italic values suggest significance at the 5% level and italic values indicate significance at the 10% level.

Table 6.13 Models of global factors for Latvia before and after announcement

Latvia	Before	B	t	Sig.	After	B	t	Sig.
Dependent	BLARTLC				ALARTLC			
Predictor 1	BINDPRD	−8.729	−2.333	***0.023***	No significant model			
Predictor 2	BWLDRET	0.749	2.347	***0.023***				
Predictor 3	BWLDCPI	−23.917	−2.395	***0.020***				
Predictor 4	BCOMMPF	0.702	1.734	*0.089*				
F-Statistic	2.977				n.a.			
Sig. of F-Statistic	***0.027***				n.a.			
Adjusted R Square	12.0%				n.a.			
Durbin-Watson Statistic	1.776				n.a.			
Breusch-Pagan Statistic	7.032 (<7.81473)				n.a.			
Condition Index, Max	4.333				n.a.			
N	59				n.a.			

Notes: B refers to the slope coefficient of the regression analysis. t refers to the t-statistic. Sig. refers to the lowest level of significance and N represents the sample size. Bolded values indicate significance at the 1% level, bolded italic values suggest significance at the 5% level and italic values indicate significance at the 10% level.

Table 6.14 Models of global factors for Slovenia before and after announcement

Slovenia	Before	B	t	Sig.	After	B	t	Sig.
Dependent	BSNRTLC				ASNRTLC			
Predictor 1	No significant model				AINDPRD	2.945	2.133	***0.039***
Predictor 2					ACOMMPR	1.563	2.281	***0.028***
Predictor 3					AOILPRIC	−1.070	−2.436	***0.020***
F-Statistic	n.a.				4.163			
Sig. of F-Statistic	n.a.				***0.012***			
Adjusted R Square	n.a.				18.8%			
Durbin-Watson Statistic	n.a.				1.986			
Breusch-Pagan Statistic	n.a.				5.150			
Condition Index, Max	n.a.				13.228 (Moderate multi-collinearity)			
N	n.a.				42			

Notes: B refers to the slope coefficient of the regression analysis. t refers to the t-statistic. Sig. refers to the lowest level of significance and N represents the sample size. Bolded values indicate significance at the 1% level, bolded italic values suggest significance at the 5% level and italic values indicate significance at the 10% level.

Table 6.15 Models of global factors for the Slovak Republic before and after announcement

Slovak Republic	Before	B	t	Sig.	After	B	t	Sig.
Dependent	BSKRTLC				ASKRTLC			
Predictor 1	No significant model				No significant model			
F-Statistic	n.a.				n.a.			
Sig. of F-Statistic	n.a.				n.a.			
Adjusted R Square	n.a.				n.a.			
Durbin-Watson Statistic	n.a.				n.a.			
Breusch-Pagan Statistic	n.a.				n.a.			
Condition Index, Max	n.a.				n.a.			
N	n.a.				n.a.			

Notes: B refers to the slope coefficient of the regression analysis. t refers to the t-statistic. Sig. refers to the lowest level of significance and N represents the sample size. Bolded values indicate significance at the 1% level, bolded italic values suggest significance at the 5% level and italic values indicate significance at the 10% level.

In each table, the dependent and the predicting variables are depicted in an abbreviated form which is described in detail in Appendix 6. In addition to the abbreviated name, details containing the B, the t-statistic and the related significance of each of the predictors are displayed. As discussed in sub-section 4.1.2.2, the tables contain the models with the highest explanatory power based exclusively on significant predictors. For each of the models, the F-statistic, the adjusted R^2, the number of observations along with three test indicators relating to the assumptions of the ordinary least square regression, Durbin-Watson, Breusch-Pagan and the condition index. Given that the condition index is a measure of the relationship between independent variables in a regression model, the models containing only one independent variable will not have a condition index value.

Table 6.8 shows the empirical test results relating to the Czech Republic. The optimal models differ across the two time periods. In the period prior to the announcement, the optimal model contains two predictors; the world return, which is positively associated with the dependent variable, and the US interest rate, which is negatively associated. In the period after the announcement, the optimal model contains a single predictor, the positively associated world return.

Despite fewer significant explanatory variables, the explanatory power of the post-announcement regression model, measured by the adjusted R^2, is twice as high compared to the pre-announcement period; 10.0% in the pre-announcement period versus 19.9% in the post-announcement period. This major difference in explanatory power supports the rejection of the null hypothesis, H0_2.1 which states that EU accession implies no change in the influence of global macroeconomic factors on the equity market returns. A model based on global factors seems to have a significantly larger influence on local equity market return levels in the period after the announcement of EU accession in the Czech Republic.

With regard to Hungary, data for which are introduced in Table 6.9, the applicable models contain only the world return as predictor in each of the time periods.

The explanatory power of the post-announcement model is higher than that of the pre-announcement period. Once again, this suggests an increasing influence of global factors after the announcement although the difference in this sample is not substantial.

The data on Poland presented in Table 6.10 suggest that the world return is a significant predictor for both time periods and that the post-announcement period model contains an additional significant predictor in the form of the global oil price. In terms of level of explanatory power, the post-announcement period model has an adjusted R^2 of 45.2% which should be compared with 19.6% for the pre-announcement model. This substantial difference in level of explanatory power across the two time periods suggests that the null hypothesis can be rejected in this sample.

The sample from the Estonian market, illustrated in Table 6.11, indicates an even larger difference in explanatory power between the two models. With an adjusted R^2 of only 1.4% based on a single predictor, the pre-announcement period model has a low explanatory level. In contrast, the post-announcement period model, which contains four significant predictors, explains 34.9% of the variability in local equity returns. Similar to the above discussed markets, this suggests that the global macroeconomic factors have a larger explanatory power in the period after the announcement and consequently that the null hypothesis can be rejected in the case of Estonian data.

With regard to the sample from Lithuania, no significant predicting model is available for the period prior to the announcement. With regard to the post-announcement period, a model based on two predicting macroeconomic factors, the world index return factor and the US interest rates, explains 15.3% of the variability. Consequently, the null hypothesis can be rejected in the case of the Lithuania sample as well.

With regard to the sample from the Latvian market in Table 6.13, the situation is the reversed. No significant model is available for the post-announcement period whereas the pre-announcement period model explains 12% of the variability. Once again it suggests that the null hypothesis can be rejected. However, in this case it seems as if the null hypothesis is rejected in favour of a lower level of influence of global macroeconomic factors after the announcement.

Regarding the Slovenian sample, illustrated in Table 6.14, no significant model can be identified for the pre-announcement period. However, in the post-announcement period, a significant predictive model containing three significant factors explains 18.8% of the variability. As in the case of the Lithuanian sample, this result suggests that the null hypothesis of no significant change in influence of global macroeconomic factors can be rejected.

Table 6.15 illustrates the findings from the Slovak market data sample. In this sample no significant model can be found in either time period which would imply that the null hypothesis cannot be evaluated.

Summary of Test of Change in Level of Influence of Global Macroeconomic Factors

The tests related to the effects of EU accession on the level of influence of global macroeconomic factors on transition economy equity returns conclude that the null hypothesis can be rejected in a majority of the samples. In six of the eight markets, the post-announcement models have larger explanatory power. Only one market sample suggests lower explanatory power and one sample is inconclusive in both time periods.

With such statistical evidence, it is feasible to conclude that the level of influence of global macroeconomic factors is significantly higher in the period after the EU accession announcement. This finding is in line with the results of the first research question where the level of co-movement with MSCI World Index was proven to have increased in association with the EU accession.

If global macroeconomic factors increase in explanatory power, it would be expected that the local macroeconomic factors decrease in explanatory power. The subsequent sub-section provides the statistical test of the influence of local macroeconomic factors on the equity returns of the European transition economies.

6.1.2.2 Test of Change in Level of Influence of Local Macroeconomic Factors

In the previous section the aim was to test changes in the level of influence of global macroeconomic factors on the local equity markets as a result of EU accession. Strong evidence to reject the null hypothesis of no change in dependence of global factors was presented. In this sub-section the focus is shifted to testing the influence of local macroeconomic factors during the same time periods.

As discussed in the sub-section 3.1.2, it is expected that the importance of local macroeconomic factors as predictors for the local equity market performance decreases as a result of the EU accession. The approach applied to test the null hypothesis of no change in level of influence is the same as that used for testing the impact of global macroeconomic factors. Initially, a broad overview of single factor regression models is introduced to provide a preliminary understanding of the data. Subsequently, the significant models with the largest level of explanatory power are compared across the two time periods.

Tables 6.16 and 6.17 contain the overview of the single factor regression analyses. Similar to the results of the global macroeconomic factors, the sample data in almost all markets meet the criteria for ordinary least square regression analysis. Durbin-Watson tests of the samples suggest that samples in three markets, Estonia, Lithuania and the Slovak Republic, contain potential issues with serial correlation. Table 6.17 provides the regression results using robust standard errors.

As with the global the macroeconomic factors, the majority of the local factors are insignificant even at the 10% level. This suggests that most local factors constitute poor predictors of the local equity market performance when studied in isolation. However, in contrast to the results of the global factors, the number of significant factors is higher in the period prior to the announcement of EU accession. In the samples prior to the announcement 12 factors are significant in total whereas the equivalent number for the post-announcement period is only four.

Table 6.16 Results of regression analyses and ordinary least square assumption tests of single local macroeconomic factors

Predictor	Dependent	B	t	Sig.	Before Adj. R Square	DW	BP	N	B	t	Sig.	After Adj. R Square	DW	BP	N
CZINT	CZRTLC	−0.17	−1.00	0.32	0.00%	2.00	1.51	83	0.39	0.12	0.90	−2.46%	1.61	2.37	42
CZINFL	CZRTLC	1.33	1.20	0.23	0.54%	1.98	0.74	83	−1.65	−0.85	0.40	−0.68%	1.54	0.01	42
CZINPR	CZRTLC	−0.12	−1.18	0.24	0.47%	1.98	**0.21**	83	0.03	0.34	0.74	−2.27%	1.81	1.41	41
CZMOSU	CZRTLC	0.10	0.43	0.67	−1.00%	1.98	2.46	83	−1.31	−2.70	***0.01***	13.30%	1.75	0.23	42
CZTRBA	CZRTLC	0.00	−1.09	0.28	0.24%	1.89	2.09	83	0.00	0.33	0.75	−2.23%	1.62	0.38	42
CZEXCH	CZRTLC	0.14	0.58	0.56	−0.82%	1.98	5.07	82	−0.17	−0.62	0.54	−1.53%	1.64	3.18	42
HUINT	HURTLC	0.71	2.75	**0.01**	7.40%	2.02	2.07	83	0.67	1.58	0.12	3.51%	1.99	2.38	42
HUINFL	HURTLC	5.38	3.97	**0.00**	15.22%	2.14	0.12	83	−1.94	−0.95	0.35	−0.26%	1.93	0.69	42
HUINPR	HURTLC	−0.12	−0.84	0.40	−0.35%	1.88	2.34	83	−0.10	−0.97	0.34	−0.14%	1.94	0.06	41
HUMOSU	HURTLC	−0.31	−0.85	0.40	−0.50%	1.86	1.61	58	−0.40	−1.42	0.16	2.39%	2.00	0.01	42
HUTRBA	HURTLC	0.00	0.32	0.75	−1.11%	1.89	0.03	83	0.00	−0.06	0.96	−2.49%	1.90	0.61	42
HUEXCH	HURTLC	−0.08	−0.17	0.87	−1.22%	2.05	3.17	82	0.29	0.97	0.34	−0.16%	1.87	0.47	42
PLINT	PLRTLC	0.17	0.75	0.46	−0.54%	1.93	0.92	83	−0.87	−0.77	0.45	−1.02%	2.29	1.94	42
PLINFL	PLRTLC	5.42	4.15	**0.00**	16.54%	2.14	0.08	83	−7.18	−2.70	***0.01***	13.27%	2.58	1.88	42
PLINPR	PLRTLC	−0.18	−1.03	0.30	0.09%	1.97	0.12	83	−0.07	−0.46	0.64	−1.95%	2.24	0.01	42
PLMOSU	PLRTLC	−0.43	−1.45	0.15	1.32%	1.94	0.64	83	0.14	0.45	0.66	−2.27%	2.30	0.02	37
PLTRBA	PLRTLC	0.00	1.55	0.13	1.68%	2.00	0.25	83	0.00	−0.55	0.59	−1.83%	2.31	0.28	40
PLEXCH	PLRTLC	1.12	3.24	**0.00**	10.49%	2.07	5.58	82	0.35	1.24	0.22	1.29%	2.16	0.05	42
ESINT	ESRTLC	−0.60	−1.50	0.14	1.60%	**1.42**	3.30	77	0.12	0.03	0.97	−2.50%	1.56	1.35	42
ESINFL	ESRTLC	3.33	0.98	0.33	−0.04%	**1.45**	0.00	77	0.43	0.16	0.87	−2.43%	1.56	**0.54**	42
ESINPR	ESRTLC	3.15	2.16	***0.03***	6.06%	**1.61**	10.73	58	1.57	0.56	0.58	−1.70%	1.55	0.53	42
ESMOSU	ESRTLC	1.66	3.22	**0.00**	10.97%	**1.59**	0.87	77	−0.39	−0.85	0.40	−0.68%	**1.63**	**1.67**	42
ESTRBA	ESRTLC	0.00	0.85	0.40	−0.37%	**1.44**	3.71	77	0.00	0.92	0.36	−0.38%	1.70	0.10	41
ESEXCH	ESRTLC	−1.48	−2.86	**0.01**	8.63%	**1.56**	0.45	77	0.46	1.01	0.32	0.07%	1.54	1.59	42
LIINT	LIRTLC	0.23	1.47	0.14	1.41%	1.79	0.44	83	−3.17	−2.37	***0.02***	10.12%	**1.49**	0.00	42
LIINFL	LIRTLC	3.78	2.93	**0.00**	8.47%	1.74	9.72	83	−4.85	−2.52	***0.02***	11.55%	**1.69**	1.11	42
LIINPR	LIRTLC	0.07	0.99	0.33	−0.04%	1.24	0.88	70	0.13	1.30	0.20	1.66%	**1.23**	0.13	42
LIMOSU	LIRTLC	−0.29	−1.17	0.25	0.44%	1.71	1.81	83	−0.22	−0.71	0.48	−1.22%	**1.30**	0.24	42

LITRBA	LIRTLC	0.00	2.04	***0.04***	3.70%	1.75	0.88	83	0.00	1.15	0.25	0.81%	1.45	0.24	42
LIEXCH	LIRTLC	−0.48	−0.43	0.67	−1.02%	1.74	1.19	82	−0.06	−0.18	0.86	−2.42%	**1.31**	0.94	42
LAINT	LARTLC	0.04	0.05	0.96	−1.75%	1.84	0.33	59	−1.38	−0.76	0.45	−1.03%	1.79	2.73	42
LAINFL	LARTLC	−3.80	−1.18	0.24	0.67%	1.75	**1.50**	59	−2.10	−1.05	0.30	0.26%	1.86	4.49	42
LAINPR	LARTLC	1.59	1.35	0.18	1.41%	2.07	0.38	59	3.10	1.75	*0.09*	4.79%	1.93	0.16	42
LAMOSU	LARTLC	1.53	2.19	***0.03***	6.17%	1.84	0.51	59	−0.40	−0.95	0.35	−0.23%	1.82	0.15	42
LATRBA	LARTLC	0.00	−1.21	0.23	0.81%	1.82	0.22	59	0.00	0.26	0.80	−2.45%	1.88	0.28	40
LAEXCH	LARTLC	−0.52	−0.40	0.69	−1.47%	1.86	0.00	59	−0.57	−1.07	0.29	0.35%	1.84	1.64	42
SNINT	SNRTLC	−0.38	−1.08	0.28	0.19%	2.00	0.07	83	0.35	0.52	0.61	−1.82%	1.70	0.53	42
SNINFL	SNRTLC	1.93	0.84	0.41	−0.37%	1.98	1.31	83	−1.88	−1.35	0.19	1.95%	1.80	2.06	42
SNINPR	SNRTLC	−0.07	−0.77	0.44	−0.50%	2.04	0.07	83	−0.02	−0.35	0.73	−2.20%	1.69	0.08	42
SNMOSU	SNRTLC	−0.44	−2.33	***0.02***	5.13%	1.94	7.32	83	−0.28	−1.14	0.26	0.74%	1.47	0.02	40
SNTRBA	SNRTLC	0.00	2.23	***0.03***	4.61%	2.07	3.54	83	0.00	0.91	0.37	−0.44%	1.61	0.03	42
SNEXCH	SNRTLC	−0.70	−1.83	*0.07*	2.83%	1.96	4.85	82	−0.20	−0.85	0.40	−0.68%	1.64	0.02	42
SKINT	SKRTLC	−0.66	−3.54	**0.00**	12.35%	**1.80**	**1.07**	83	−0.36	−0.37	0.72	−2.16%	1.81	1.92	42
SKINFL	SKRTLC	−1.54	−1.75	*0.08*	2.45%	**1.53**	0.05	83	−0.43	−0.37	0.71	−2.14%	1.82	0.00	42
SKINPR	SKRTLC	−0.23	−1.82	*0.07*	2.74%	**1.50**	**0.06**	83	0.15	0.84	0.41	−0.73%	1.81	0.02	42
SKMOSU	SKRTLC	0.34	1.65	0.10	2.06%	**1.57**	0.23	83	0.11	0.59	0.56	−1.60%	1.78	0.39	42
SKTRBA	SKRTLC	0.00	−1.11	0.27	0.28%	1.57	0.39	83	0.00	−0.55	0.58	−1.72%	1.86	0.16	42
SKEXCH	SKRTLC	0.04	0.12	0.90	−1.23%	**1.62**	**0.12**	82	0.35	0.88	0.39	−0.57%	1.75	2.15	42

Notes: B refers to the slope coefficient of the regression analysis. t refers to the t-statistic. Sig. refers to the lowest level of significance. Adj. R Square refers to the value of the adjusted R square of the regression model. DW and BP refer to the Durbin-Watson and Breusch-Pagan test statistics and N represents the sample size

In the case of the Sig. column, bolded values imply significance at the 1% level, bolded italic values suggest significance at the 5% level and italic values indicate significance at the 10% level. Bolded values in the DW column imply that there are possible issues with serial correlation whereas bolded values in the BP column suggest that the assumption of homoskedasticity can not be confirmed.

Table 6.17 Results of regression analyses of single local macroeconomic factors with robust standard errors

Predictor	Dependent	B	t	Sig.	Before adj. R square	DW	BP	N	B	t	Sig.	After adj. R square	DW	BP	N
CZINT	CZRTLC	−0.17	−1.00	0.32	0.00%	2.00	1.51	83	0.39	0.12	0.90	−2.46%	1.61	2.37	42
CZINFL	CZRTLC	1.33	1.20	0.23	0.54%	1.98	0.74	83	−1.65	−0.85	0.40	−0.68%	1.54	0.01	42
CZINPR	CZRTLC	−0.12	−1.18	0.24	0.47%	1.98	**0.21**	83	0.03	0.34	0.74	−2.27%	1.81	1.41	41
CZMOSU	CZRTLC	0.10	0.43	0.67	−1.00%	1.98	2.46	83	−1.31	−2.70	***0.01***	13.30%	1.75	0.23	42
CZTRBA	CZRTLC	0.00	−1.09	0.28	0.24%	1.89	2.09	83	0.00	0.33	0.75	−2.23%	1.62	0.38	42
CZEXCH	CZRTLC	0.14	0.51	0.61	−0.82%	Robust std. err.		82	−0.17	−0.62	0.54	−1.53%	1.64	3.18	42
HUINT	HURTLC	0.71	2.75	**0.01**	7.40%	2.02	2.07	83	0.67	1.58	0.12	3.51%	1.99	2.38	42
HUINFL	HURTLC	5.38	3.97	**0.00**	15.22%	2.14	0.12	83	−1.94	−0.95	0.35	−0.26%	1.93	0.69	42
HUINPR	HURTLC	−0.12	−0.84	0.40	−0.35%	1.88	2.34	83	−0.10	−0.97	0.34	−0.14%	1.94	0.06	41
HUMOSU	HURTLC	−0.31	−0.85	0.40	−0.50%	1.86	1.61	58	−0.40	−1.42	0.16	2.39%	2.00	0.01	42
HUTRBA	HURTLC	0.00	0.32	0.75	−1.11%	1.89	0.03	83	0.00	−0.06	0.96	−2.49%	1.90	0.61	42
HUEXCH	HURTLC	−0.08	−0.17	0.87	−1.22%	2.05	3.17	82	0.29	0.97	0.34	−0.16%	1.87	0.47	42
PLINT	PLRTLC	0.17	0.75	0.46	−0.54%	1.93	0.92	83	−0.87	−0.77	0.45	−1.02%	2.29	1.94	42
PLINFL	PLRTLC	5.42	4.15	**0.00**	16.54%	2.14	0.08	83	−7.18	−2.79	**0.01**	13.27%	Robust std. err.		42
PLINPR	PLRTLC	−0.18	−1.03	0.30	0.09%	1.97	0.12	83	−0.07	−0.46	0.64	−1.95%	2.24	0.01	42
PLMOSU	PLRTLC	−0.43	−1.45	0.15	1.32%	1.94	0.64	83	0.14	0.45	0.66	−2.27%	2.30	0.02	37
PLTRBA	PLRTLC	0.00	1.55	0.13	1.68%	2.00	0.25	83	0.00	−0.55	0.59	−1.83%	2.31	0.28	40
PLEXCH	PLRTLC	1.12	2.55	***0.01***	10.49%	Robust std. err.		82	0.35	1.24	0.22	1.29%	2.16	0.05	42
ESINT	ESRTLC	−0.60	−1.33	0.19	1.60%	Robust std. err.		77	0.12	0.03	0.97	−2.50%	1.56	1.35	42
ESINFL	ESRTLC	3.33	1.23	0.22	−0.04%	Robust std. err.		77	0.43	0.16	0.87	−2.43%	1.56	**0.54**	42
ESINPR	ESRTLC	3.15	1.51	0.14	6.06%	Robust std. err.		58	1.57	0.56	0.58	−1.70%	1.55	0.53	42
ESMOSU	ESRTLC	1.66	2.94	**0.00**	10.97%	Robust std. err.		77	−0.39	−0.85	0.40	−0.68%	**1.63**	**1.67**	42
ESTRBA	ESRTLC	0.00	0.96	0.34	−0.37%	Robust std. err.		77	0.00	0.92	0.36	−0.38%	1.70	0.10	41
ESEXCH	ESRTLC	−1.48	−2.93	**0.00**	8.63%	Robust std. err.		77	0.46	1.01	0.32	0.07%	1.54	1.59	42
LIINT	LIRTLC	0.23	1.47	0.14	1.41%	1.79	0.44	83	−3.17	−2.37	***0.02***	10.12%	**1.49**	0.00	42
LIINFL	LIRTLC	3.78	1.33	0.19	8.47%	Robust std. err.		83	−4.85	−2.52	***0.02***	11.55%	**1.69**	1.11	42
LIINPR	LIRTLC	0.07	1.00	0.32	−0.04%	Robust std. err.		70	0.13	1.09	0.20	1.66%	Robust std. err.		42
LIMOSU	LIRTLC	−0.29	−1.17	0.25	0.44%	1.71	1.81	83	−0.22	−0.81	0.42	−1.22%	Robust std. err.		42

LITRBA	LIRTLC	0.00	2.04	***0.04***	3.70%	1.75	0.88	83	0.00	1.15	0.25	0.81%	1.45	0.24	42
LIEXCH	LIRTLC	−0.48	−0.43	0.67	−1.02%	1.74	1.19	82	−0.06	−0.18	0.86	−2.42%	Robust std. err.		42
LAINT	LARTLC	0.04	0.05	0.96	−1.75%	1.84	0.33	59	−1.38	−0.76	0.45	−1.03%	1.79	2.73	42
LAINFL	LARTLC	−3.80	−1.18	0.24	0.67%	1.75	**1.50**	59	−2.10	−0.97	0.34	0.26%	Robust std. err.		42
LAINPR	LARTLC	1.59	1.35	0.18	1.41%	2.07	0.38	59	3.10	1.75	*0.09*	4.79%	1.93	0.16	42
LAMOSU	LARTLC	1.53	2.19	***0.03***	6.17%	1.84	0.51	59	−0.40	−0.95	0.35	−0.23%	1.82	0.15	42
LATRBA	LARTLC	0.00	−1.21	0.23	0.81%	1.82	0.22	59	0.00	0.26	0.80	−2.45%	1.88	0.28	40
LAEXCH	LARTLC	−0.52	−0.40	0.69	−1.47%	1.86	0.00	59	−0.57	−1.07	0.29	0.35%	1.84	1.64	42
SNINT	SNRTLC	−0.38	−1.08	0.28	0.19%	2.00	0.07	83	0.35	0.52	0.61	−1.82%	1.70	0.53	42
SNINFL	SNRTLC	1.93	0.84	0.41	−0.37%	1.98	1.31	83	−1.88	−1.35	0.19	1.95%	1.80	2.06	42
SNINPR	SNRTLC	−0.07	−0.77	0.44	−0.50%	2.04	0.07	83	−0.02	−0.35	0.73	−2.20%	1.69	0.08	42
SNMOSU	SNRTLC	−0.44	−1.43	0.16	5.13%	Robust std. err.		83	−0.28	−1.14	0.26	0.74%	1.47	0.02	40
SNTRBA	SNRTLC	0.00	2.23	***0.03***	4.61%	2.07	3.54	83	0.00	0.91	0.37	−0.44%	1.61	0.03	42
SNEXCH	SNRTLC	−0.70	−1.38	0.17	2.83%	Robust std. err.		82	−0.20	−0.85	0.40	−0.68%	1.64	0.02	42
SKINT	SKRTLC	−0.66	−3.54	**0.00**	12.35%	**1.80**	**1.07**	83	−0.36	−0.37	0.72	−2.16%	1.81	1.92	42
SKINFL	SKRTLC	−1.54	−2.15	***0.03***	2.45%	Robust std. err.		83	−0.43	−0.37	0.71	−2.14%	1.82	0.00	42
SKINPR	SKRTLC	−0.23	−2.12	***0.04***	2.74%	Robust std. err.		83	0.15	0.84	0.41	−0.73%	1.81	0.02	42
SKMOSU	SKRTLC	0.34	1.52	0.13	2.06%	Robust std. err.		83	0.11	0.59	0.56	−1.60%	1.78	0.39	42
SKTRBA	SKRTLC	0.00	−1.18	0.24	0.28%	Robust std. err.		83	0.00	−0.55	0.58	−1.72%	1.86	0.16	42
SKEXCH	SKRTLC	0.04	0.17	0.87	−1.23%	Robust std. err.		82	0.35	0.88	0.39	−0.57%	1.75	2.15	42

Notes: B refers to the slope coefficient of the regression analysis. t refers to the t-statistic. Sig. refers to the lowest level of significance. Adj. R Square refers to the value of the adjusted R square of the regression model. DW and BP refer to the Durbin-Watson and Breusch-Pagan test statistics and N represents the sample size. Bolded values indicate significance at the 1% level, bolded italic values suggest significance at the 5% level and italic values indicate significance at the 10% level.

While this is not evidence enough to draw conclusions about the null hypothesis, it does suggest that local factors tend to more often constitute significant predictors in the period prior to the announcement compared to the post-announcement period.

With the initial single factor regression analyses presented, the focus is now shifted to the core part of the hypothesis test. The following tables illustrate the results of the empirical tests of the null hypothesis of no change in the level of influence of local macroeconomic factors on the performance of local equity markets.

Table 6.18 presents the regression result of the most optimal regression models in the two time periods derived from the Czech samples. No significant model is available for the pre-announcement period. However, in the post-announcement period, the model contains a single explanatory variable in the form of money supply which explains 13.3% of the variability in the dependent variable.

The regression models based on the Hungarian sample presented in Table 6.19 suggest a different outcome. The model for the pre-announcement period, based on a single significant explanatory variable in the form of the inflation rate, explains 15.2% of the variability in local market index. This is to be compared with the 9.2% adjusted R^2 of the post-announcement model which is based on two explanatory variables, the inflation rate and the level of money supply. The difference in adjusted R^2 suggests that the local factors in the Hungarian sample contain a larger portion of explanatory power before the announcement compared to after.

Table 6.18 Models of local factors for the Czech Republic before and after announcement

Czech Republic	Before	B	t	Sig.	After	B	t	Sig.
Dependent	BCZRTLC				ACZRTLC			
Predictor 1	No significant model				ACZMOSU	−1.310	−2.700	***0.010***
F-Statistic	n.a.				4.069			
Sig. F-Statistic	n.a.				0.025			
Adjusted R Square	n.a.				13.30%			
Durbin-Watson Statistic	n.a.				1.754			
Breusch-Pagan Statistic	n.a.				0.226			
Condition Index, Max	n.a.				n.a.			
N	n.a.				42			

Notes: B refers to the slope coefficient of the regression analysis. t refers to the t-statistic. Sig. refers to the lowest level of significance and N represents the sample size. Bolded values indicate significance at the 1% level, bolded italic values suggest significance at the 5% level and italic values indicate significance at the 10% level.

Table 6.19 Models of local factors for Hungary before and after announcement

Hungary	Before	B	t	Sig.	After	B	t	Sig.
Dependent	BHURTLC				AHURTLC			
Predictor 1	BHUINFL	5.379	3.965	**0.000**	AHUINFL	–4.514	–2.004	*0.052*
Predictor 2				AHUMOSU	–0.710	–2.277	***0.028***	
F-Statistic	15.725				3.087			
Sig. F-Statistic	0.000				0.057			
Adjusted R Square	15.2%				9.2%			
Durbin-Watson Statistic	2.144				2.113			
Breusch-Pagan Statistic	0.117				0.491			
Condition Index, Max	n.a.				2.746			
N	83				42			

Notes: B refers to the slope coefficient of the regression analysis. t refers to the t-statistic. Sig. refers to the lowest level of significance and N represents the sample size. Bolded values indicate significance at the 1% level, bolded italic values suggest significance at the 5% level and italic values indicate significance at the 10% level.

Similar to the Hungarian sample, the Polish sample, introduced in Table 6.20, suggests that the local factors have a higher level of explanatory power before the announcement of EU accession. The explanatory variables include the inflation rate and the exchange rate in both time periods. However, in the period before the announcement the adjusted R^2 is 22.3% compared with 18.3% in the period after the announcement.

In the Estonian sample, depicted in Table 6.21, no significant model based on local macroeconomic factors exists for the post-announcement period. In the pre-announcement period, a model based on the money supply factor explains 11.0% of the variability in the local equity market index.

In Table 6.22, models based on the Lithuanian sample suggest that local macroeconomic factors explain a larger portion of the local equity market variability in the post-announcement period compared to the pre-announcement period. The difference in adjusted R^2 is large, 20.5% in the post-announcement period versus 3.7% in the pre-announcement period. While this finding is in line with that of the Czech sample, it is opposite to the findings in all remaining country samples.

The Latvian sample of Table 6.23 provides empirical evidence that the local factors explain a somewhat larger portion of the local equity market variability in the pre-announcement period. However, the difference in adjusted R^2 between the two optimal significant models is small, 6.2% before the announcement versus 4.8% after.

In the Slovenian sample, presented in Table 6.24, only the pre-announcement period contains a significant model. The model contains two predictors in the form

Table 6.20 Models of local factors for Poland before and after announcement

Poland	Before	B	t	Sig.	After	B	t	Sig.
Dependent	BPLRTLC				APLRTLC			
Predictor 1	BPLINFL	4.567	3.622	**0.001**	APLINFL	−7.997	−3.051	**0.004**
Predictor 2	BPLEXCH	1.263	3.892	**0.000**	APLEXCH	0.490	1.856	*0.071*
F-Statistic	12.600				5.582			
Sig. F-Statistic	0.000				0.007			
Adjusted R Square	22.3%				18.3%			
Durbin-Watson Statistic	2.235				2.544			
Breusch-Pagan Statistic	5.683				1.467			
Condition Index, Max	2.426				1.808			
N	82				42			

Notes: B refers to the slope coefficient of the regression analysis. t refers to the t-statistic. Sig. refers to the lowest level of significance and N represents the sample size. Bolded values indicate significance at the 1% level, bolded italic values suggest significance at the 5% level and italic values indicate significance at the 10% level.

Table 6.21 Models of local factors for Estonia before and after announcement

Estonia	Before	B	t	Sig.	After	B	t	Sig.
Dependent	BESRTLC				AESRTLC			
Predictor 1	BESMOSU	1.656	2.942	**0.004**	No significant model			
F-Statistic	8.650				n.a.			
Sig. F-Statistic	0.004				n.a.			
Adjusted R Square	11.0%				n.a.			
Durbin-Watson Statistic	Robust std. error				n.a.			
Breusch-Pagan Statistic	Robust std. error				n.a.			
Condition Index, Max	n.a.				n.a.			
N	77				n.a.			

Notes: B refers to the slope coefficient of the regression analysis. t refers to the t-statistic. Sig. refers to the lowest level of significance and N represents the sample size. Bolded values indicate significance at the 1% level, bolded italic values suggest significance at the 5% level and italic values indicate significance at the 10% level.

Table 6.22 Models of local factors for Lithuania before and after announcement

Lithuania	Before	B	t	Sig.	After	B	t	Sig.
Dependent	BLIRTLC				ALIRTLC			
Predictor 1	BLITRBA	0.000107	2.03664	***0.045***	ALIINFL	−4.566	−2.499	***0.017***
Predictor 2					ALIINT	−2.960	−2.351	***0.024***
F-Statistic	4.148				6.3			
Sig. F-Statistic	0.045				0.004			
Adjusted R Square	3.7%				20.5%			
Durbin-Watson Statistic	1.746				1.877			
Breusch-Pagan Statistic	0.885				1.541			
Condition Index, Max	n.a.				6.648			
N	83				42			

Notes: B refers to the slope coefficient of the regression analysis. t refers to the t-statistic. Sig. refers to the lowest level of significance and N represents the sample size. Bolded values indicate significance at the 1% level, bolded italic values suggest significance at the 5% level and italic values indicate significance at the 10% level.

Table 6.23 Models of local factors for Latvia before and after announcement

Latvia	Before	B	t	Sig.	After	B	t	Sig.
Dependent	BLARTLC				ALARTLC			
Predictor 1	BLAMOSU	1.534	2.194	***0.032***	ALAINPR	3.102	1.750	*0.088*
F-Statistic	4.813				3.063			
Sig. F-Statistic	0.032				0.088			
Adjusted R Square	6.2%				4.8%			
Durbin-Watson Statistic	1.837				1.929			
Breusch-Pagan Statistic	0.513				0.164			
Condition Index, Max	n.a.				n.a.			
N	59				42			

Notes: B refers to the slope coefficient of the regression analysis. t refers to the t-statistic. Sig. refers to the lowest level of significance and N represents the sample size. Bolded values indicate significance at the 1% level, bolded italic values suggest significance at the 5% level and italic values indicate significance at the 10% level.

Table 6.24 Models of local factors for Slovenia before and after announcement

Slovenia	Before	B	t	Sig.	After	B	t	Sig.
Dependent	BSNRTLC				ASNRTLC			
Predictor 1	BSNTRBA	0.000	2.588	***0.011***	No significant model			
Predictor 2	BSNEXCH	−0.964	−1.665	*0.100*				
F-Statistic	2.840				n.a.			
Sig. F-Statistic	0.043				n.a.			
Adjusted R Square	11.3%				n.a.			
Durbin-Watson Statistic	Robust std error				n.a.			
Breusch-Pagan Statistic	Robust std error				n.a.			
Condition Index, Max	3.750				n.a.			
N	82				n.a.			

Notes: B refers to the slope coefficient of the regression analysis. t refers to the t-statistic. Sig. refers to the lowest level of significance and N represents the sample size. Bolded values indicate significance at the 1% level, bolded italic values suggest significance at the 5% level and italic values indicate significance at the 10% level.

of the trade balance and exchange rate variables. Jointly these two predictors explain 11.3% of the local equity market variability.

Also in the Slovak sample, described in Table 6.25, only the pre-announcement period offers a significant model based on two predictors. The predictors, however, are different from those in the Slovenian model. The significant predictors include the factors related to interest rates and to industrial production. The model based on these two predictors explains 15.6% of the local equity market variability.

Summary of Test of Change in Level of Influence of Local Macroeconomic Factors

The statistical tests of the level of influence of local macroeconomic factors before and after the EU accession announcement provide results which are in line with expectations formulated in Chap. 3. In six of the eight samples, the pre-announcement regression models provide a higher level of explanatory power, measured by the adjusted R^2, than the post-announcement models. This emphasises the findings suggesting a shift in influence from local to global macroeconomic factors.

Table 6.25 Models of local factors for the Slovak Republic before and after announcement

Slovak Republic	Before	B	t	Sig.	After	B	t	Sig.
Dependent	BSKRTLC				ASKRTLC			
Predictor 1	BSKINT	–0.670	–3.656	**0.000**	No significant model			
Predictor 2	BSKINPR	–0.237	–2.035	***0.045***				
F-Statistic	8.589				n.a.			
Sig. F-Statistic	0.000				n.a.			
Adjusted R Square	15.6%				n.a.			
Durbin-Watson Statistic	1.719				n.a.			
Breusch-Pagan Statistic	0.911				n.a.			
Condition Index, Max	5.841				n.a.			
N	83				n.a.			

Notes: B refers to the slope coefficient of the regression analysis. t refers to the t-statistic. Sig. refers to the lowest level of significance and N represents the sample size. Bolded values indicate significance at the 1% level, bolded italic values suggest significance at the 5% level and italic values indicate significance at the 10% level.

6.1.2.3 Summary of Test of Change in Influence of Macroeconomic Factors

The objective of the previous two sub-sections was to empirically test whether there are any changes in terms of influence of global as well as local macroeconomic factors on the local equity index of transition economies as the EU accession is announced. The tests were conducted based on regression models specified exclusively with significant independent factors. Since the models and the size of the sample sizes vary significantly across the markets and the time periods, the statistic used for comparison is the adjusted R^2.

As is clear from Table 6.26, there are indications that the null hypotheses of no change across the two time periods can be rejected with regard to both the global and local macroeconomic models. In the case of the global macroeconomic factor models, six out of eight markets demonstrate a higher, in most markets a substantially higher, level of explanatory power of the global factors in the period after the announcement compared to the period prior to the announcement. Only one market shows the opposite trend while the eighth market contained no significant model for any of the time periods. The average explanatory power is 8.5% for the models in the period before the announcement while the corresponding value after the announcement is 20.0%.

With regard to the local macroeconomic factor models, there is a shift in the opposite direction, although not as large. The local macroeconomic factor models

Table 6.26 Summary of adjusted R squares of all regression models

	Global macroeconomic factor model		Local macroeconomic factor model	
Country	Adjusted R square-Before	Adjusted R square-After	Adjusted R square-Before	Adjusted R square-After
Czech Republic	10.0%	19.9%	0.0%	13.3%
Estonia	1.4%	34.9%	11.0%	0.0%
Hungary	25.1%	25.9%	15.2%	9.2%
Latvia	12.0%	0.0%	6.2%	4.8%
Lithuania	0.0%	15.3%	3.7%	20.5%
Poland	19.6%	45.2%	22.3%	18.3%
Slovak Republic	0.0%	0.0%	15.6%	0.0%
Slovenia	0.0%	18.8%	11.3%	0.0%
Average All Markets	8.5%	20.0%	10.7%	8.3%

Notes: The average of all markets is calculated by taking the unweighted arithmetic mean of the values of the eight markets.

demonstrate a larger level of explanatory power in the period before the announcement in six out of eight cases. While the difference is distinctive, with 10.7% in the period prior to the announcement versus 8.3% in the period after announcement, it is not as large as the difference found for the global macroeconomic factors.

In conclusion it can be said that the null hypotheses of no change in the level of influence by global and local macroeconomic factors can be rejected based on the empirical tests conducted within this study. These empirical findings suggest that transition economies enter into an accelerated phase of integration with global markets as a result of accession to an established economic union. Further interpretations of these empirical results will be discussed in Chap. 7.

6.2 Findings on Impact of EU Accession on Equity Market Performance

The two research hypotheses related to equity market performance are explored with a combination of statistical and graphical methods as described in Sect. 4.2. The initial sub-section includes the findings on the impact of EU accession on the volatility of equity markets in European transition economies while the second sub-section addresses the findings on return.

6.2.1 Findings on Impact of EU Accession on Equity Market Volatility

The findings relating to the impact of EU accession on equity market volatility are based on two analyses including one analysis of the time-varying trends in the standard deviation of equity returns and one statistical test of significant differences in the level of variance across pre- and post-announcement periods. The subsequent sub-section presents the findings from the analysis of the time-varying trends.

6.2.1.1 Time-Varying Trends of Standard Deviation

As with the analysis of the correlation coefficient in the first research hypothesis, it can be useful to graphically illustrate the key variables, which in this case is the volatility, over time before entering into a discussion of the actual test results. Figures 6.4–6.6 provide graphical illustrations of the rolling 26-week average standard deviation of equity market indices in the eight studied markets. The average standard deviations are calculated for returns based on both local currencies and on USD.

When studying the trends in Fig. 6.4, there is an indication of higher volatility in the Polish and Hungarian equity indices during periods prior to the accession announcement. With regard to the Czech index, differences are not as obvious although the highest volatility is seen in 1998. From the figure it is also apparent that the differences related to the currency in which the returns are calculated plays only a limited role.

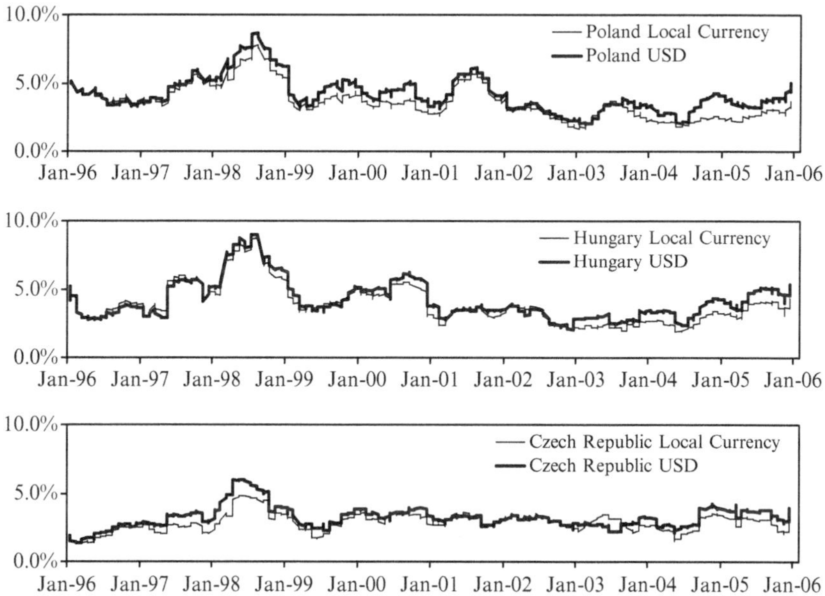

Fig. 6.4 Rolling 26-week standard deviation of equity market returns in Poland, Hungary and the Czech Republic
Notes: Standard deviations are recalculated on a weekly basis based on a rolling 26-week time horizon
Sources: Standard deviations are calculated based on data from Bloomberg

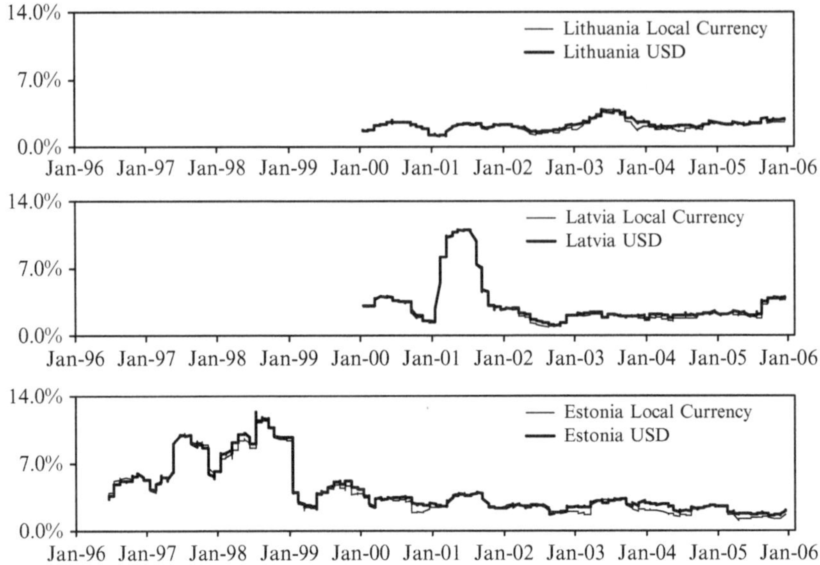

Fig. 6.5 Rolling 26-week standard deviation of equity index returns in Lithuania, Latvia and Estonia
Notes: Standard deviations are recalculated on a weekly basis based on a rolling 26-week time horizon
Sources: Standard deviations are calculated based on data from Bloomberg

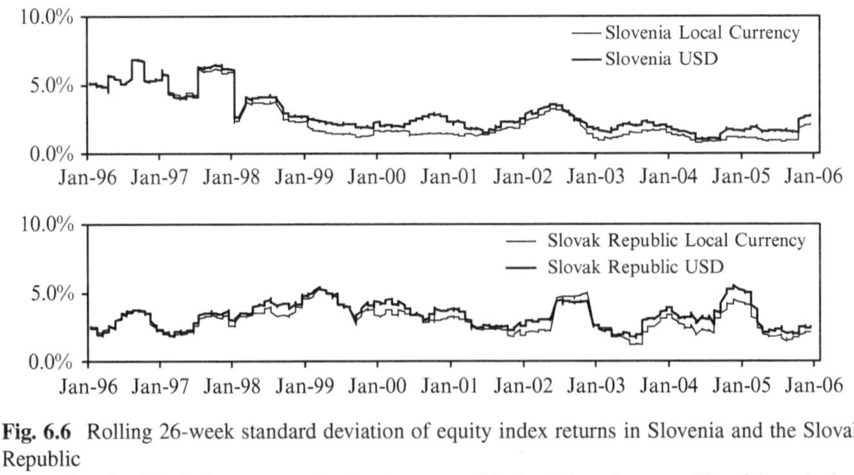

Fig. 6.6 Rolling 26-week standard deviation of equity index returns in Slovenia and the Slovak Republic
Notes: Standard deviations are recalculated on a weekly basis based on a rolling 26-week time horizon
Sources: Standard deviations are calculated based on data from Bloomberg

With regard to index volatility in the markets of the three Baltic economies depicted in Fig. 6.5, a distinctly lower post-announcement overall level is detected in Estonia and Latvia. However, the return volatility in the Lithuanian market index is rather stable with a possible peak appearing in 2003.

Turning the attention to volatility in the Slovenian and Slovak indices presented in Fig. 6.6, it is clear that also these markets demonstrate a declining trend. This is particularly obvious for the Slovenian index where the standard deviation of the return levels has declined from around 5% in 1996 and 1997 to levels below 3% in the period between 2003 and 2005. With regard to the index in the Slovak Republic, there is no equivalently clear trend. However, the rolling 26-week standard deviation level in the period before January 2003 is frequently higher than that after January 2003.

6.2.1.2 Test of Significant Difference in Volatility of Returns

The graphical analyses of the historical trends indicate that there are differences in the level of volatility before and after the EU accession announcement for several markets. The question that arises then is whether these differences are statistically significant which would imply that the null hypothesis can be rejected.

Tables 6.27 and 6.28 illustrate the findings of the statistical tests conducted. The tables include data on the mean weekly return, the variance of the weekly return, the number of observations and the degrees of freedom as well as the F-statistic and the critical two-tail F-value for both pre- and post-announcement periods. Table 6.27 contains the test results of the test using returns based on local currencies whereas Table 6.28 contains the results of the USD-based return data.

Appendix 6 offers a detailed key to the abbreviations applied in the subsequent tables. However, to facilitate the interpretation at this stage, it can be stated that the two initial letters in the variable name refer to the country code. The subsequent two letters refer to whether the data relate to the pre- or post-period. The letters AN refer to which cutting point that has been used, which in this case is the announcement of the EU accession details. The two final letters in the abbreviation refer to whether the return levels have been based on local currencies or on USD.

As is clear from the data in Table 6.27, all market indices, except the Lithuanian index, demonstrate a lower level of variance in the period after the accession announcement compared with before the announcement. For some of the markets, including Estonia, Slovenia and Latvia, the difference is substantial. This is in line with expectations concluded from the graphical illustrations in the previous sub-section.

However, the result of the F-test suggests that the difference in variance is not significantly different over the two time periods for all markets. The volatility changes in the indices of the Czech Republic and Lithuania are not substantial enough to be considered significant at the 5% level.

When measuring the volatility of the index returns based on US currency, illustrated in Table 6.28, the result is largely similar to that of the above analysis in the

Table 6.27 F-Test of differences in return variances by market in local currency

	PLPRANLC	PLPOANLC	HUPRANLC	HUPOANLC	CZPRANLC	CZPOANLC	LTPRANLC	LTPOANLC
Mean	0.0028	0.0046	0.0056	0.0056	0.0009	0.0069	–0.0009	0.0085
Variance	0.0020	0.0007	0.0023	0.0010	0.0009	0.0008	0.0004	0.0007
Observations	363	184	363	184	358	183	152	184
df	362	183	362	183	357	182	151	183
F	2.6683		2.3645		1.0789		0.6002	
P(F≤*f*) two-tail	0.0000		0.0000		0.2835		0.0006	
F Critical two-tail	1.2935		1.2935		1.2948		0.7349	

	LVPRANLC	LVPOANLC	ESPRANLC	ESPOANLC	SVPRANLC	SVPOANLC	SKPRANLC	SKPOANLC
Mean	0.0053	0.0060	0.0039	0.0059	0.0026	0.0025	0.0003	0.0057
Variance	0.0025	0.0005	0.0033	0.0005	0.0012	0.0002	0.0011	0.0007
Observations	153	184	338	184	360	180	343	164
df	152	183	337	183	359	179	342	163
F	4.8291		7.0198		6.3338		1.5390	
P(F≤*f*) two-tail	0.0000		0.0000		0.0000		0.0010	
F Critical two-tail	1.3540		1.2970		1.2966		1.3111	

Table 6.28 F-Test of differences in return variances by market in USD

	PLPRANUS	PLPOANUS	HUPRANUS	HUPOANUS	CZPRANUS	CZPOANUS	LTPRANUS	LTPOANUS
Mean	0.0018	0.0058	0.0042	0.0062	0.0007	0.0088	0.0001	0.0098
Variance	0.0024	0.0012	0.0024	0.0014	0.0012	0.0010	0.0004	0.0007
Observations	363	184	363	184	358	183	152	184
df	362	183	362	183	357	182	151	183
F	1.9395		1.6430		1.1113		0.5722	
P(F≤f)two-tail	0.0000		0.0001		0.2119		0.0002	
F Critical two-tail	1.2935		1.2935		1.2948		0.7349	
	LVPRANUS	LVPOANUS	ESPRANUS	ESPOANUS	SVPRANUS	SVPOANUS	SKPRANUS	SKPOANUS
Mean	0.0052	0.0064	0.0033	0.0072	0.0012	0.0032	–0.0005	0.0073
Variance	0.0026	0.0006	0.0033	0.0006	0.0014	0.0004	0.0013	0.0011
Observations	153	184	338	184	360	180	343	164
df	152	183	337	183	359	179	342	163
F	4.3438		5.6029		3.8134		1.2484	
P(F≤*f*) two-tail	0.0000		0.0000		0.0000		0.0539	
F Critical two-tail	1.3540		1.2970		1.2966		1.3111	

sense that the majority of the markets have significantly different volatility levels over the two time periods. The one detectable difference in the USD-based sample is that the decline in volatility of the index of the Slovak Republic is not statistically significant.

The above tests have been conducted for each market on an individual basis. However, the objective of the research question is not necessarily to explore each market separately but rather all markets jointly. This can be done by collapsing the pre-announcement data samples from all markets into a combined sample and all post-announcement samples into a second combined sample and subsequently conduct the statistical test.

The results of such a test are presented in Table 6.29. The difference in volatility levels over the two time periods is significant. This suggests that even if two or three markets might not provide data that reject the null hypothesis on an individual basis, the overall conclusion using the complete data set is that the null hypothesis of equal variance can be rejected.

6.2.1.3 Summary of test of significant difference in volatility of returns

The analysis of whether the level of equity market volatility is affected by the EU accession is explored using two related approaches. The initial approach is based on a graphical review of the 26-week rolling averages of the standard deviation of equity index returns. The rolling standard deviation averages suggest declining volatility in the period after the EU accession announcement in most markets. In fact, with the exception of the Czech Republic, Lithuania and the Slovak Republic, all markets demonstrate a decreasing level of return volatility.

In the approach containing the statistical test, the indications from the graphical analyses are confirmed. With the exception of the Czech Republic and Lithuania, all markets demonstrate a statistically significant decrease in the level of volatility across the two time periods. Furthermore, when analysing all markets as a joint sample, there is strong evidence of a significant reduction in the level of volatility independent of whether the returns are calculated in local currencies or in USD.

Table 6.29 F-Test of differences in return variance of all markets in local currency and USD

	ALPRANLC	ALPOANLC	ALPRANUS	ALPOANUS
Mean	0.0026	0.0057	0.0019	0.0068
Variance	0.0018	0.0006	0.0019	0.0009
Observations	2,430	1,447	2,430	1,447
df	2,429	1,446	2,429	1,446
F	2.7314		2.1836	
P(F<=*f*) two-tail	0.0000		0.0000	
F Critical two-tail	1.0971		1.0971	

6.2.2 *Findings on Impact of EU Accession on Return Levels*

The aim of the analysis in this sub-section is to test whether any potential difference in mean returns before and after the EU accession announcement is statistically significant. The analysis can be conducted on a country-by-country level or at a level that includes weekly pre-announcement returns from all eight transition economies in a single sample and compare it to the returns of the post-announcement period. Furthermore, the analysis can be conducted using return data derived from either local currencies or from USD and with or without adjustments for the risk level. This sub-section includes a presentation and description of the empirical results for all of the above suggested analyses.

6.2.2.1 Time-Varying Trends in Closing Prices

Prior to applying statistical methods to test the null hypothesis, it is appropriate to graphically review each of the indices to evaluate whether any overall trends can be determined. The graphical review is also potentially helpful to explain the statistical test results. The graphical illustrations of relevant country indices are presented in Figs. 6.7–6.14.

While several observations from each individual market will be discussed in the subsequent paragraphs, certain observations are worth noting separately since they tend to reoccur across the markets.

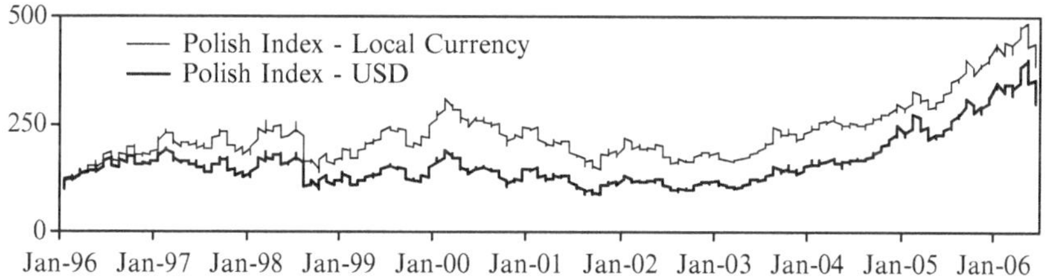

Fig. 6.7 Polish equity index – weekly closing values indexed to 100 as of January 1996
Sources: Bloomberg

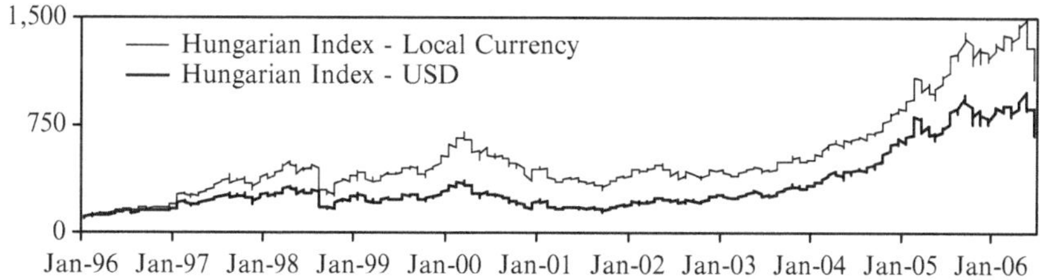

Fig. 6.8 Hungarian equity index – weekly closing values indexed to 100 as of January 1996
Sources: Bloomberg

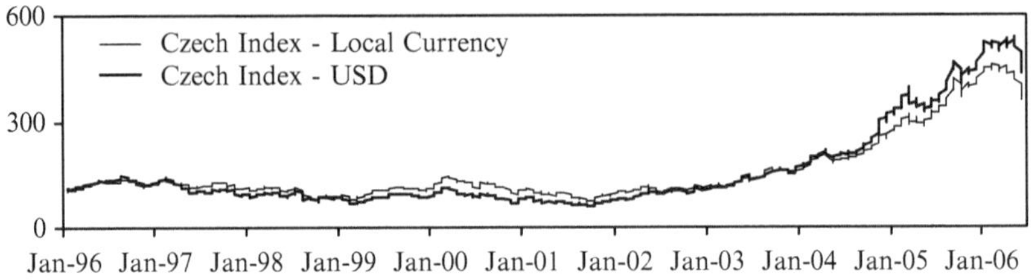

Fig. 6.9 Czech equity index – weekly closing values indexed to 100 as of January 1996
Sources: Bloomberg

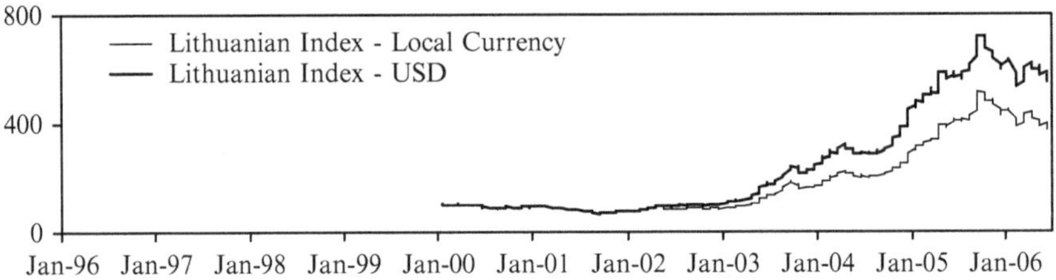

Fig. 6.10 Lithuanian equity index – weekly closing values indexed to 100 as of January 2000
Sources: Bloomberg

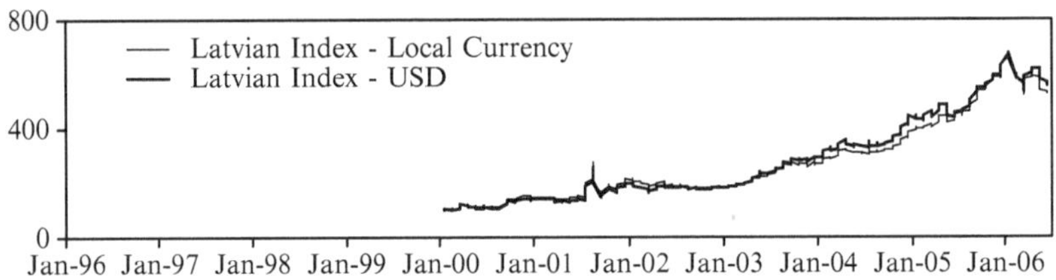

Fig. 6.11 Latvian equity index – weekly closing values indexed to 100 as of January 2000
Sources: Bloomberg

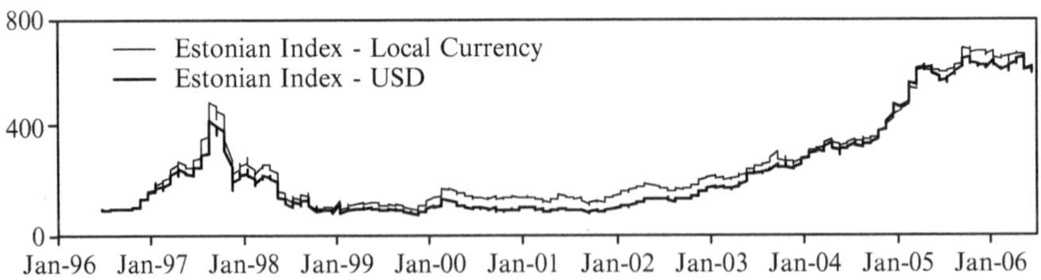

Fig. 6.12 Estonian equity index – weekly closing values indexed to 100 as of June 1996
Sources: Bloomberg

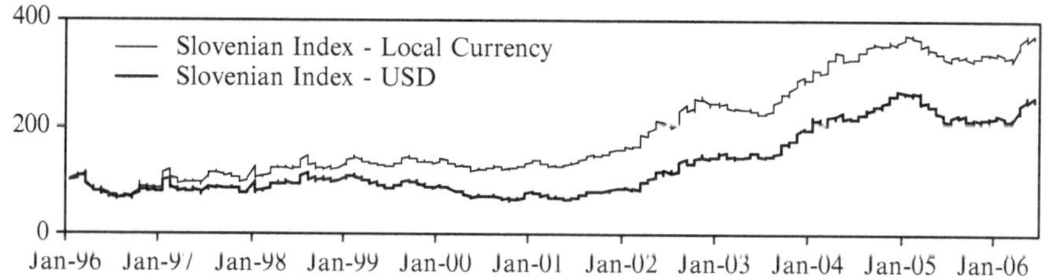

Fig. 6.13 Slovenian equity index – weekly closing values indexed to 100 as of January 1996
Sources: Bloomberg

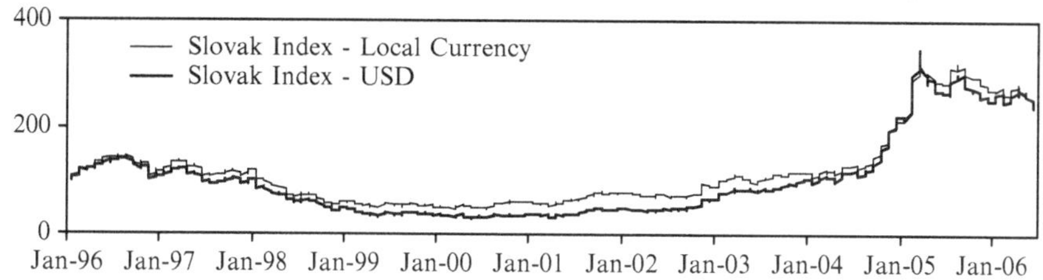

Fig. 6.14 Slovak equity index – weekly closing values indexed to 100 as of January 1996
Sources: Bloomberg

First, most of the eight equity indices show a positive trend in index closing values starting around the beginning of 2003. For some of the markets, the rise in closing values was quite substantial. The Estonian index went from just over 200 in December 2002 to close to 700 in December 2005 when measured in the local currency.

Second, the Russian financial crisis, which involved a devaluation of the Russian Rouble and a flight of foreign capital from the market in August 1998, has had an effect on some but not all of the markets within this study. Analysing the closing prices for the indices of the Czech Republic, Slovenia and the Slovak Republic, no effect can be determined during the autumn of 1998. The Estonian equity index experienced both a strongly positive and strongly negative development during 1997 along with a negative adjustment in the first half of 1998. However, there was no particular change directly associated with the Russian events of August 1998. At the same time, a review of the index closing prices in the Polish and Hungarian markets suggests that there is a distinct negative change in the month of August 1998.

The Polish and Hungarian equity indices displayed in Figs. 6.7 and 6.8 demonstrate a homogenous development. A long trend of negative or flat closing values beginning in early 2000 was interrupted in the first half of 2003. The subsequent positive trend lasted until May 2006 with occasional interruptions in 2005. The one difference that is worth highlighting is that the while the Polish equity index rose 2.89 times in the entire time period, the Hungarian index rose 10.15 times.

The historical development of the closing values of the Czech index, illustrated in Fig. 6.9, is similar to that in Poland when looking at the period after 2002. The period prior to 2002 is represented by a steadily declining trend.

The trends in the closing values of the Lithuanian, Latvian and Estonian equity indices, displayed in Figs. 6.10–6.12, are somewhat similar when observing the period after 2000. One thing that separates them is the difference in performance denominated in local versus US currency. The difference is a result of alternative currency policies. The Lithuanian currency was pegged to the USD until January 2002 and only thereafter pegged to the EUR while the Estonian currency has been pegged to the EUR since the beginning of 1999 and the Latvian currency has been floating freely against both currencies.

The performance of the Slovenian and Slovak equity indices illustrated in Figs. 6.13 and 6.14, suggest very different trends. While the Slovenian index has been steadily increasing since the end of 2001, with certain exceptions particularly in first half of 2005, the Slovak index experienced a subtle increase as of the end of 2002 followed by a steep increase in the second half of 2004. Both the Slovenian Tolar and the Slovak Koruna have been kept loosely pegged to the EUR.

6.2.2.2 Test of Significant Difference in Mean Returns

With a brief review of the historical trends in the equity index closing prices conducted, it is appropriate to explore whether the changes which appear graphically are large enough to be statistically significant.

The subsequent tables contain the detailed data and test results. In Table 6.30, the t-test of significant difference in mean returns is explored using the local currencies for each of the markets. In line with the graphical illustrations discussed above, the data for the return mean in the first row suggest a higher return for each of the markets subsequent to the EU accession announcement. However, in order to reject the null hypothesis of equal means, the difference needs to be statistically significant. The t-statistic is calculated for each market and compared with the two-tailed critical t value at the 5% significance level.

The hypothesis of equal means can be rejected if the t-statistic is less than the negative value or more than the positive value of the critical t number. As is clear from Table 6.30, the null hypothesis, H0_4 can only be rejected for two markets, the Czech Republic and Lithuania, when based on local currency returns.

In Table 6.31, the same analysis is conducted using the return data denominated in USD. The findings are largely similar to those found with the local currency analysis. However, when measuring the return in USD, one more market, the Slovak Republic, demonstrates significantly different market returns before and after the EU accession announcement.

With less than half of the market samples providing data rejecting the null hypothesis, there is insufficient evidence to reject the null hypothesis when studying the markets on an individual basis.

Table 6.30 t-test of significant difference in mean returns by market in local currency

	PLPRANLC	PLPOANLC	HUPRANLC	HUPOANLC	CZPRANLC	CZPOANLC	LTPRANLC	LTPOANLC
Mean	0.0028	0.0046	0.00564	0.00565	0.0009	0.0069	−0.0009	0.0085
Variance	0.0020	0.0007	0.0023	0.0010	0.0009	0.0008	0.0004	0.0007
Observations	363	184	363	184	358	183	152	184
Hyp. Mean Diff.	0		0		0		0	
df	526		512		379		333	
t Stat	−0.5852		−0.0032		−2.2483		−3.7911	
P(*T*<=*t*) two-tail	0.5587		0.9974		0.0251		0.0002	
t Critical two-tail	1.9645		1.9646		1.9662		1.9671	
	LVPRANLC	**LVPOANLC**	**ESPRANLC**	**ESPOANLC**	**SVPRANLC**	**SVPOANLC**	**SKPRANLC**	**SKPOANLC**
Mean	0.0053	0.0060	0.0039	0.0059	0.0026	0.0025	0.0003	0.0057
Variance	0.0025	0.0005	0.0033	0.0005	0.0012	0.0002	0.0011	0.0007
Observations	153	184	338	184	360	180	343	164
Hyp. Mean Diff.	0		0		0		0	
df	204		476		518		390	
t Stat	−0.1582		−0.5873		0.0418		−1.9299	
P(T<=*t*) two-tail	0.8745		0.5573		0.9667		0.0543	
t Critical two-tail	1.9717		1.9650		1.9646		1.9661	

Table 6.31 t-test of significant difference in mean returns by market in USD

	PLPRANUS	PLPOANUS	HUPRANUS	HUPOANUS	CZPRANUS	CZPOANUS	LTPRANUS	LTPOANUS
Mean	0.0018	0.0058	0.0042	0.0062	0.0007	0.0088	0.0001	0.0098
Variance	0.0024	0.0012	0.0024	0.0014	0.0012	0.0010	0.0004	0.0007
Observations	363	184	363	184	358	183	152	184
Hyp. Mean Diff.	0		0		0		0	
df	483		455		384		332	
t Stat	−1.1210		−0.5076		−2.7042		−3.6957	
$P(T<=t)$ two-tail	0.2628		0.6119		0.0072		0.0003	
t Critical two-tail	1.9649		1.9652		1.9662		1.9671	

	LVPRANUS	LVPOANUS	ESPRANUS	ESPOANUS	SVPRANUS	SVPOANUS	SKPRANUS	SKPOANUS
Mean	0.0052	0.0064	0.0033	0.0072	0.0012	0.0032	−0.0005	0.0073
Variance	0.0026	0.0006	0.0033	0.0006	0.0014	0.0004	0.0013	0.0011
Observations	153	184	338	184	360	180	343	164
Hyp. Mean Diff.	0		0		0		0	
df	209		496		538		355	
t Stat	−0.2722		−1.0551		−0.7923		−2.4397	
$P(T<=t)$ two-tail	0.7857		0.2919		0.4285		0.0152	
t Critical two-tail	1.9714		1.9648		1.9644		1.9667	

Table 6.32 t-Test of significant difference in mean returns for all markets in local currency and USD

	ALPRANLC	ALPOANLC	ALPRANUS	ALPOANUS
Mean	0.0026	0.0057	0.0019	0.0068
Variance	0.0018	0.0006	0.0019	0.0009
Observations	2,430	1,447	2,430	1,447
Hyp. Mean Diff.	0		0	
df	3,874		3,813	
t Stat	−2.8750		−4.1547	
P(T<=t) two-tail	0.0041		0.0000	
t Critical two-tail	1.9606		1.9606	

However, the aim of this study is not to draw conclusions exclusively about single markets although these insights are relevant. Instead, the aim is to understand whether overall return levels in European transition economies change as a result of the EU accession announcement. The more appropriate way to analyse this is to combine the data for all markets into two categories and conduct the t-test. This analysis is presented in Table 6.32.

With this approach there is clear evidence to reject the null hypothesis of equal means before and after. The mean weekly returns increase from 0.26% prior to the announcement to 0.57% subsequent to the announcement when measured in local currencies. The equivalent values for the USD-based return rates are 0.19% and 0.68% respectively.

With the above return calculations completed it is appropriate to address the complementary analysis of risk-adjusted returns described in the previous sub-section. For these calculations, the differential returns are calculated using index returns based on local currencies. The results of the analysis are presented in Table 6.33.

The results presented in Table 6.33 are clearly indicating that the Sharpe Ratio is substantially higher in the period after the announcement of the EU accession details. This provides a strong argument in favour of rejecting the null hypothesis of no significant change in the level of returns as a consequence of EU accession when taking risk-adjusted returns into consideration.

6.2.2.3 Summary of Tests of Significant Difference in Mean Returns

Three related analyses are conducted to explore the effects of EU accession on the return levels of equity markets in transition economies. The initial test is based on a graphical illustration of the respective equity index to explore any dynamics suggesting the presence of distinct changes in the level of returns around the time of the accession or the announcement of the accession details. While all of the eight market indices demonstrate a positive trend starting around 2003, there are negative or stabilising trends in several markets for the period starting in 2005. Statistically this graphical analysis cannot provide any concluding results despite the positive trends.

Table 6.33 Results of Sharpe ratio analyses

	Poland	Hungary	Czech Republic	Lithuania	Latvia	Estonia	Slovenia	Slovak Republic
Pre-Announcement Period								
Number of Weekly Observations	362	362	362	152	152	339	360	343
Average Differential Return	0.032%	0.327%	–0.018%	–0.142%	0.449%	0.288%	0.072%	–0.099%
Standard Deviation of Differential Return	0.044	0.047	0.030	0.020	0.051	0.057	0.035	0.034
Pre-Announcement Sharpe Ratio	0.007	0.069	–0.006	–0.071	0.089	0.050	0.020	–0.029
Post-Announcement Period								
Number of Weekly Observations	185	185	185	185	185	185	181	167
Average Differential Return	0.383%	0.425%	0.674%	0.816%	0.533%	0.555%	0.161%	0.499%
Standard Deviation of Differential Return	0.027	0.031	0.029	0.026	0.023	0.022	0.014	0.027
Post-Announcement Sharpe Ratio	0.141	0.138	0.233	0.318	0.233	0.258	0.114	0.183

The second analysis involves statistically testing whether the return levels are significantly different across two time periods, one relating to before the announcement of the EU accession details and the other relating to after the announcement. The analysis is conducted with returns in both local currencies and in USD. When studying the markets individually, there is not sufficient evidence to reject the null hypothesis given that data samples from only two or three markets, dependent on the currency used for the return calculations, provide statistically significant changes. However, when comparing the combined sample in the pre-announcement period with that of the post-announcement period, the null hypothesis of no change can be rejected.

Finally, when adjusting the return levels for the changing risk levels and comparing a risk-adjusted measure in the form of the Sharpe Ratio across the two time periods there is clear evidence arguing for higher return levels in the period after the EU accession announcement.

6.3 Concluding Remarks on Findings and Discussion

Chapter 6 provided a detailed description of the empirical methods and the associated test results applied to address the four research hypothesis introduced in Chap. 3. Each research hypothesis has been addressed in multiple ways in order to ensure a more extensive understanding. While the research hypotheses are unique from an academic point of view, the methods applied to test them have largely been explored and used in previous academic research.

The test results have been discussed within the preceding chapter. However, a broader and more detailed interpretation of the conclusions as well as a discussion of their implications in academia and in practice will be provided in the next chapter.

Chapter 7
Conclusions

The aim of this study has been to provide empirical evidence regarding four research questions related to the effects on equity market integration and performance of EU accession among European transition economies. The four research questions are derived from existing academic research and address areas which have not yet been explored. The first research question empirically tests the effect on the level of co-movement between equity markets in European transition economies and global as well as European equity indices. The second research question investigates whether there is an impact of the EU accession on the level of influence global and local macroeconomic factors have on equity markets in European transition economies. Jointly, these two questions contribute to the understanding of the later stages of market integration. The last two questions explore the effects of EU accession on the volatility and the return levels of equity markets in transition economies.

As described in Chap. 4, the methods applied to test the research hypotheses derived from the four questions are empirical in nature. The methods incorporate statistical methods which, in most cases, have been applied in previous research. The data applied in the empirical tests cover a time period of 10 years from 1996 to 2006 for most markets. The statistical test results presented in Chap. 6 provide evidence of significant changes in the level of integration with global markets, partly explained by a shift in influence from local to global macroeconomic factors. Furthermore, the test results indicate a decline in equity market volatility and, to a certain extent, an increase in return levels as a result of EU accession.

This chapter offers an interpretation of the overall empirical findings and outlines how these findings contribute to parties in practice, including asset managers and policy makers, as well as to academia. The chapter is structured into five sections. The first section outlines a detailed interpretation of the statistical findings for each of the research questions. The second section highlights limitations which should be taken into consideration when interpreting the results. The third section specifies how this research contributes to the understanding relevant for academia and in practice. The fourth section explores additional research which could be conducted to extend the insights generated from this study. Finally, the last section contains the concluding remarks of the study.

7.1 Interpretation of Results

The statistical test results in Chap. 6 offer findings which clarify some of the effects on equity markets in European transition economies as a result of EU accession. The aim of this section is to further elaborate on these test results and put them into a broader context.

7.1.1 EU Accession and Level of Co-movement of Equity Returns

The statistical tests of the initial research hypothesis suggest that there is evidence of a significant increase in the level of co-movement between local equity market returns and global equity market returns, measured by the MSCI World Index, when comparing a time period before the EU accession with one after. However, the tests also suggest that there is no evidence of increasing co-movement or even weak indications of declining co-movement when comparing with indices that include exclusively companies in the EU.

While these seemingly contradicting findings might appear surprising at first, there is logic when putting them into a broader context. However, before proceeding with the discussion of this logic it is important to once again mention that correlation coefficients from all but one market were positive across both the global and the European reference indices before and after the EU accession. This implies that there is positive co-movement between the equity returns and in certain cases the co-movement is strong with several correlation coefficients between 0.40 and 0.57.

Returning to the logic for the different findings between global and European reference indices, the results indicate that the correlation coefficients relating to the European indices are high already in the initial period. This could be explained by the fact that the integration with European markets is likely to have occurred largely in the 1990s, when initial trade agreements between the EU and the EU candidate countries were implemented. As discussed in Chap. 5, privatisations of companies in the European transition economies were often targeted at investors within the EU during the second half of the 1990s. In addition, foreign direct investment, mostly from EU 15 members, steadily increased well before the EU accession actually occurred, as can be seen in Table 7.1.

Furthermore, the increasing imports and exports were largely related to existing EU members as can be detected in Table 7.2. The combination of foreign direct investment and international trade concentrated to existing EU members is likely to have contributed to the high levels of equity return co-movement with EU markets well before the EU accession announcement.

Further integration between transition economy and Western European equity indices is likely to occur over time as the economies become increasingly interlinked economically and as remaining trade barriers are removed. However, it is

Table 7.1 Foreign direct investment inflow in the period 1994-2004

USD Million	1994	1995	1996	1997	1998	1999	2000	2004
Czech Republic	868.9	2,561.9	1,428.2	1,301.1	3,716.4	6,326.2	4,980.2	4,975.0
Estonia	214.6	201.5	150.3	266.7	580.6	305.0	387.0	972.0
Hungary	1,143.5	5,101.9	3,300.4	4,170.9	3,337.1	3,313.1	2,763.0	4,508.2
Latvia	214.0	180.0	382.0	521.0	357.0	348.0	407.0	671.8
Lithuania	31.3	72.6	152.4	354.5	925.5	486.5	379.0	n.a.
Poland	1,874.8	3,658.1	4,499.7	4,913.8	6,368.0	7,275.8	9,446.1	12.484.0
Slovak Republic	272.9	241.4	395.7	230.6	706.8	428.5	2,383.1	1,107.5
Slovenia	128.1	177.4	194.0	375.2	247.9	181.2	175.5	903.4
Total	4,748.1	12,194.8	10,502.7	12,133.8	16,239.3	18,664.3	20,920.9	25,621.9

Source: OECD International Direct Investment Database, 2007

Table 7.2 Exports by destination and imports by region of origin in 2005

	Exports 2005		Imports 2005	
EUR Billion	Intra-EU	Extra-EU	Intra-EU	Extra-EU
Czech Republic	53.1	10.0	50.0	11.7
Estonia	4.8	1.4	6.1	1.9
Hungary	38.3	11.9	35.8	17.3
Latvia	3.2	1.0	5.3	1.7
Lithuania	6.2	3.3	7.3	5.1
Poland	55.5	16.4	60.6	20.5
Slovak Republic	22.0	3.8	22.4	6.0
Slovenia	10.2	5.2	12.7	3.6
Total	193.3	53.0	200.2	67.8
Total in %	100.0%	27.4%	100.0%	33.9%

Source: European Commission, 2007

unlikely that there will be any large and distinct shifts in the level of equity market co-movement.

With regard to the co-movement with the MSCI World Index, an index which comprises over 1,400 companies from Europe, the US, Canada, Australia, New Zealand, Japan and other Far East markets, the test results suggest a significant increase for the period starting 2004. The significant increase in level of co-movement between this broad global index and the European transition economies could be related to a number of local and global economic drivers.

First, the level of economic interaction outside the European markets could have increased. If extra-European trade increases after the expansion of intra-European trade, the positive effects on equity market correlation with markets outside Europe could be somewhat delayed in comparison with effects on the correlation with European markets.

Second, the decline in the value of the USD in the period starting from 2002 also seems to be a factor which affects the co-movement. Given that the MSCI World Index is denominated in USD, all the non-US equities in the World Index as well as the equity markets in the transition economies have received a positive boost which may have increased the level of correlation in the post-2002 period.

Finally, there might be further global as well as local macroeconomic factors affecting the equity return levels. These will be explored further in the subsequent sub-section.

With regard to the conclusions related to market integration, the above test results suggest that the European transition economies which accessed the EU in 2004 had already largely been integrated with European markets before the EU accession occurred or even was announced. This is particularly the case for the larger transition economies, which all demonstrated high levels of co-movement both before and after the announcement of the EU accession details.

However, the completion of the EU accession does seem to have significant implications on the level of co-movement between the equity returns of the transition economies and the overall world market returns. While this is partly a result of the currency denomination used for the calculations as discussed above, it nevertheless highlights an important and relevant observation. In order to further understand the underlying drivers for this co-movement, the findings from the analyses of macroeconomic factors are interpreted in the next sub-section.

7.1.2 EU Accession and Influence of Macroeconomic Factors on Equity Returns

The statistical tests of the research hypotheses related to the influence of global and local macroeconomic variables on transition economy equity markets suggest that there are statistically significant changes in how equity returns in transition economies are affected by macroeconomic factors before and after the EU accession announcement. The results indicate that global macroeconomic factors increase in importance while the local factors become less influential.

Regarding the global macroeconomic factors the unweighted arithmetic mean of the adjusted R^2 increases from 8.5% in the pre-announcement period to 20.0% in the post-announcement period. When excluding the models where there are no significant independent variables, the adjusted R^2 ranges from 15.3% for Lithuania to 45.2% for Poland in the post-announcement period.

As discussed in sub-section 4.1.2.1, the macroeconomic factors included in this study have, in previous research, proven to have significant relationships with equity returns in emerging markets (Bodurtha et al., 1989; Fifield et al., 2002; Harvey, 1995b, 1995a). Table 7.3 indicates that far from all global macroeconomic factors are significant in each of the market models covered in this study. In the post-announcement period each of the included global macroeconomic factors is significant in at least one model. In the pre-announcement period this is true for all factors except the one related to the oil price.

When comparing the models of one country across the two time periods it is clear from Table 7.3 that they rarely contain the exact same combination of global

Table 7.3 Summary of significant global macroeconomic factors in regression model

Global macroeconomic factors		Pre-announcement period	Post-announcement period
Czech Republic	Adjusted R square:	10.0%	19.9%
	Significant factors:	World equity return US interest rate	World equity return
Estonia	Adjusted R square:	1.4%	34.9%
	Significant factors:	Industry production	Industry production World equity return World inflation US interest rate
Hungary	Adjusted R square:	25.1%	25.9%
	Significant factors:	World equity return	World equity return
Latvia	Adjusted R square:	12.0%	0.0%
	Significant factors:	World equity return Industry production World inflation Commodity price	No significant factor
Lithuania	Adjusted R square:	0.0%	15.3%
	Significant factors:	No significant factor	World equity return US interest rate
Poland	Adjusted R square:	19.6%	45.2%
	Significant factors:	World equity return	World equity return Oil price
Slovak Republic	Adjusted R square:	0.0%	0.0%
	Significant factors:	No significant factor	No significant factor
Slovenia	Adjusted R square:	0.0%	18.8%
	Significant factors:	No significant factor	Industry production Commodity price Oil price
Summary of global macroeconomic factors			
World equity return		4	5
Industry production		2	2
World inflation		1	1
US interest rate		1	2
Commodity price		1	1
Oil price		0	2

macroeconomic factor models as independent variables. However, in the case where the models are different there is at least one macroeconomic factor in common across the two models.

The most common significant predicting factor across the models is the world equity return measured by the monthly return in the MSCI World Index. This global macroeconomic factor appears as a significant predictor in four pre-announcement models and in five post-announcement models. In the cases where the models contain only the world equity return as a significant predictor, such as in the post-announcement models for the Czech Republic and Hungary as well as in the pre-announcement models for Hungary and Poland, the models explain between 19.6% and 25.9% of the equity return variability in the transition economies. Given the results from the previous research question, which indicated a high level of co-movement between the returns of the transition economy equity markets and the weekly returns of MSCI World Index, these findings are not unexpected.

Other significant and reoccurring global macroeconomic factors include global industry production rate which is a proxy for global GDP. While not as frequent a predictor as the world equity return factor, it does appear in two models for each time period. The explanatory power of the world industry production seems more limited than the world equity return factor. In the single case where the industry production factor appears as the only explanatory variable, which is the case in the pre-announcement period in Estonia, the model results in an adjusted R^2 of only 1.4%. Finally, US interest rates and global oil prices are the remaining global macroeconomic factors which occur more than once in a single time period.

While many of the global macroeconomic factors are industry independent, factors such as commodity prices and oil price can be associated more strongly to specific industries. What could be seen as surprising when studying Tables 5.10 and 7.3 is that while certain markets, including Latvia, Lithuania and Hungary, have a large portion of oil-related businesses in their indices there is no significant influence of the oil price. However, keeping in mind that these markets are not oil producing nations and that the listed companies mostly relate to transit operations of oil and gas from Russia and other oil producing countries, the relative indifference to the global oil prices is more understandable.

With regard to the local macroeconomic factors, illustrated in Table 7.4, there is evidence of a decrease in the level of explanatory power across the two time periods. The unweighted arithmetic means of the adjusted R^2 for the models decreases from 10.7% in the pre-announcement period to 8.3% in the post-announcement period. While the difference between the unweighted arithmetic means of the two periods for the local macroeconomic factors is not as substantial as that for the global factors, the fact that samples from six of the eight markets show a higher adjusted R^2 in the pre-announcement period suggests that the null hypothesis can be rejected.

Given the influence of exchange rates on the research question related to market integration, the test of the research hypothesis related to local macroeconomic factors is particularly interesting since it is based on local currency returns, thus eliminating the direct impact of exchange rates on the equity index returns. What is clear from Table 7.4 is that while the exchange rate between the local currencies and the USD occasionally appears as a significant factor in the regression models, as in the samples for Poland and Slovenia, it does not constitute a dominant factor influencing returns in all markets.

The most frequently reoccurring local factor in the significant regression models is the local currency inflation rate, which appears in three occasions in the post-announcement period and at two occasions in the pre-announcement period. An increase in consumer price index suggests a decrease in the value of a currency which is likely to be reflected in a higher share price when measured in local currency. Since the return is calculated as the difference in share price, a higher inflation rate is likely to imply a higher equity returns. In real terms, however, the inflation does not imply any positive effects on equity market returns.

The second most frequently appearing local macroeconomic factor is the level of money supply. As the quantity of local currency increases, the interest rates tend to decrease which in turn implies a more attractive environment for corporate credit rates and a basis for higher share prices.

Table 7.4 suggests that changes in the local market industrial production has limited impact on the level of equity returns. Given that industrial output is a driver of revenue and cash flows, it would have been expected to play a more dominant role in the equity returns. In general it seems as the three most frequent local macroeconomic factors are related to the financial or nominal aspects of the economy.

Overall it can be concluded that while some global macroeconomic factors become more important as predictors of equity market returns in European transition economies after the announcement of the timing and details of the EU acces-

Table 7.4 Summary of significant local macroeconomic factors in regression model

Local macroeconomic factors		Pre-announcement period	Post-announcement period
Czech Republic	Adjusted R square:	0.0%	13.3%
	Significant factors:	No significant factor	Money supply
Estonia	Adjusted R square:	11.0%	0.0%
	Significant factors:	Money supply	No significant factor
Hungary	Adjusted R square:	15.2%	9.2%
	Significant factors:	Inflation rate	Inflation rate Money supply
Latvia	Adjusted R square:	6.2%	4.8%
	Significant factors:	Money supply	Industrial production
Lithuania	Adjusted R square:	3.7%	20.5%
	Significant factors:	Trade balance	Inflation rate Interest rate
Poland	Adjusted R square:	22.3%	18.3%
	Significant factors:	Inflation rate Exchange rate with USD	Inflation rate Exchange rate with USD
Slovak Republic	Adjusted R square:	15.6%	0.0%
	Significant factors:	Interest rate Industrial production	No significant factor
Slovenia	Adjusted R square:	11.3%	0.0%
	Significant factors:	Trade balance Exchange rate with USD	No significant factor
Summary of local macroeconomic factors			
Inflation rate		2	3
Money supply		2	2
Exchange rate with USD		2	1
Trade balance		2	0
Interest rate		1	1
Industrial production		1	1

sion, this is not the case for all global factors included in this study. The most frequently occurring global macroeconomic factors in terms of significant predictors for transition economy equity performance are changes in world equity returns, changes in global industry production levels, changes in US interest rates and changes in the oil price. Furthermore, the findings of the study also suggest that local macroeconomic factors become less influential in predicting the performance of equity markets in EU transition economies after the announcement of EU accession.

7.1.3 EU Accession and Equity Market Volatility and Return

The study incorporates empirical tests exploring the effect of EU accession on equity market volatility. With data samples from six of the eight markets indicating statistically significant declines in volatility when comparing time periods before and after the EU accession announcement, the findings of this study suggest the presence of reduced volatility levels. This conclusion is further supported by the 26-week rolling average of the standard deviations. In six of the eight markets there is a clear trend towards lower standard deviations in the time period after the accession announcement.

These empirical and graphical results related to changes in the volatility of equity indices provide an argument for the conclusion that the volatility of equity markets in the European transition economies is reduced in the period subsequent to the announcement of the EU accession. While the drivers of this change are not explicitly explored within the scope of this study, it is possible to identify a few likely influencing factors.

First, the underlying drivers of country risk have become less negative. As illustrated in Fig. 3.1 and in Appendix 2, the credit rating of the eight transition economies for foreign investors has improved. The political components described in Table 3.1 have improved in several cases as measures against corruption and steps enhancing democracy are part of the reforms related to the EU accession. In terms of economic factors there are clear indications of improved investment environment. For example, real GDP growth has increased, as is clear from Table 3.2.

Second, the EU accession implied an increasing interest among accession countries in improving corporate governance policies to levels which are more harmonised with those of Western European markets. As voluntary standards were introduced, awareness of corporate governance improved and as a result, a more stable involvement of foreign as well as domestic capital was established.

Third, the foreign direct investments have steadily arrived in an increasing pattern, as can be concluded from Table 7.1. While these funds do not include investments into equity markets, they result in a more stable environment for foreign and local equity investors.

Regarding the effects of EU accession on equity market return levels in European transition economies, the conclusions differ depending on whether each market is evaluated independently or whether all markets are evaluated jointly. When testing each market as an independent sample, there is only limited evidence to suggest a significant change in the level of weekly equity returns. Using local currencies as the basis for the weekly return calculations, the results suggest that only two of eight samples support a conclusion of significant changes in the return levels. If the local currencies are exchanged for USD, the number of samples supporting the conclusion of significant changes in return levels increases to three. In either case, less than a majority of the samples support this conclusion.

However, when consolidating all market data into a single sample and dividing it into two time periods, the result is different. In this case, the statistical results, independent of base currency, strongly suggest the presence of a statistically significant change in the return levels between the two time horizons.

Furthermore, taking the risk-adjusted performance into account, the study provides clear evidence of more attractive risk-adjusted returns in the period after the announcement of the EU accession compared to that before the announcement. Applying the Sharpe ratio (Sharpe, 1994) as the risk-adjusted measure, the analyses suggest that all markets have experienced a substantial improvement in the return levels.

7.2 Limitations of Study

As with most empirical research, there are certain limitations that must be taken into considerations when evaluating the empirical findings of this study. In this case, the limitations can be divided into two categories; limitations related to the data samples and limitations related to the applied test methods. Relevant limitations in the respective categories are explored in the subsequent sub-sections.

7.2.1 Limitations Related to Data Samples

Limitations related to the samples cover the source, the scope and the definition of the qualitative information and the quantitative data samples selected for the analyses. In this study the number of markets included in the empirical tests has been limited by the fact that only a small number of Central European transition economies have accessed the EU to date. Emerging markets accessing the EU in January 2007 could not be included due to the lack of data in the post-accession period. With eight markets incorporated in the test, a sufficient number of markets are included to draw conclusions which could be generalised to a certain degree, particularly in the Central European setting. However, further considerations might be required before drawing major conclusions outside the European context.

Furthermore, the indices included in the study are often of limited scope and might contain biases in terms of industry or company size. However, by selecting to start the time series no earlier than in January 1996, and later for some less developed markets, the effects of these biases have been reduced. Furthermore, several of the analyses include tests based on a combination of all indices in the form of panel data samples. This often results in a reduction of the biases although a certain level of bias will remain.

Also, in line with common research practice, costs associated with transactions in the transition economies are excluded from the definition of market returns. While this has limited impact on analyses which focus on a single market at a time, it can distort the relative performance when comparing with global and European reference indices where cost of investing is often lower. Comparisons between reference indices and local equity market indices appear in only two research questions. In addition, as the European transition economies become more integrated, the costs associated with investing in these equity markets will continue to decline. As a result, the overall implications of the differing investment costs for this study are likely to be limited.

7.2.2 Limitations Related to Research Methodology

In addition to the research limitations associated with the data samples, there are also limitations which relate to the applied research methodology. One methodology limitation which has influenced the results of the tests is the selection of point in time relating to when the EU accession effects should be considered to occur. There is a rationale for applying the date of the announcement as the point of measure as this is when the details and the exact timing of the accession were clarified. However, as is explored in sub-section 6.1.1, it is clear that when a different time period is applied, it is possible that the findings regarding some of the research hypotheses would be different.

Another limitation relates to the fact that there are a reduced number of macroeconomic factors applied within the scope of this study. However, by incorporating six global and six local macroeconomic factors, all of which have been proven to contain significant relationships with the equity returns in emerging markets in previous academic research, the study incorporates a comprehensive scope. Still, it is possible that other predictive macroeconomic factors exist which could have been relevant for this study.

Finally, some of the analyses applied within the study, including those based on the graphical illustrations do not provide statistical accuracy in their conclusions. This implies that the weight of the findings from these analyses should be taken more lightly. In this study, the graphical analyses have been allocated functions related to establishing an understanding of the background and providing support in the derivation of statistical and economic conclusions.

Despite limitations related to the data sample and the research methodology, the conclusions of this study are relevant for the investment community and academia. The subsequent section outlines the main contributions of this work.

7.3 Contributions and Implications of Research

The findings of this study are relevant for several parties within and outside the academic community. In addition to empirically exploring dimensions of market integration theory, the study provides evidence which is largely relevant in the investment community as well as for policy makers. The following sub-sections detail how the results of this study contribute to the knowledge base of practitioners and academia.

7.3.1 Contribution to Academia

As discussed in Sect. 2.2, existing market integration research has been focused primarily on the early stages of integration, in particular market liberalisation. A model introduced by Bekaert and Harvey (2003) theoretically predicts the effects of a successful market liberalisation announcement on emerging equity markets. The model suggests that as an emerging market transitions from a segmented to integrated state, equity prices should increase at the announcement. The size of the increase is dependent on a combination of the credibility of the announcement, the potential diversification benefits and the level to which liberalisation had already been expected.

The empirical findings of this study are in line with the market integration theory suggested by Bekaert and Harvey (2003). The study concludes that while the level of co-movement between Western European equity indices and equity indices in the transition economies increases over time, it is clear that a large portion of integration has already occurred prior to the accession announcement and was, for certain countries, present in the second half of the 1990s. This implies that it is possible that the market integration theory suggested by Bekaert and Harvey (2003) sufficiently describes the empirical occurrences for the intra-European integration in the case of European transition economies.

However, when observing the market integration effects on a more global basis, there is evidence of further integration effects with regard to the level of co-movement with global equity markets. This suggests that the study also provides empirical evidence which is complementary to the existing liberalisation research in the sense that it indicates the presence of further effects on market integration when an already liberalised market accesses the EU.

In addition to an increased level of co-movement with global markets, factors related to global rather than local factors are increasingly important as predictors of equity market returns after the EU accession announcement. Together with the increased co-movement findings, this implies that while models which incorporate successful and effective market liberalisation possibly describe the market integration effects on a regional basis, they do not describe the complete integration process related to European transition economies and equity markets outside the European region.

This study contributes to existing market integration theory by providing empirical evidence which suggests that successful liberalisation might not constitute the end phase in the market integration process. Given the statistically significant evidence suggesting an impact of EU accession on the level of integration, measured by co-movement, a more complete model would be achieved by adding variables describing accession to economic unions to the model measuring successful market liberalisation.

7.3.2 Contribution to Practice

From the perspective of practitioners, this study contributes with several important and relevant insights which have implications on for example how investment portfolios should be adapted as countries included in the portfolio transition into an economic union.

The first insight relates to the change in level of co-movement with the world indices as a result of the EU accession. While this change might have positive implications for certain portfolios focusing exclusively on emerging markets, it also implies that there is a reduced opportunity for portfolio diversification available for global investors when including the transition economies in a globally diversified portfolio. This reduction in diversification benefits should be taken into consideration when configuring the structure of portfolios to ensure that the risk level remains within the portfolio requirements.

The second insight relates to the indication provided by this research that co-movement with European markets tends to occur before the announcement of EU accession. This emphasises that the diversification opportunities offered by European transition economies with regard to European equity portfolios might in fact be reduced ahead of the announcement of the final details and timing of the EU accession and must be carefully considered in European equity portfolios.

The third insight relates to the evidence which suggests that global macroeconomic factors become increasingly useful as equity market performance predictors while the local macroeconomic factors become less applicable. This suggests that models related to active portfolio management might require revision with regard to the applied predictors. In this context it is also worthwhile to note another result from this study. Despite geographical proximity, it is rarely the case that an identical set of macroeconomic factors can be applied to the transition economies. Each market requires a unique combination of macroeconomic factors although the return of the MSCI World Index tends to appear as a significant predictor in several markets.

The fourth relevant contribution derived from this study is that while EU accession results in a statistically significant decline in the level of equity market volatility, it does not result in any significant changes in the return levels when observing the transition markets on an individual basis. However, when studying all markets jointly or when applying a risk-adjusted measure of return, there is evidence of a statistically significant upward shift in the period subsequent to the announcement of the EU accession.

Jointly, these insights contribute valuable information which can support portfolio managers in delivering improved risk-adjusted returns to investors. In addition, the insights are relevant for policy makers, in the sense that it offers evidence that measures and reforms promoting dimensions required for the EU accession result in positive effects for financial markets.

7.4 Further Research

The focus of this study has exclusively been on the effects of the EU accession of eight Central and Eastern European transition economies on three characteristics of the equity markets in the respective economies. The study has provided insights into the market integration process of equity markets in transition economies as well as the effects of EU accession on the volatility and return levels of equity markets. There are, however, additional areas that would deserve attention in terms of establishing an even more comprehensive understanding of the market integration process and the effects on financial markets as a result of EU accession.

First, the scope of financial markets could be extended to include fixed income instruments as well as pricing spreads such as term spreads, which refer to pricing difference of short- and long-term government bonds, and junk bond spreads, which refer to the spread difference of gradable and non-gradable bonds.

Second, an area that has received attention with regard to emerging financial markets in general is that of contagion. Contagion effects imply that events in one country have an impact on financial markets in other countries. Events studied include the impact of the Mexican devaluation in 1994 and the Asian economic crisis in 1997 (Dahiya, 1997). However, limited research has been conducted with regard to determining how the level of contagion is affected by the EU accession and related events.

Third, the lack of data has limited the depth and scope of analysis of the interesting and relevant area of how corporate governance measures in general, and at the level of financial exchanges in particular, affect the performance of emerging market performance. However, given the structure of reporting companies meeting the voluntary corporate governance recommendations separately from companies that do not, rewarding empirical studies should be possible as soon as the sample size of conforming companies increases.

Finally, findings and predictions relating to the effects of EU accession developed within this study could be further tested with data from Greece and Portugal as well as more recent EU member states as data become available.

7.5 Concluding Remarks

This study includes empirical tests of four research questions relating to the effects of EU accession on the level of integration and performance of equity markets in European transition economies. The conclusions of the study are that EU accession seems to be associated with a distinct increase in the level of co-movement with global but not necessarily European equity indices. Furthermore, the EU accession also seems to result in a decline in the level of equity market volatility for acceding countries while the market return levels increase temporarily when measured on a risk-adjusted basis.

The findings of this study both confirm and complement existing market integration theory in the sense that models containing market liberalisation are found to be largely sufficient in describing the integration process in a regional perspective. However, in terms of integration with global equity indices, models aiming to fully explain the market integration process should also include the effects of a transition into an economic trade union. The findings of this study are also relevant for both investment professionals and policy makers by improving the understanding of effects on portfolios containing equities from European transition economies.

References

Aggarwal, Reena, Carla Inclan, and Ricardo Leal (1999), "Volatility in Emerging Financial Markets," *Journal of Quantitative Analysis*, 34, 33–55.

Agrawal, Anup and Charles R. Knoeber (1996), "Firm Performance and Mechanisms to Control Agency Problems Between Managers and Shareholders," *Journal of Financial and Quantitative Analysis*, 31 (3), 377–97.

Alexander, Gordon J., Cheol S. Eun, and Sundaram Janakiramanan (1987), "Asset Pricing and Dual Listing on Foreign Capital Markets: A Note," *Journal of Finance*, 42 (1), 151–58.

Aydogan, Kursat and Guner Gursoy (2001), "P/E and PBV Ratios as Predictors of Stock Returns in Emerging Equity Markets," *Emerging Markets Quarterly*, 4, 60–67.

Bai, Jushan, Robin L. Lumsdaine, and James H. Stock (1998), "Testing For and Dating Common Breaks in Multivariate Time Series," *Review of Economic Studies*, 65 (3), 395–432.

Baldwin, Richard E., Joseph F. Francois, Richard Portes, Dani Rodrik and Istvan P. Szekely (1997), "The Costs and Benefits of Eastern Enlargement: The Impact on the EU and Central Europe," *Economic Policy*, 12 (24), 125–76.

Baldwin, Richard E. and Anthony J. Venables (2004), "Regional Economic Integration," Graduate Institute of International Studies, Geneva London School of Economics.

Barberis, Nicholas, Andrei Shleifer, and Jeffrey Wurgler (2005), "Comovement," *Journal of Financial Economics*, 75 (2), 283–317.

Barry, Christopher B., John W. Peavy III, and Mauricio Rodriguez (1997), *Emerging Stock Markets: Risk, Return, and Performance*. Charlottesville, VA: The Research Foundation of the Institute of Chartered Financial Analysts.

Barry, Christopher B., John W. Peavy III, and Mauricio Rodriguez (1998), "Performance Characteristics of Emerging Capital Markets," *Financial Analysts Journal*, 54 (1), 72–80.

Basu, Parantap, Hiroyuki Kawakatsu, and Matthew Morey (2000), "Liberalization and Emerging Markets Stock Prices," *Emerging Markets Quarterly*, 4 (3), 7–17.

Baur, Dirk (2003), "What is Co-movement?," European Commission, Joint Research Center, Ispra (VA), Italy.

Bekaert, Geert (2000), "Emerging Equity Markets and Market Integration," *NBER Reporter*, Winter 1999-2000, 8–11.

Bekaert, Geert (1995), "Market Integration and Investment Barriers in Emerging Equity Markets," *The World Bank Economic Review*, 9 (1), 75–107.

Bekaert, Geert, Claude B. Erb, Campbell R. Harvey, and Tadas E. Viskanta (1997), "The Behavior of Emerging Market Returns," in *The Future of Emerging Market Capital Flows*, Edward Altman and Richard Levich and Jianping Mei, Eds. Boston: Kluwer Academic Publishers.

Bekaert, Geert, Claude B. Erb, Campbell R. Harvey, and Tadas E. Viskanta (1998), "Distributional Characteristics of Emerging Market Returns and Asset Allocation," *Journal of Portfolio Management*, 24 (2), 102–16.

Bekaert, Geert and Campbell R. Harvey (2001), "Economic Growth and Financial Liberalization," *NBER Reporter*, Spring 2001, 8–11.

Bekaert, Geert and Campbell R. Harvey (1997), "Emerging Equity Market Volatility," *Journal of Financial Economics*, 43 (1), 29–77.

Bekaert, Geert and Campbell R. Harvey (2003), "Emerging Markets Finance," *Journal of Empirical Finance*, 10 (1/2), 3–56.

Bekaert, Geert and Campbell R. Harvey (2000), "Foreign Speculators and Emerging Equity Markets," *Journal of Finance*, 55 (2), 565–613.

Bekaert, Geert and Campbell R. Harvey (1995), "Time-Varying World Market Integration," *Journal of Finance*, 50 (2), 403–44.

Bekaert, Geert, Campbell R. Harvey, and Robin L. Lumsdaine (2002), "Dating the Integration of World Equity Markets," *Journal of Financial Economics*, 65 (2), 203–47.

Bekaert, Geert, Campbell R. Harvey, and Christian T. Lundblad (2003), "Equity Market Liberalization in Emerging Markets," *Journal of Financial Research*, 26 (3), 275–99.

Bekaert, Geert, Campbell R. Harvey, and Angela Ng (2005), "Market Integration and Contagion," *Journal of Business*, 78 (1), 39–70.

Bekaert, Geert and Michael S. Urias (1999), "Is There a Free Lunch in Emerging Market Equities?," *Journal of Portfolio Management*, 25 (3), 83–95.

Berle, Adolf and Gardiner C. Means (1932), *The Modern Corporation and Private Property*. New York: MacMillan.

Best Practices Committee at the Corporate Governance Forum (2004), "Best Practices in Public Companies 2005." Warsaw.

Bhagat, Sanjai, Dennis C. Carey, and Charles M. Elson (1999), "Director Ownership, Corporate Performance, and Management Turnover," *Corporate Governance Advisor*, 7 (5), 10–12.

Bhagwati, Jagdish N. (1998), "The Capital Myth," *Foreign Affairs*, 77 (3), 7–12.

Bilson, Chris M., Tim J. Brailsford, and Vince J. Hooper (2000), "Selecting Macroeconomic Variables as Explanatory Factors of Emerging Stock Market Returns," *Working Paper Series in Finance, Australia National University*, 00-04, 1–31.

Bodurtha Jr., James N., D. Chinhyung Cho, and Lemma W. Senbet (1989), "Economic Forces and the Stock Market: An International Perspective," *Global Finance Journal*, 1 (1), 21–46.

Bratislava Stock Exchange (2006), "Important Events in the History of the Bratislava Stock Exchange," Bratislava Stock Exchange.

Breuss, Fritz (2002), "Consequences of EU Enlargement for Macroeconomic Stability in Euroland," in Policy Modeling EcoMod 2002. Brussels: EcoMod.

Breuss, Fritz (2001), "Macroeconomic Effects of EU Enlargement for Old and New Members," Austrian Institute of Economic Research.

Brown, Drusilla, Alan Deardorff, Simeon Djankov, and Robert Stern (1997), "An Economic Assessment of the Integration of Czechoslovakia, Hungary and Poland into the European Union," in Europe's Economy Looks East: Implications for Germany and the European Union, Stanley W. Black, Ed. Cambridge: Cambridge University Press.

Budapest Stock Exchange (2006), "BSE Event Calendar." Warsaw: Budapest Stock Exchange.

Budapest Stock Exchange, Ernst & Young Advisory Ltd., and Kapolyi Law Office (2004), "Corporate Governance Recommendations." Budapest.

Burda, Michael C. (1998), "The Consequences of EU Enlargement for Central and Eastern European Labor Markets," in CEPR Discussion Paper Series Vol. 1881: Centre for Economic Policy Research.

Chen, Nai-Fu (1991), "Financial Investment Opportunities and the Macroeconomy," *Journal of Finance*, 46 (2), 529–54.

Chen, Nai-Fu, Richard Roll, and Stephen A. Ross (1986), "Economic Forces and the Stock Market," *Journal of Business*, 59 (3), 383–403.

Cheung, Yin-Wong and Lilian K. Ng (1998), "International Evidence on the Stock Market and Aggregate Economic Activity," *Journal of Empirical Finance*, 5 (3), 281–96.

Claessens, Stijn, Susmita Dasgupta, and Jack Glen (1995), "Return Behavior in Emerging Stock Markets," *World Bank Economic Review*, 9 (1), 131–51.

Claessens, Stijn and Simeon Djankov (1999), "Enterprise Performance and Management Turnover in the Czech Republic," *European Economic Review*, 43, 1115–24.

Claessens, Stijn, Simeon Djankov, Joseph P. H. Fan, and Lamy H. P. Lang (2002), "Disentangling the Incentive and Entrenchment Effects of Large Shareholdings," *Journal of Finance*, 57 (6), 2741–71.
Claessens, Stijn, Susmita Dasgupta, and Jack Glen (1998), "The Cross-Section of Stock Returns: Evidence from Emerging Markets," *Emerging Markets Quarterly*, 2 (4), 4–13.
Cottrell, Robert (2005), "Meet the Neighbours: A Survey of the EU's Eastern Borders," in The Economist.
Dahiya, Sandeep (1997), "The Risks and Returns of Brady Bonds in a Portfolio Framework," *Financial Markets, Institutions & Instruments*, 6 (5), 45–60.
Dally, Kevin (2006), "Sovereign Ratings History since 1975." London: Standard & Poor's.
De Santis, Giorgio and Selahattin Imrohoroglu (1997), "Stock Returns and Volatility in Emerging Financial Markets," *Journal of International Money and Finance*, 16 (4), 561–79.
DeFusco, Richard A., Dennis W. McLeavey, Jerald E. Pinto, and David E. Runkle (2004), *Quantitative Methods for Investment Analysis* (2 ed.). Charlottesvill, VA: CFA Institute.
Deutsche Boerse (2006), "Fact Book 2005." Frankfurt.
Divecha, A.B., J. Drach, and D. Stefek (1992), "Emerging Markets: A Quantitative Perspective," *Journal of Portfolio Management*, 19 (1), 41–56.
EBRD (2000), "Lietuvos Telekomas IPO—Project Summary Document." London: European Bank for Reconstruction and Development.
EFTA (2004), "The European Economic Area Agreement." Geneva.
Engardio, Pete (2002), "The Era of Blind Investment is Over," *Business Week*, March 11, 2002, 50.
Erb, Claude B., Campbell R. Harvey, and Tadas E. Viskanta (1996), "Political Risk, Economic Risk and Financial Risk," *Financial Analysts Journal*, 52 (6), 28–46.
Errunza, Vihang and Etienne Losq (1989), "Capital Flow Controls, International Asset Pricing, and Investor Welfare: A Multi-Country Framework," *Journal of Finance*, 44 (4), 1025–37.
Errunza, Vihang and Etienne Losq (1985), "International Asset Pricing Under Mild Segmentation: Theory and Test," *Journal of Finance*, 40 (1), 105–24.
Errunza, Vihang, Lemma Senbet, and Ked Hogan (1998), "The Pricing of Country Funds from Emerging Markets: Theory and Evidence," *International Journal of Theoretical and Applied Finance*, 1 (1), 111–43.
Eun, Cheol and Sundaram Janakiramanan (1986), "A Model of International Asset Pricing with a Constraint on the Foreign Equity Ownership," *Journal of Finance*, 41 (4), 897–914.
European Commission (2000), "EU Stabilisation and Association Process for Countries of South-Eastern Europe." Brussels.
European Commission (2007), "The European Neighbourhood Policy." Brussels.
European Commission (2006), "The History of the European Union," European Commission.
European Commission, Directorate General for Enlargement (2005), "2005 Enlargement Strategy Paper," in Communication from the Commission. Brussels.
European Council (1993), "Conclusions of the Presidency–Copenhagen 21-22 June 1993." Copenhagen.
European Council (2002), "Consolidated Version of the Treaty on European Union," *Official Journal of the European Communities*, C (325), 5–32.
European Council (1995), "Presidency Conclusions—15 and 16 December 1995." Madrid.
Eurostat (2006), "Harmonized Indices of Consumer Prices, 1996 = 100," European Commission.
Fama, Eugene F. (1965), "Random Walks in Stock Market Prices," *Financial Analysts Journal*, 21 (5), 55–59.
Fama, Eugene F (1990), "Stock Returns, Expected Returns, and Real Activity," *Journal of Finance*, 45 (4), 1089–108.
Fama, Eugene F (1981), "Stock Returns, Real Activity, Inflation and Money," *American Economic Review*, 71 (4), 545–65.
Fama, Eugene F. and Kenneth R. French (1992), "The Cross-Section of Expected Stock Returns," *Journal of Finance*, 47 (2), 427–65.
Ferson, Wayne E. and Campbell R. Harvey (1991a), "Sources of Predictability in Portfolio Returns," *Financial Analysts Journal*, 47 (3), 49–56.

Ferson, Wayne E. and Campbell R. Harvey (1991b), "The Variation of Economic Risk Premiums," *Journal of Political Economy*, 99 (2), 385–415.

Ferson, Wayne and Campbell R. Harvey (1993), "The Risk and Predictability of International Equity Returns," *Review of Financial Studies*, 6 (3), 527–66.

Fifield, S. G. M., D. M. Power, and C. D. Sinclair (2002), "Macroeconomic Factors and Share Returns: An Analysis Using Emerging Market Data," *International Journal of Finance & Economics*, 7 (1), 51–62.

Fisher, Ronald A. (1921), "On the 'probable error' of a coefficient of correlation deduced from a small sample," *Metron*, 1, 3–32.

Frenkel, Michael and Lukas Menkhoff (2004), "Are Foreign Institutional Investors Good for Emerging Markets?" *World Economy*, 27 (8), 1275–93.

Garcia, Rene and Eric Ghysels (1998), "Structural Change and Asset Pricing in Emerging Markets," *Journal of International Money and Finance*, 17 (3), 455–73.

Goetzmann, William N. and Philippe Jorion (1999), "Re-emerging Markets," *Journal of Financial and Quantitative Analysis*, 34 (1), 1–32.

Gompers, Paul A., Joy I. Ishii, and Andrew Metrick (2003), "Corporate Governance and Equity Prices," *Quarterly Journal of Economics*, 118 (1), 107–55.

Gordon, Myron J. (1982), *The Investment, Financing and Valuation of the Corporation*. Oxford: Greenwood Publishing Group.

Gottschalk, Ricardo (2005), "Can It Be Both Economically and Morally Rewarding to Invest in Developing Countries?" *Global Economy Journal*, 5 (2), receding p1–18.

Greenwood, John G. (1993), "Portfolio Investment in Asian and Pacific Economies: Trends and Prospects," *Asian Development Review*, 11 (1), 120–50.

Gujarati, Damodar N. (1995), *Basic Econometrics* (3 ed.). New York: McGraw-Hill.

Hambrick, Donald and Eric Jackson (2000), "Outside Directors with a Stake: The Linchpin in Improving Governance," *California Management Review*, 42 (4), 108–27.

Harris, James W. (2000), "Weighing Emerging Market Risk: The Supply of Capital," *Business Economics*, 35 (1), 52.

Harvey, Campbell R. (1995a), "The Risk Exposure of Emerging Equity Markets," *World Bank Economic Review*, 9, 19–50.

Harvey, Campbell R. (1995b), "Predictable Risk and Returns in Emerging Markets," *Review of Financial Studies*, 773–816.

Heijdra, Ben J., Christian Keuschnigg, and Wilhelm Kohler (2002), "Eastern Enlargement of the EU: Jobs, Investment and Welfare in Present Member Countries." Munich: CESifo.

Henry, Peter Blair (2000), "Stock Market Liberalization, Economic Reform, and Emerging Market Equity Prices," *Journal of Finance*, 55 (2), 529–564.

IMF (2006a), "IMF Primary Commodity Prices," IMF.

IMF (2006b), "International Financial Statistics," IMF.

International Finance Corporation (1999), *Emerging Stock Markets Fact Book 1999*. Washington, D.C.: International Finance Corporation.

Jensen, Michael C. and William H. Meckling (1976), "Theory of the Firm: Managerial Behavior, Agency Costs and Ownership Structure," *Journal of Financial Economics*, 3 (4), 305-60.

Johnson, Robert R., Gerald W. Buetow, and Gerald R. Jensen (1999), "International Mutual Fund Returns and Federal Reserve Policy," *Financial Services Review*, 8 (3), 199–210.

Johnson, Simon, Peter Boone, Alasdair Breach, and Eric Friedman (2000), "Corporate Governance in the Asian Financial Crisis," *Journal of Financial Economics*, 58, 141–86.

Jorion, Philippe (1985), "International Portfolio Diversification with Estimation Risk," *Journal of Business*, 58 (3), 259–78.

Karolyi, G. Andrew (1998), "Why Do Companies List Shares Abroad?: A Survey of the Evidence and Its Managerial Implications," in Financial Markets, Institutions & Instruments. Malden, MA: Blackwell Publishers.

Karolyi, G. Andrew and Rene M. Stulz (2003), *International Capital Markets Volume I*. Cheltenham: Edward Elgar Publishing Limited.

Keuschnigg, Christian, Mirela Keuschnigg, and Wilhelm Kohler (2001), "The German Perspective on Eastern EU Enlargement," *The World Economy*, 24 (4), 513–42.

Keuschnigg, Christian and Wilhelm Kohler (2002), "Eastern Enlargement of the EU: How Much Is It Worth For Austria?" *Review of International Economics*, 10 (2), 324–42.
Kim, E. Han and Vijay Singal (2000), "Stock Market Openings: Experience of Emerging Economies," *Journal of Business*, 73 (1), 25–66.
Kohler, Wilhelm (2000), "Wer Gewinnt Wer Verliert Durch Die Osterweiterung der EU?," in Jahrestagung 1999: Erweiterung der EU, L Hoffmann, Ed. Berlin: Duncker and Humblot.
Kyle, Albert S. and Wei Xiong (2001), "Contagion as a Wealth Effect," *Journal of Finance*, 56 (4), 1401–40.
La Porta, Rafael, Florencio Lopez-de-Silanes, and Andrei Shleifer (1999), "Corporate Ownership Around the World," *Journal of Finance*, 54 (2), 471–517.
Lintner, John (1965), "The Valuation of Risk Assets and the Selection of Risky Investments in Stock Portfolios and Capital Budgets," *Review of Economics and Statistics*, 47 (1), 13–37.
Lipsey, Richard G. (1957), "The Theory of Custom Unions: Trade Diversion and Welfare," *Economica*, 24 (93), 40–46.
Ljubljana Stock Exchange (2005), "Corporate Governance Code." Ljubljana.
Ljubljana Stock Exchange (2006), "LJSE From 1989 to 2005," Ljubljana Stock Exchange.
Lo, Andrew W. and A. Craig MacKinlay (1988), "Stock Market Prices Do Not Follow Random Walks: Evidence from a Simple Specification Test," *Review of Financial Studies*, 1 (1), 41–66.
London Stock Exchange (2006), "Main Market Fact Sheet—September 2006." London.
Lowenstein, Roger (2000), *When Genius Failed: The Rise and Fall of Long-Term Capital Management*. New York: Random House Inc.
Lyn, Esmeralda O. and Edward J. Zychowicz (2004), "Predicting Stock Returns in the Developing Markets of Eastern Europe," *Journal of Investing*, 13 (2), 63–71.
Markowitz, Harry M. (1952), "Portfolio Selection," *Journal of Finance*, 7 (1), 77–91.
Markowitz, Harry M. (1959), *Portfolio Selection: Efficient Diversification of Investments*. New York: John Wiley & Sons.
Masters, Seth J. (2002), "Emerging Markets," *Journal of Portfolio Management*, 28 (3), 96–101.
McMillan, John and Ewen McCann (1981), "Welfare Effects in Customs Unions," *Economic Journal*, 91 (363), 697–703.
Meade, James (1955), *The Theory of Customs Unions*. Amsterdam: North Holland Publishing Co.
Miller, Darius (1999), "The Market Reaction to International Cross-listings: Evidence from Depositary Receipts," *Journal of Financial Economics*, 51 (1), 103–23.
Morck, Randall, Andrei Shleifer, and Robert W. Vishny (1988), "Management Ownership and Market Valuation: An Empirical Analysis," *Journal of Financial Economics*, 20, 293–315.
MSCI (2006), "Index Definitions," Morgan Stanley International Capital Inc.
Newbold, Paul (1991), *Statistics for Business and Economics* (3 ed.). Englewood Cliffs, NJ: Prentice-Hall.
Obstfeld, Maurice (1994), "Risk Taking, Global Diversification and Growth," *American Economic Review*, 84 (5), 1310–29.
OECD (2006), "OECD Country Statistical Profiles 2006," OECD.
OECD (2004), *OECD Principles of Corporate Governance*. Paris: OECD Publications Service.
OMX Group (2006), "About Securities Market—History," OMX Group.
Prague Stock Exchange (2006), "History of the Exchange," Prague Stock Exchange.
Price, M. P. (1994), *Emerging Stock Markets*. New York: McGraw-Hill.
Roll, Richard and Stephen A. Ross (1980), "An Empirical Investigation of the Arbitrage Pricing Theory," *Journal of Finance*, 35 (5), 1073–103.
Ross, Stephen A. (1976), "The Arbitrage Theory of Capital Asset Pricing," *Journal of Economic Theory*, 13, 341–60.
Sharpe, William F. (1964), "Capital Asset Prices: A Theory of Market Equilibrium Under Conditions of Risk," *Journal of Finance*, 19 (3), 425–42.
Sharpe, William F. (1966), "Mutual Fund Performance," *Journal of Business*, 39 (1), 119–38.
Sharpe, William F. (1994), "The Sharpe Ratio," *Journal of Portfolio Management*, Fall 1994.
Sinn, Hans-Werner (2004), "EU Enlargement, Migration and the New Constitution," *CESifo Economic Studies*, 50 (4), 685–707.

Sinn, Hans-Werner and Martin Werding (2001), "Immigration Following EU Enlargement," *CESifo Forum*, 2 (2), 40–47.
Sohinger, Jasminka (2005), "Growth and Convergence in European Transition Economies: The Impact of Foreign Direct Investment," *Eastern European Economics*, 43 (2), 73–94.
Solnik, Bruno and Bernard Noetzlin (1982), "Optimal International Asset Allocation," *Journal of Portfolio Management*, Fall, 11–21.
Soubbotina, Tatyana P. (2004), *Beyond Economic Growth—An Introduction to Sustainable Development*. Washington D.C.: The International Bank for Reconstruction and Development.
Standard & Poor's (2006), "Standard & Poor's Ratings Definitions," McGraw-Hill.
Stanley, M.T. (1995), *Guide to Investing in Emerging Markets*. Chicago: Richard D. Irwin.
Stapleton, Richard and Marti Subrahmanyam (1977), "Market Imperfections, Capital Market Equilibrium, and Corporate Finance," *Journal of Finance*, 32, 307–19.
Stulz, Rene M. (1999), "International Portfolio Flows and Security Markets.", Unpublished working paper, The Ohio State University, Columbus, OH.
Tesar, Linda and Ingrid Werner (1995), "Home Bias and High Turnover," *Journal of International Money and Finance*, 14, 467–92.
Tesar, Linda and Ingrid Werner (1992), *Home Bias and the Globalisation of Securities Markets*. Cambridge, MA: National Bureau of Economic Research.
Tobin, James (2003), "A Proposal for Monetary Reform," *Eastern Economic Journal*, 29 (4), 519–26.
Trichet, Jean-Claude (2004), "EU Enlargement: Challenges and Opportunities," in Europe's Frontiers: EU Enlargement—Its Implications and Consequences. Lisbon: European Central Bank.
Viner, Jacob (1950), *The Customs Union Issue*. New York: Carnegie Endowment for International Peace.
Walter, Ingo (1993), "Emerging Equity Market," *ASEAN Economic Bulletin*, 10 (1), 1–19.
Warsaw Stock Exchange (2006), "15 Years of WSE," Warsaw Stock Exchange.

Appendix

Appendix 1 Index Constituents by Market as of End of Year 2005

Appendix 1A Index constituents in the Czech market

Company name	Industry	Market capitalisation year end 2005, MEUR
ČEZ	Utilities	7,951
Telefonica O2 C.R.	ICT and Media	5,716
Erste Bank	Banking	5,615
Komercni Banka	Banking	4,516
Zentiva	Pharmaceuticals	1,496
CETV	ICT and Media	1,483
Unipetrol	Oil and Gas	1,456
Philip Morris	Food, Beverage and Tobacco	1,206
Severoceske Doly	Mining	488
Orco	Financial Investments	345
SČ ENERGETIKA	Utilities	235
STČ ENERGETICKÁ	Utilities	220
SSŽ	Construction	201
Paramo	Oil and Gas	44

Source: Local Stock Exchange

Appendix 1B Index constituents in the Estonian market

Company name	Industry	Market capitalisation year end 2005, MEUR
Eestic Telekom	Communications and Media	1,048
Tallink Group	Transportation	676
Merko Ehitus	Construction	305
Tallinna Vesi	Utilities	270
Tallinna Kaubamaja	Retail Trade	152
Eesti Ehitus	Construction	131
Norma	Industrial Manufacturing	87
Saku Olletehas	Food, Beverage and Tobacco	77
Baltika	Retail Trade	76
Harju Elekter	Industrial Manufacturing	69
Starman	ICT and Media	50
Kalev	Textile and Furniture	34
Viisnurk	Textile and Furniture	12
Tallinna Farmaatsiateehas	Pharmaceuticals	5
PTA Group	Textile and Furniture	4

Source: Local Stock Exchange

Appendix 1C Index constituents in the Hungarian market

Company name	Industry	Market capitalisation year end 2005, MEUR
Mol	Oil and Gas	8,603
OTB	Banking	7,719
Matav	ICT and Media	3,941
Richter	Pharmaceuticals	2,825
Bchem	Chemicals	693
Egis	Pharmaceuticals	692
TVK	Chemicals	503
FHB	Banking	300
Demasz	Utility	250
Antenna Hungaria	ICT and Media	244
Fotex	Trade	97
Synergon	ICT and Media	19

Source: Local Stock Exchange

Appendix 1D Index constituents in the Latvian market

Company name	Industry	Market capitalisation year end 2005, MEUR
Latvijas Gaze	Oil and Gas	546
Ventspils Nafta	Transportation	401
Latvijas Kugnieciba	Transportation	370
Valmieras Stikla Skiedra	Industrial Manufacturing	90
SAF Tehnika	Manufacturing Electric Goods	51
Liepajas Metaljurgs	Industrial Manufacturing	51
Latvijas Balzams	Food, Beverage and Tobacco	48
Grindeks	Pharmaceuticals	40
Olainfarm	Pharmaceuticals	29
Rigas Kugu Buvetava	Industrial Manufacturing	24
Ditton Pievadjkezu Rupnica	Industrial Manufacturing	10

Source: Local Stock Exchange

Appendix 1E Index constituents in the Lithuanian market

Company name	Industry	Market capitalisation year end 2005, MEUR
Mazeikiu Nafta	Oil and Gas	1,940
TEO LT	ICT and Media	640
Lietuvos Dujos	Oil and Gas	535
Lietuvos Energija	Utilities	467
VST	Utilities	430
Rytu Skirstomieji Tinklai	Utilities	401
Lifosa	Chemicals	278
DnB NORD Bankas	Banking	238
Lietuvos Elektrine	Utilities	170
Invalda	Financial Investments	167
Snoras	Banking	143
Stumbras	Food, Beverage and Tobacco	115
Snaige	Manufacturing Electric Goods	115
Klaipedo Nafta	Oil and Gas	106
Rokiskio Suris	Food, Beverage and Tobacco	103
Apranga	Retail Trade	102
Klaipedos Juru Kroviniu Kompanja	Transportation	97
Siauliu Bankas	Banking	87
DFDS LISCO	Transportation	74
Pieno Zvaigzdes	Food, Beverage and Tobacco	70
Panevezio Statybos Trestas	Construction	66
Limarko Laivinin.	Transportation	65
Ukio Bankas	Banking	65
Utenos Trikatazas	Textile and Furniture	51
Alita	Food, Beverage and Tobacco	47
Sanitas	Pharmaceuticals	45
Grigiskes	Pulp and Paper	42
Vilniaus Baldai	Textile and Furniture	41
Lietuvos Juru Laivininkyste	Transportation	34
Zemaitijos Pienas	Food, Beverage and Tobacco	27
Kauno Energija	Utilities	23
Vilniaus Degtine	Food, Beverage and Tobacco	21
Klaipedos Baldai	Textile and Furniture	21
Mazeikiu Elektrine	Utilities	17
Vilkyskiu Pienine	Food, Beverage and Tobacco	14
Anyksciu Vynas	Food, Beverage and Tobacco	13
Dvarcioniu Keramika	Industrial Manufacturing	12
Vilniaus Vingis	Manufacturing Electric Goods	11
Gubernija	Food, Beverage and Tobacco	9
Linas	Textile and Furniture	7
Pramprojektas	Construction	6
Alytaus Tekstile	Textile and Furniture	5
Kauno Tiekimas	Transportation	5

Source: Local Stock Exchange

Appendix 1F Index constituents in the Polish market, part 1

Company name	Industry	Market capitalisation year end 2005, MEUR
PKNORLEN	Oil and Gas	2,324
TPSA	ICT and Media	2,268
PEKAO	Transportation	2,261
PKOBP	Banking	2,029
KGHM	Mining	1,635
BANKBPH	Banking	990
PGNIG	Oil and Gas	810
AGORA	ICT and Media	707
BZWBK	Banking	554
NETIA	ICT and Media	552
LOTOS	Oil and Gas	537
TVN	ICT and Media	489
GTC	Textile and Furniture	442
PROKOM	ICT and Media	390
MOL	Oil and Gas	369
INGBSK	Banking	333
KETY	Packaging Material	283
BRE	Banking	252
CERSANIT	Textile and Furniture	247
ECHO	ICT and Media	237
ORBIS	Hotel	234
POLIMEXMS	Construction	223
GETIN	Financial Investments	196
GRAJEWO	ICT and Media	182
HANDLOWY	Banking	168
BIOTON	Pharmaceuticals	165
MILLENNIUM	Banking	162
CIECH	Chemicals	161
LPP	Textile and Furniture	157
SWIECIE	Packaging Material	156
SOFTBANK	ICT and Media	152
COMPLAND	ICT and Media	150
PGF	Pharmaceuticals	145
FARMACOL	Pharmaceuticals	121
BORYSZEW	Mining	113
APATOR	Manufacturing Electric Goods	110
BUDIMEX	Construction	104
PBG	Oil and Gas	101
KREDYTB	Banking	101
DEBICA	Manufacturing	93
ALCHEMIA	Oil and Gas	93
KOELNER	Manufacturing	90
DWORY	Chemicals	89
DUDA	Packaging Material	89
KOGENERA	Utilities	87
SANOK	Industrial Manufacturing	86
JELFA	Pharmaceuticals	84

Source: Local Stock Exchange

Appendix 1F Index constituents in the Polish market, part 2

Company name	Industry	Market capitalisation year end 2005, MEUR
OPOCZNO	Construction	80
CCC	Textile and Furniture	79
PULAWY	Chemicals	78
AMREST	Restauration	78
EUROCASH	Retailer	76
STALPROD	Industrial Manufacturing	69
COMARCH	ICT and Media	59
WSIP	ICT and Media	59
BACA	Banking	58
FORTE	Textile and Furniture	56
EMAX	ICT and Media	55
ASSECOPOL	ICT and Media	53
BARLINEK	Flooring	50
PRATERM	Utilities	47
ABG	ICT and Media	46
RAFAKO	Industrial Manufacturing	45
GROCLIN	Logistics	42
ELBUDOWA	Industrial Manufacturing	38
RMFFM	ICT and Media	37
JCAUTO	Automotive Spare Parts	36
VISTULA	Textile and Furniture	36
ELSTAROIL	Oil and Gas	35
SNIEZKA	Chemicals	34
ZELMER	Manufacturing Electric Goods	34
STALEXP	Metals	32
POLICE	Chemicals	32
ATM	ICT and Media	32
WAWEL	Food, Beverage and Tobacco	31
NOWAGALA	Flooring	30
PROVIMROL	Agriculture	30
ELDORADO	Retailing	30
JUTRZENKA	Food, Beverage and Tobacco	29
ELEKTRIM	n.a.	29
DECORA	Textile and Furniture	28
POLMOSLBN	Food, Beverage and Tobacco	27
GRUPAONET	ICT and Media	27
KROSNO	Glassworks	27
BCHEM	Chemicals	27
PEKAES	Transportation	27
IMPEXMET	Metals	25

Source: Local Stock Exchange

Appendix 1F Index constituents in the Polish market, part 3

Company name	Industry	Market capitalisation year end 2005, MEUR
SOKOLOW	Food, Beverage and Tobacco	24
POLCOLOR	Flooring	23
IMPEL	Facility Management	23
AMICA	Manufacturing Electric Goods	23
MENNICA	Metals	22
PAGED	Textile and Furniture	20
PROCHEM	Construction	20
STALPROFI	Metals	19
TECHMEX	ICT and Media	19
TIM	Distribution of Electric Goods	18
AMBRA	Food, Beverage and Tobacco	18
IVAXCORP	Pharmaceuticals	18
COMP	ICT and Media	18
LUBAWA	Military Equipment	17
MNI	ICT and Media	16
INDYKPOL	Food, Beverage and Tobacco	16
KRUSZWICA	Food, Beverage and Tobacco	15
GRAAL	Food, Beverage and Tobacco	14
PEP	Utilities	14
BOS	Banking	14
SPIN	ICT and Media	14
LENA	Manufacturing Electric Goods	14
INTERIA.PL	ICT and Media	14
HOOP	Food, Beverage and Tobacco	13
MPECWRO	Utilities	12
HUTMEN	Metals	12
ZREW	Industrial Manufacturing	11
MIESZKO	Food, Beverage and Tobacco	10
ATMGRUPA	ICT and Media	10
TORFARM	Pharmaceuticals	8
ENERGOPN	Industrial Manufacturing	8
KOPEX	Industrial Manufacturing	8
BMPAG	Financial Investments	1
SKYEUROPE	Transportation	0.5

Source: Local Stock Exchange

Appendix 1G Index constituents in the Slovak market

Company name	Industry	Market capitalisation year end 2005, MEUR
Slovnaft, a.s.	Oil and Gas	1,435
Všeobecná úverová banka, a.s.	Banking	402
OTP Banka Slovensko, a.s.	Banking	159
Slovenské energetické strojárne, a.s.	Industrial Manufacturing	18
Biotika, a.s.	Pharmaceuticals	6

Source: Local Stock Exchange

Appendix 1H Index constituents in the Slovenian market

Company name	Industry	Market capitalisation year end 2005, MEUR
KRKA	Pharmaceuticals	281
Sava	Industrial Manufacturing	253
Petrol	Oil and Gas	234
Pivovarna Laško	Food, Beverage and Tobacco	215
Mercator	Retail Trade	195
Gorenje	Manufacturing Electric Goods	171
Merkur	Retail Trade	154
Luka Koper	Transportation	131
Istrabenz	Industrial Manufacturing	128
Intereuropa	Transportation	108
Aerodrom Ljubljana	Transportation	90
Terme Čatež	Health Care	49
Delo	Publishing	47
Etol	Chemicals	39
Žito	Food, Beverage and Tobacco	28

Source: Local Stock Exchange

Appendix 2 Detailed Sovereign Credit Rating Data

Appendix 2A Czech Republic, Estonia, Hungary and Latvia

		Local currency			Foreign Currency		
Sovereign	Date	Long-Term	Outlook	Short-Term	Long-Term	Outlook	Short-Term
Crech Republic	30-Nov-05	A	Positive	A-1	A–	Positive	A-2
	03-Sep-04	A	Stable	A-1	A–	Stable	A-2
	05-Nov-02	A+	Stable	A-1	A–	Stable	A-2
	05-Nov-98	AA–	Stable	A-1+	A–	Stable	A-2
	30-Jun-98	AA	Stable	A-1+	A	Stable	A-1
	07-Nov-95				A	Stable	A-1
	18-Jul-94				BBB+	Positive	—
	28-Jul-93				BBB	Positive	—
Estonia	17-Jul-06	A	Stable	A-1	A	Stable	A-1
	21-Jul-05	A	Positive	A-1	A	Positive	A-1
	17-Nov-04	A	Stable	A-1	A	Stable	A-1
	18-Dec-03	A–	Positive	A-2	A–	Positive	A-2
	20-Nov-01	A–	Stable	A-2	A–	Stable	A-2
	21-Dec-00	A–	Positive	A-2	BBB+	Positive	A-2
	11-Dec-97	A–	Stable	A-2	BBB+	Stable	A-2
Hungary	15-Jun-06	BBB+	Negative	A-2	BBB+	Negative	A-2
	26-Jan-06	A–	Negative	A-2	A–	Negative	A-2
	27-May-05	A–	Stable	A-2	A–	Stable	A-2
	19-Nov-02	A	Stable	A-1	A–	Stable	A-2

Appendix 2A (continued)

Sovereign	Date	Local currency Long-Term	Outlook	Short-Term	Foreign Currency Long-Term	Outlook	Short-Term
	19-Dec-00	A+	Stable	A-1	A–	Stable	A-2
	02-Feb-00	A	Positive	A-1	BBB+	Positive	A-2
	11-Dec-98	A	Stable	A-1	BBB	Positive	A-3
	22-Jan-98	A–	Positive	A-1	BBB–	Positive	A-3
	27-Jul-97	A–	Stable	A-1	BBB–	Stable	A-3
	28-Oct-96	A–	Stable	A-1	BBB–	Stable	—
	31-Jan-96				BB+	Stable	—
	06-Feb-95				BB+	Negative	—
	15-Apr-94				BB+	Stable	—
	20-Apr-92				BB+	Positive	—
Latvia	29-Jul-04	A–	Stable	A-2	A–	Stable	A-2
	29-Jul-03	A–	Stable	A-2	BBB+	Positive	A-2
	20-Aug-02	A–	Stable	A-2	BBB+	Stable	A-2
	09-Aug-01	A–	Stable	A-2	BBB	Positive	A-3
	16-Jan-97	A–	Stable	A-2	BBB	Stable	A-3

Source: Standard & Poor's (2006)

Appendix 2B Lithuania, Poland, Slovak Republic and Slovenia

Sovereign	Date	Local Currency Long-Term	Outlook Term	Short-Term	Foreign Currency - Long	Outlook Term	Short-
Lithuania	18-May-06	A	Stable	A-1	A	Stable	A-1
	05-Dec-05	A	Positive	A-1	A	Positive	A-1
	01-Feb-05	A–	Positive	A-2	A–	Positive	A-2
	05-Feb-04	A–	Stable	A-2	A–	Stable	A-2
	29-Jul-03	A–	Stable	A-2	BBB+	Positive	A-2
	17-Feb-03	A–	Stable	A-2	BBB+	Stable	A-2
	22-Apr-02	BBB+	Stable	A-2	BBB	Stable	A-3
	09-Jun-97	BBB+	Stable	A-2	BBB–	Stable	A-3
Poland	24-Apr-06	A–	Stable	A-2	BBB+	Stable	A-2
	22-Mar-05	A–	Positive	A-2	BBB+	Positive	A-2
	07-Oct-04	A–	Stable	A-2	BBB+	Stable	A-2
	05-Nov-03	A–	Negative	A-2	BBB+	Negative	A-2
	23-Jun-03	A	Negative	A-1	BBB+	Negative	A-2
	31-Jul-02	A	Stable	A-1	BBB+	Stable	A-2
	22-Aug-01	A+	Stable	A-1	BBB+	Stable	A-2
	12-Apr-01	A+	Stable	A-1	BBB+	Positive	A-2
	15-May-00	A+	Stable	A-1	BBB+	Stable	A-2
	10-Jun-99	A	Positive	A-1	BBB	Positive	A-3
	03-Jun-97	A–	Positive	A-1	BBB–	Positive	A-3

Appendix 2B (continued)

		Local Currency			Foreign Currency		
Sovereign	Date	Long-Term	Outlook Term	Short-Term	- Long	Outlook Term	Short-
	10-Apr-96	A–	Stable	A-1	BBB–	Stable	—
	01-Jun-95				BB	Positive	—
Slovak Republic	19-Dec-05	A	Stable	A-1	A	Stable	A-1
	13-Dec-04	A–	Positive	A-2	A–	Positive	A-2
	02-Mar-04	A–	Stable	A-2	BBB+	Positive	A-2
	19-Dec-02	A–	Stable	A-2	BBB	Positive	A-3
	30-Oct-01	A–	Stable	A-2	BBB–	Positive	A-3
	09-Nov-00	BBB+	Positive	A-2	BB+	Positive	B
	12-Nov-99	BBB+	Stable	A-2	BB+	Stable	B
	17-Sep-98	BBB+	Negative	A-2	BB+	Negative	B
	07-Apr-98	A	Negative	A-1	BBB–	Negative	A-3
	24-Jun-97	A	Stable	A-1	BBB–	Stable	A-3
	11-Apr-96	A	Stable	A-1	BBB–	Stable	—
	05-Apr-95				BB+	Stable	—
	15-Feb-94				BB–	Stable	—
Slovenia	16-May-06	AA	Stable	A-1+	AA	Stable	A-1+
	13-May-04	AA	Stable	A-1+	AA–	Stable	A-1+
	26-Mar-03	AA	Stable	A-1+	A+	Positive	A-1+
	23-Oct-02	AA	Stable	A-1+	A	Positive	A-1
	15-Jan-98	AA	Stable	A-1+	A	Stable	A-1
	08-May-96	AA	Stable	—	A	Stable	—

Source: Standard & Poor's (2006)

Appendix 3 Exchange Rates Applied in the Analysis

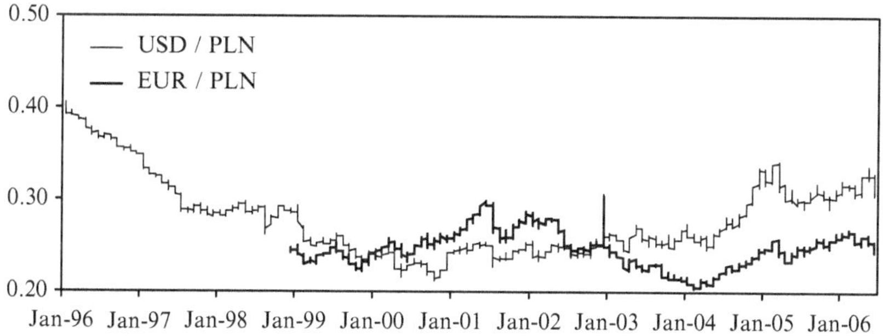

Appendix 3A USD and EUR per Polish Zloty
Source: Oanda

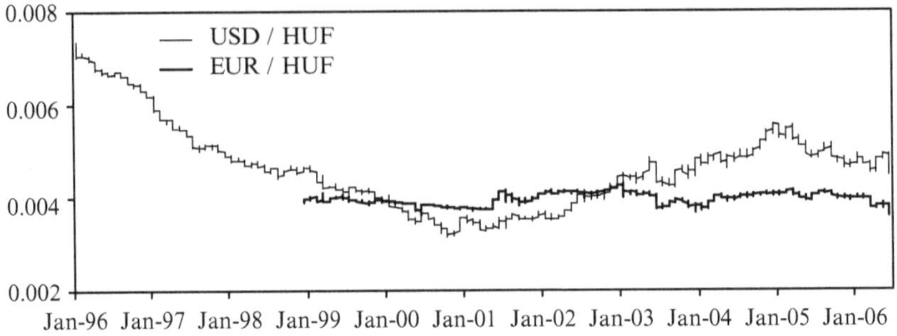

Appendix 3B USD and EUR per Hungarian Forint
Source: Oanda

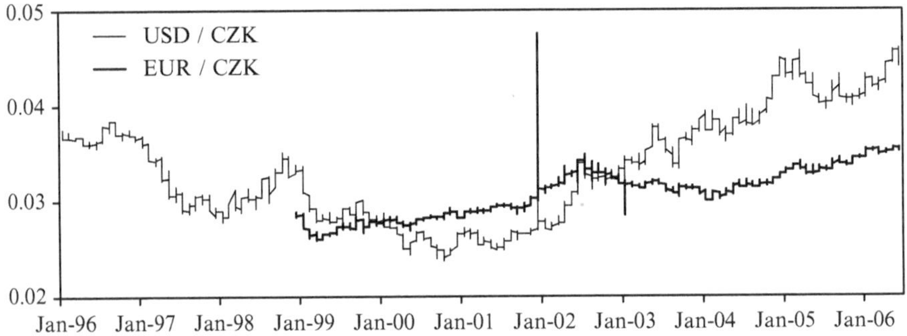

Appendix 3C USD and EUR per Czech Koruna
Source: Oanda

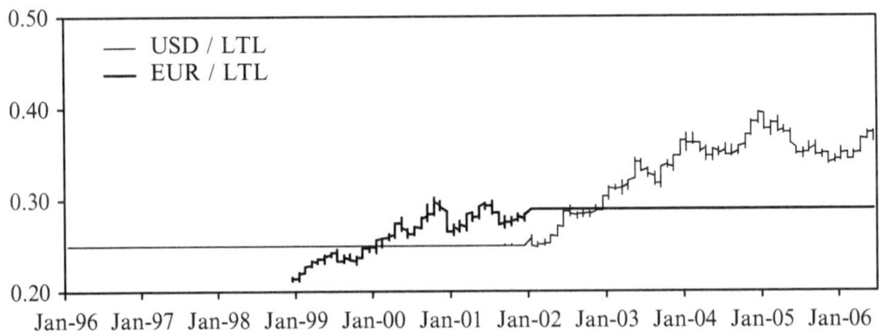

Appendix 3D USD and EUR per Lithuanian Litas
Source: Oanda

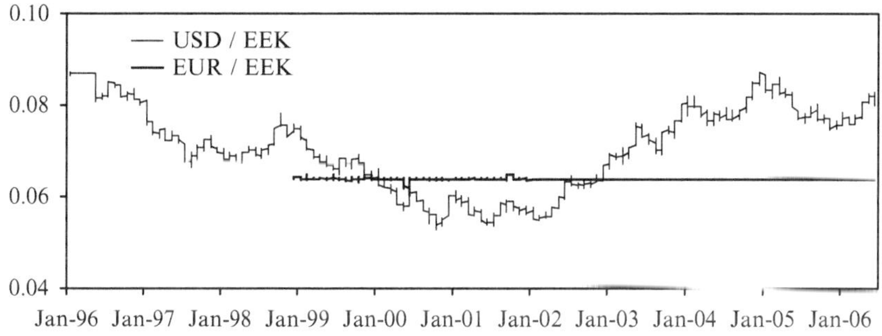

Appendix 3F USD and EUR per Estonian Kroon
Source: Oanda

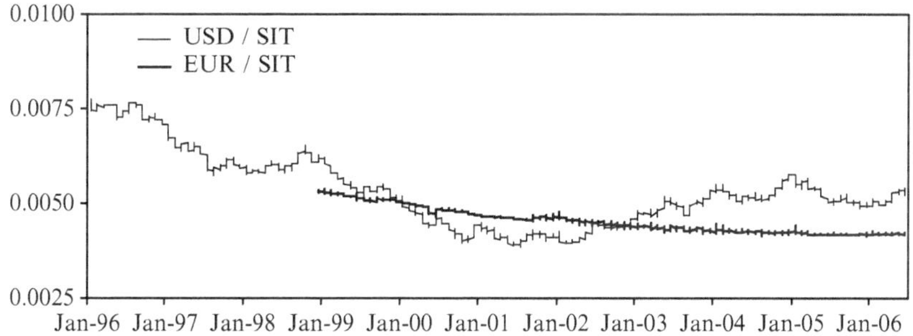

Appendix 3G USD and EUR per Slovenian Tolar
Source: Oanda

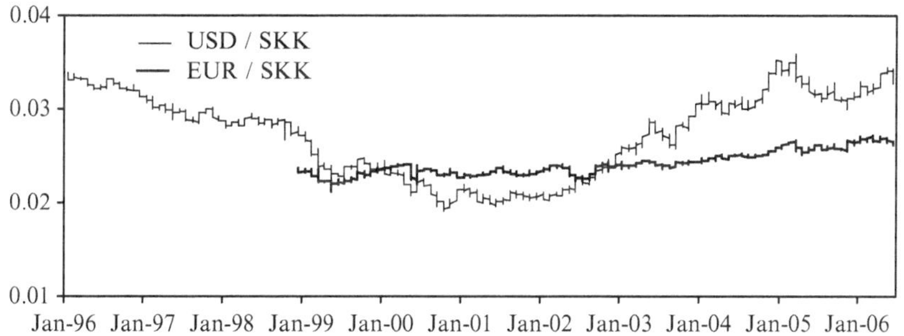

Appendix 3H USD and EUR per Slovak Koruna
Source: Oanda

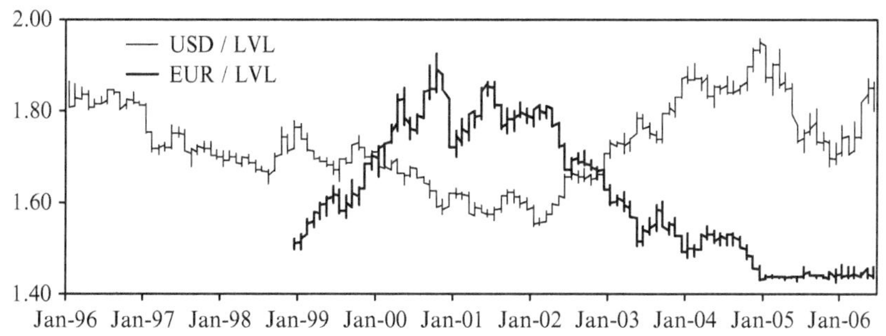

Appendix 3E USD and EUR per Latvian Lats
Source: Oanda

Appendix 4 Rolling 26-Week Correlation Coefficients of Global and Local Equity Market Indices

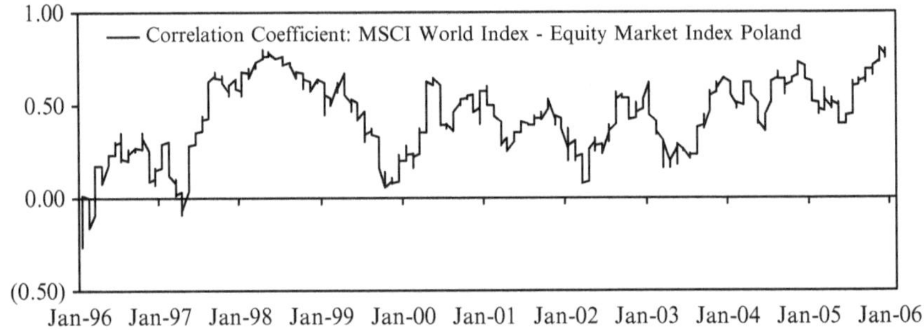

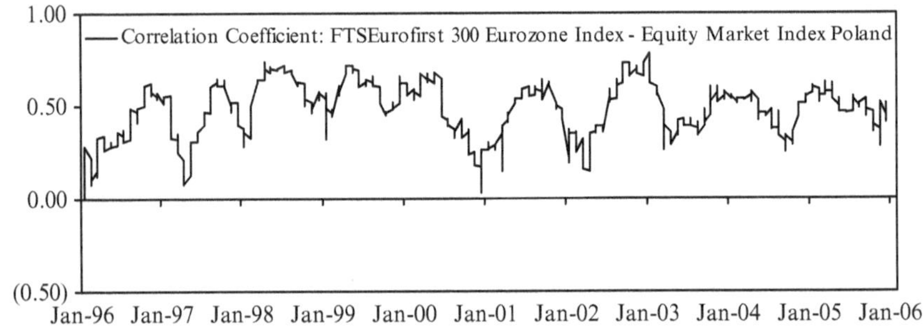

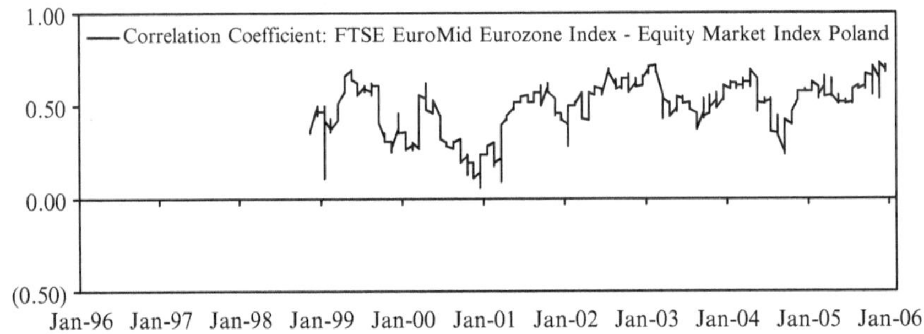

Appendix 4A Poland

Notes: Correlation coefficients are recalculated on a weekly basis based on a rolling 26-week time horizon

Source: Correlation coefficients are calculated based on data from Bloomberg

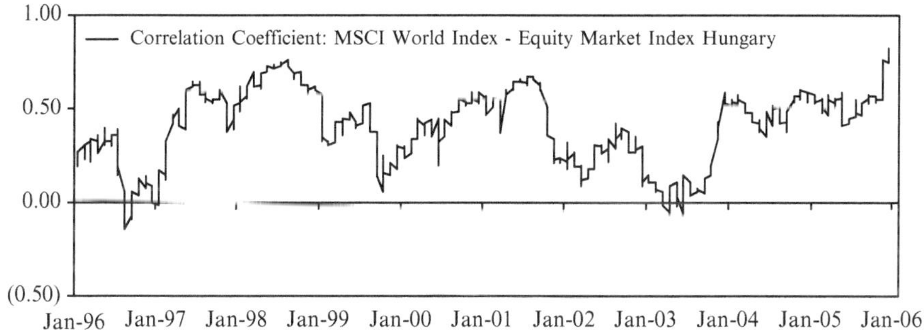

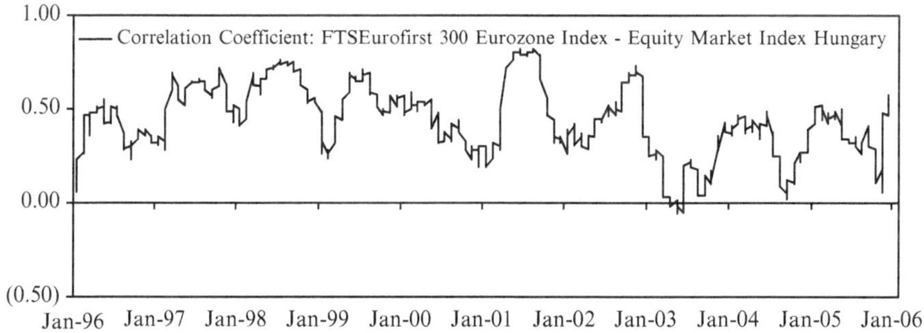

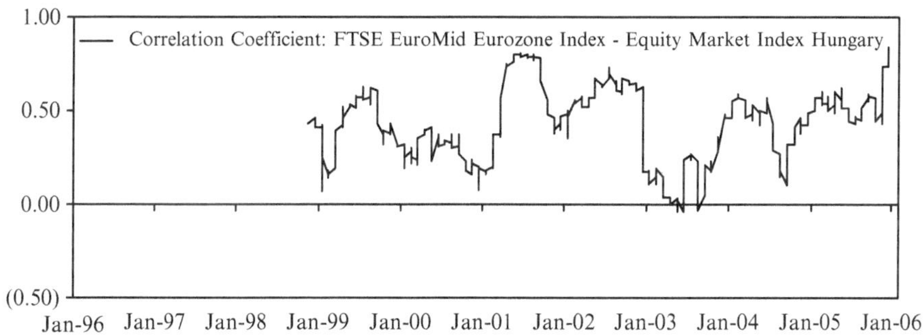

Appendix 4B Hungary

Notes: Correlation coefficients are recalculated on a weekly basis based on a rolling 26-week time horizon

Source: Correlation coefficients are calculated based on data from Bloomberg

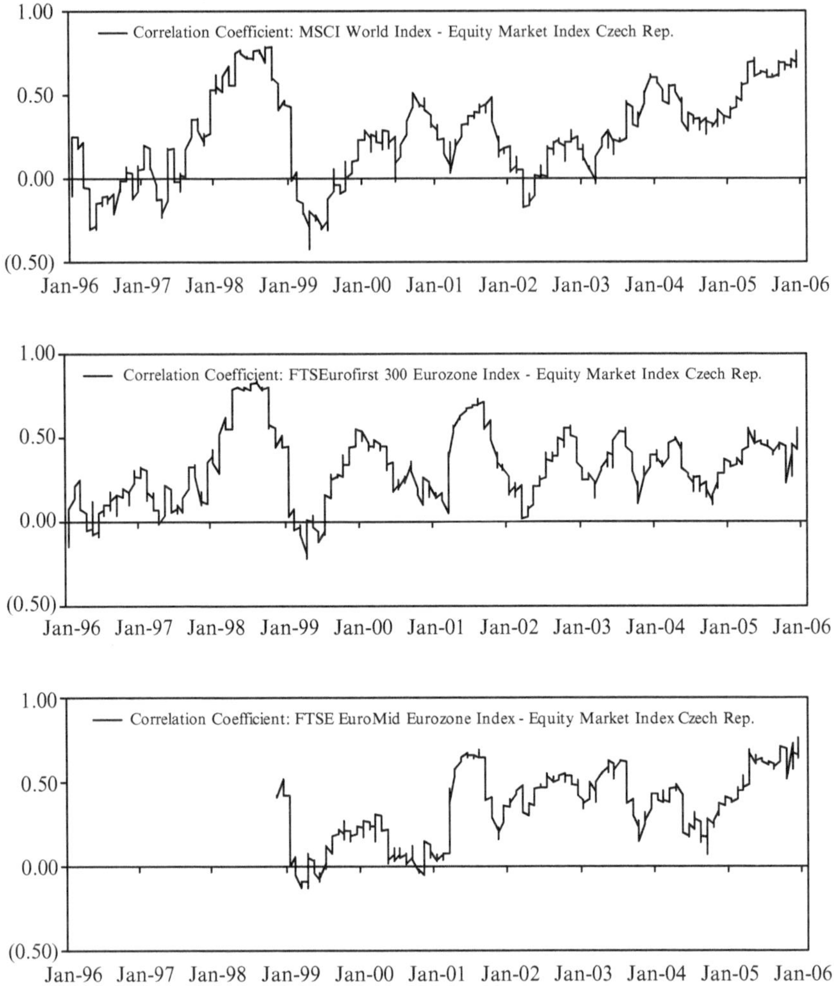

Appendix 4C Czech Republic

Notes: Correlation coefficients are recalculated on a weekly basis based on a rolling 26-week time horizon

Source: Correlation coefficients are calculated based on data from Bloomberg

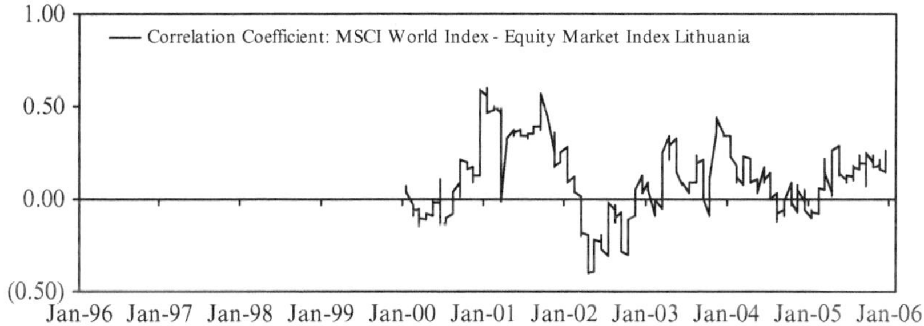

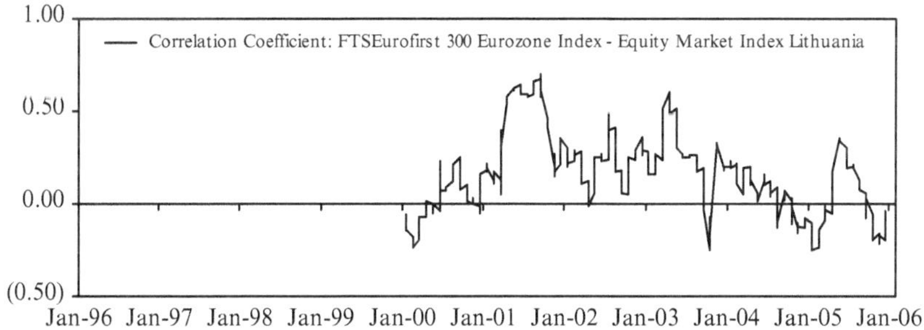

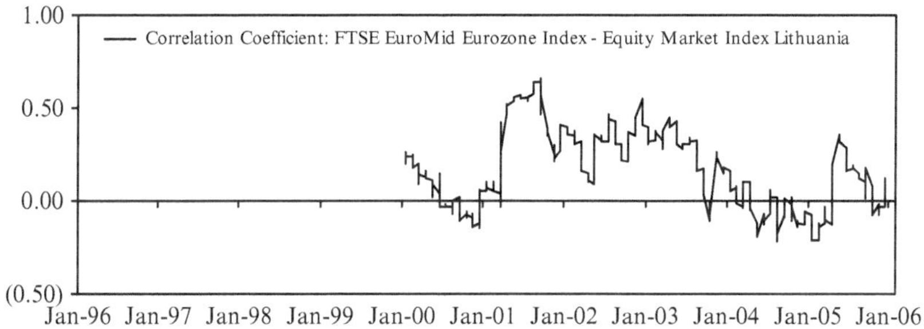

Appendix 4D Lithuania

Notes: Correlation coefficients are recalculated on a weekly basis based on a rolling 26-week time horizon

Source: Correlation coefficients are calculated based on data from Bloomberg

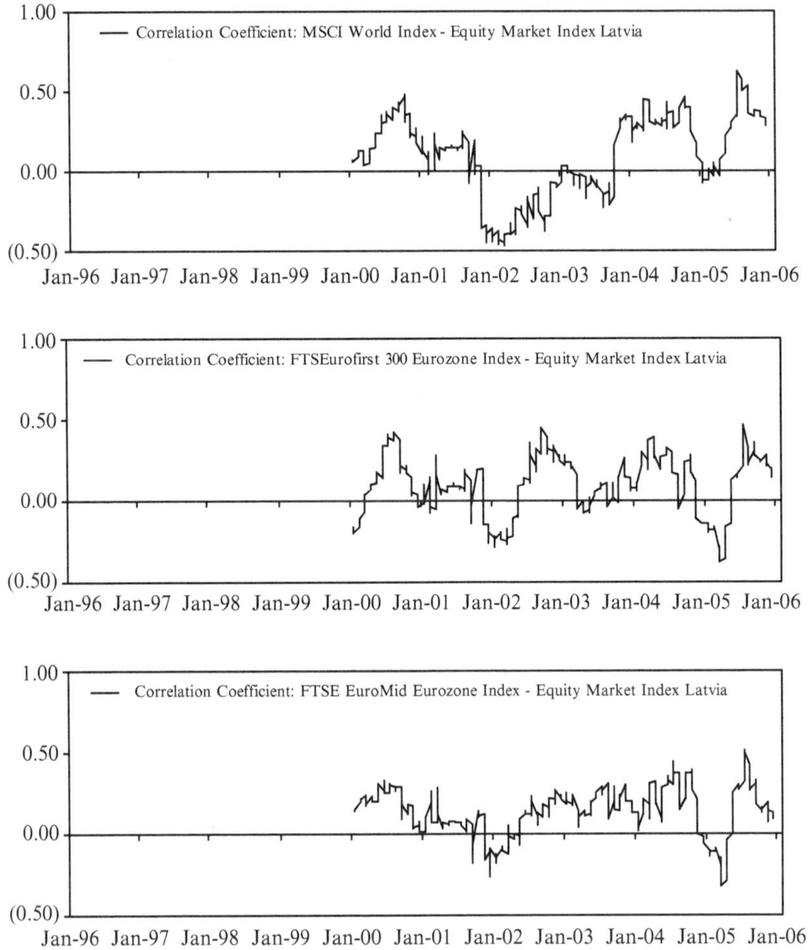

Appendix 4E Latvia

Notes: Correlation coefficients are recalculated on a weekly basis based on a rolling 26-week time horizon

Source: Correlation coefficients are calculated based on data from Bloomberg

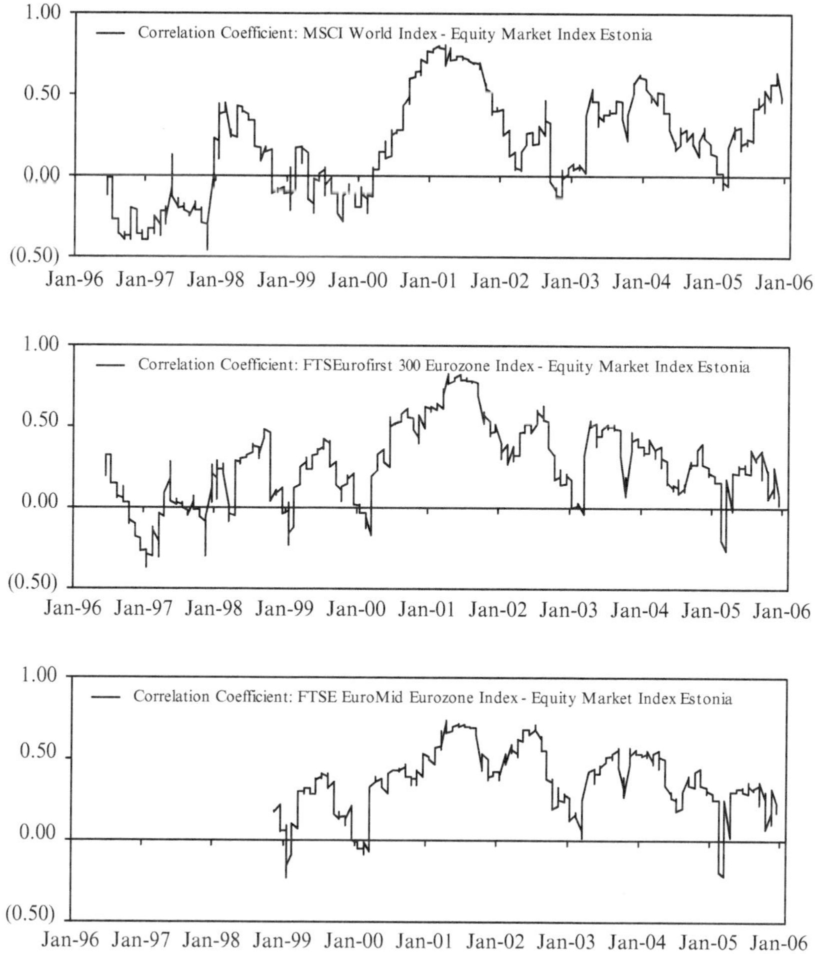

Appendix 4F Estonia

Notes: Correlation coefficients are recalculated on a weekly basis based on a rolling 26-week time horizon

Source: Correlation coefficients are calculated based on data from Bloomberg

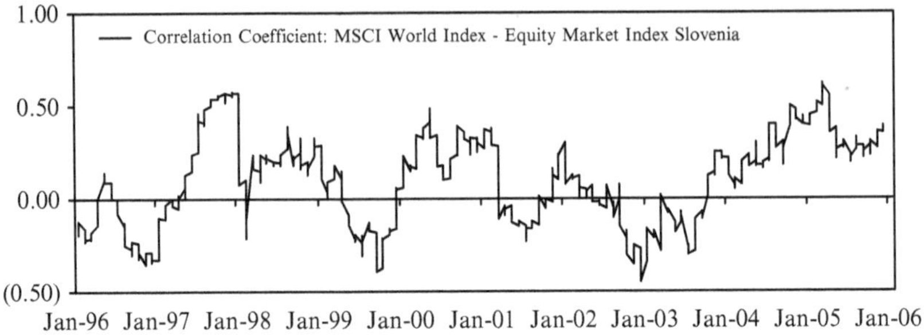

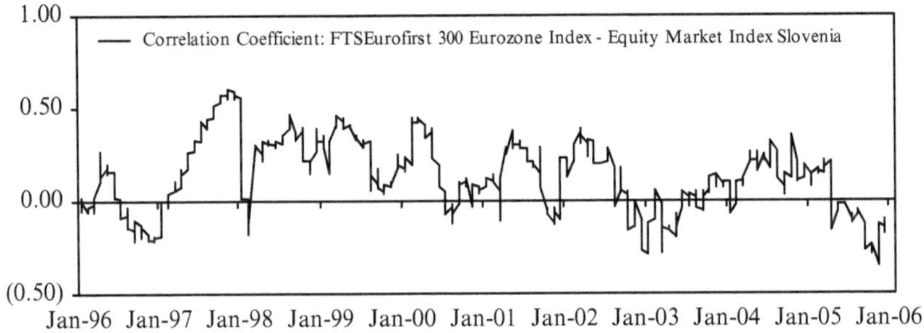

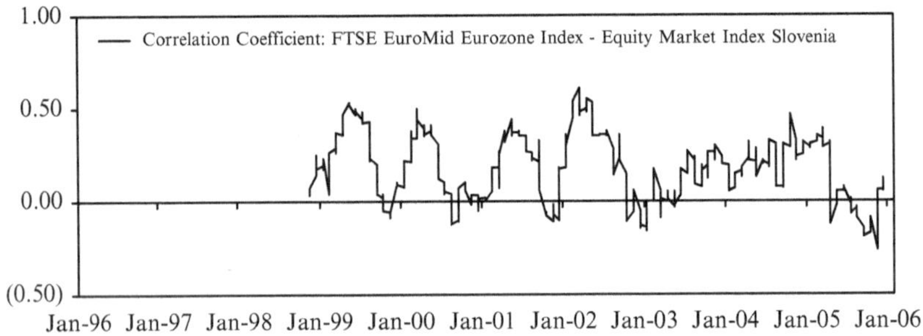

Appendix 4G Slovenia

Notes: Correlation coefficients are recalculated on a weekly basis based on a rolling 26-week time horizon

Source: Correlation coefficients are calculated based on data from Bloomberg

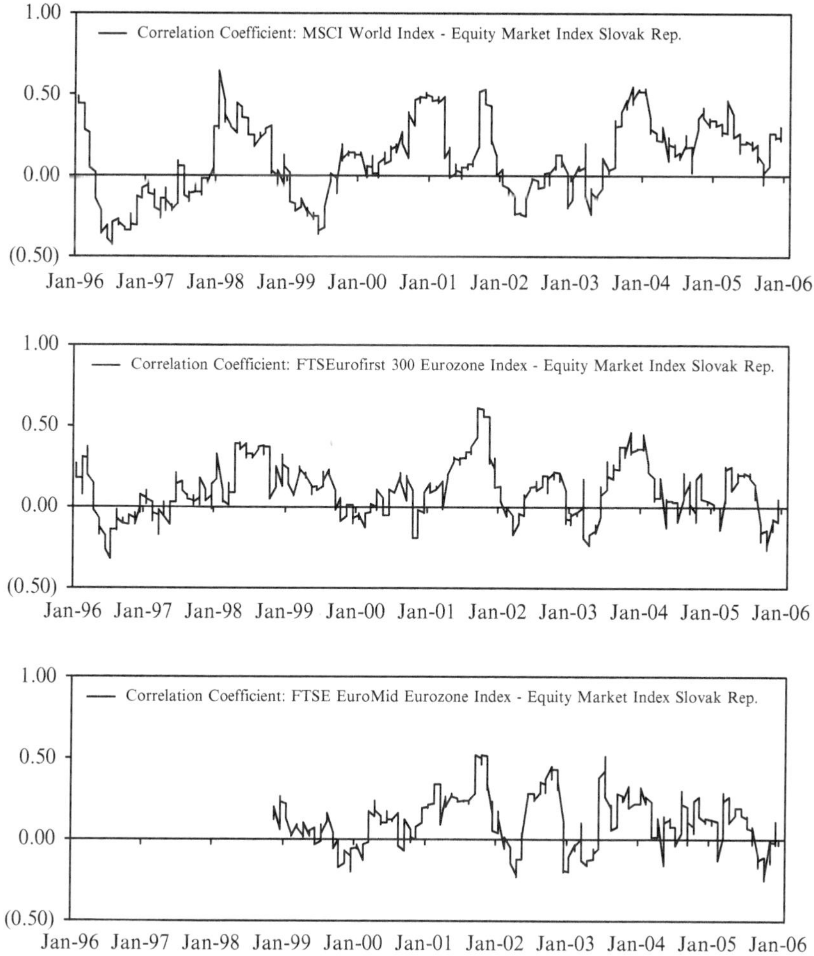

Appendix 4H Slovak Republic

Notes: Correlation coefficients are recalculated on a weekly basis based on a rolling 26-week time horizon

Source: Correlation coefficients are calculated based on data from Bloomberg

Appendix 5 List of Abbreviations Applied in Text

ADR	American Depositary Receipts
APT	Arbitrage Pricing Theory
BSE	Budapest Stock Exchange
BSSE	Bratislava Stock Exchange
CAPM	Capital Asset Pricing Model
CPI	Harmonised Consumer Price Index;
DEM	German Marks
Dec	December
DW	Durbin-Watson Statistic
D_1	Dividend in Period 1
EEA	European Economic Area
EFTA	European Free Trade Area
EMDB	Emerging Market Database
EMU	European Monetary Union
EU	European Union
EUR	Euro
EU15	15 Member States of the EU before the Enlargement of May 2004
FDI	Foreign Direct Investment
g	Expected Annual Dividend Growth Rate
GDP	Gross Domestic Product
GNP	Gross National Product
ICRG	International Country Risk Guide
ICT	Information and Communication Technology
IFC	International Finance Corporation
IMF	International Monetary Fund
Jan	January
Jun	June
k	Required Rate of Risk-Adjusted Return for an Asset
LJSE	Ljubljana Stock Exchange
ln	Natural Logarithm
Max	Maximum
Min	Minimum
MNC	Multinational Corporation
MSCI	Morgan Stanley Capital International
N	Number; NA / n.a. Not Available
OECD	Organisation for Economic Co-operation and Development
Post Ann	Post-Announcement;
Pre Ann	Pre-Announcement
PSE	Prague Stock Exchange
r	Pearson's Correlation Coefficient

r′	Transformed Correlation Coefficient as per Fisher's z-transformation
Rep	Republic
RFR	Risk Free Rate of Interest
RIA	Regional Market Integration Agreements
Std dev	Standard Deviation
S&P	Standard & Poor's
-bills	Treasury Bills
US	United States of America
USD	United States Dollar
WSE	Warsaw Stock Exchange;

Appendix 6 List of Variable Acronyms

Appendix 6A Acronyms related to independent global macroeconomic variables

Acronym: Eonomic Factor		Time Period
BCOMMPR	Commodity price change	Pre Ann.
BINDPRD	Change in industry production	Pre Ann.
BOILPRIC	Oil price change	Pre Ann.
BUSINT	US interest rate	Pre Ann.
BWLDCPI	Inflation rate	Pre Ann.
BWLDRET	Equity return rate	Pre Ann.
ACOMMPR	Commodity price change	Post Ann.
AINDPRD	Change in industry production	Post Ann.
AOILPRIC	Oil price change	Post Ann.
AUSINT	US interest rate	Post Ann.
AWLDCPI	Inflation rate	Post Ann.
AWLDRET	Equity return rate	Post Ann.

Notes: Ann. refers to Announcement of EU accession

Appendix 6B Acronyms related to independent local macroeconomic variables

Acronym	Economic Factor	Market	Time Period	Variable	Economic Factor	Market	Time Period
BCZINT	Interest rate	Czech Rep.	Pre Ann.	ACZINT	Interest rate	Czech Rep.	Post Ann.
BCZINFL	Inflation	Czech Rep.	Pre Ann.	ACZINFL	Inflation	Czech Rep.	Post Ann.
BCZINPR	Industrial prod.	Czech Rep.	Pre Ann.	ACZINPR	Industrial prod.	Czech Rep.	Post Ann.
BCZMOSU	Money supply	Czech Rep.	Pre Ann.	ACZMOSU	Money supply	Czech Rep.	Post Ann.
BCZTRBA	Trade balance	Czech Rep.	Pre Ann.	ACZTRBA	Trade balance	Czech Rep.	Post Ann.
BCZEXCH	Exchange rate	Czech Rep.	Pre Ann.	ACZEXCH	Exchange rate	Czech Rep.	Post Ann.
BESINT	Interest rate	Estonia	Pre Ann.	AESINT	Interest rate	Estonia	Post Ann.
BESINFL	Inflation	Estonia	Pre Ann.	AESINFL	Inflation	Estonia	Post Ann.
BESINPR	Industrial prod.	Estonia	Pre Ann.	AESINPR	Industrial prod.	Estonia	Post Ann.
BESMOSU	Money supply	Estonia	Pre Ann.	AESMOSU	Money supply	Estonia	Post Ann.
BESTRBA	Trade balance	Estonia	Pre Ann.	AESTRBA	Trade balance	Estonia	Post Ann.
BESEXCH	Exchange rate	Estonia	Pre Ann.	AESEXCH	Exchange rate	Estonia	Post Ann.
BHUINT	Interest rate	Hungary	Pre Ann.	AHUINT	Interest rate	Hungary	Post Ann.
BHUINFL	Inflation	Hungary	Pre Ann.	AHUINFL	Inflation	Hungary	Post Ann.
BHUINPR	Industrial prod.	Hungary	Pre Ann.	AHUINPR	Industrial prod.	Hungary	Post Ann.
BHUMOSU	Money supply	Hungary	Pre Ann.	AHUMOSU	Money supply	Hungary	Post Ann.
BHUTRBA	Trade balance	Hungary	Pre Ann.	AHUTRBA	Trade balance	Hungary	Post Ann.
BHUEXCH	Exchange rate	Hungary	Pre Ann.	AHUEXCH	Exchange rate	Hungary	Post Ann.
BLAINT	Interest rate	Latvia	Pre Ann.	ALAINT	Interest rate	Latvia	Post Ann.
BLAINFL	Inflation	Latvia	Pre Ann.	ALAINFL	Inflation	Latvia	Post Ann.
BLAINPR	Industrial prod.	Latvia	Pre Ann.	ALAINPR	Industrial prod.	Latvia	Post Ann.
BLAMOSU	Money supply	Latvia	Pre Ann.	ALAMOSU	Money supply	Latvia	Post Ann.
BLATRBA	Trade balance	Latvia	Pre Ann.	ALATRBA	Trade balance	Latvia	Post Ann.
BLAEXCH	Exchange rate	Latvia	Pre Ann.	ALAEXCH	Exchange rate	Latvia	Post Ann.
BLIINT	Interest rate	Lithuania	Pre Ann.	ALIINT	Interest rate	Lithuania	Post Ann.
BLIINFL	Inflation	Lithuania	Pre Ann.	ALIINFL	Inflation	Lithuania	Post Ann.
BLIINPR	Industrial prod.	Lithuania	Pre Ann.	ALIINPR	Industrial prod.	Lithuania	Post Ann.
BLIMOSU	Money supply	Lithuania	Pre Ann.	ALIMOSU	Money supply	Lithuania	Post Ann.
BLITRBA	Trade balance	Lithuania	Pre Ann.	ALITRBA	Trade balance	Lithuania	Post Ann.

BLIEXCH	Exchange rate	Lithuania	Pre Ann.	ALIEXCH	Exchange rate	Lithuania	Post Ann.
BPLINT	Interest rate	Poland	Pre Ann.	APLINT	Interest rate	Poland	Post Ann.
BPLINFL	Inflation	Poland	Pre Ann.	APLINFL	Inflation	Poland	Post Ann.
BPLINPR	Industrial prod.	Poland	Pre Ann.	APLINPR	Industrial prod.	Poland	Post Ann.
BPLMOSU	Money supply	Poland	Pre Ann.	APLMOSU	Money supply	Poland	Post Ann.
BPLTRBA	Trade balance	Poland	Pre Ann.	APLTRBA	Trade balance	Poland	Post Ann.
BPLEXCH	Exchange rate	Poland	Pre Ann.	APLEXCH	Exchange rate	Poland	Post Ann.
BSKINT	Interest rate	Slovak Rep.	Pre Ann.	ASKINT	Interest rate	Slovak Rep	Post Ann.
BSKINFL	Inflation	Slovak Rep.	Pre Ann.	ASKINFL	Inflation	Slovak Rep	Post Ann.
BSKINPR	Industrial prod.	Slovak Rep.	Pre Ann.	ASKINPR	Industrial prod.	Slovak Rep.	Post Ann.
BSKMOSU	Money supply	Slovak Rep.	Pre Ann.	ASKMOSU	Money supply	Slovak Rep.	Post Ann.
BSKTRBA	Trade balance	Slovak Rep.	Pre Ann.	ASKTRBA	Trade balance	Slovak Rep.	Post Ann.
BSKEXCH	Exchange rate	Slovak Rep.	Pre Ann.	ASKEXCH	Exchange rate	Slovak Rep.	Post Ann.
BSNINT	Interest rate	Slovenia	Pre Ann.	ASNINT	Interest rate	Slovenia	Post Ann.
BSNINFL	Inflation	Slovenia	Pre Ann.	ASNINFL	Inflation	Slovenia	Post Ann.
BSNINPR	Industrial prod.	Slovenia	Pre Ann.	ASNINPR	Industrial prod.	Slovenia	Post Ann.
BSNMOSU	Money supply	Slovenia	Pre Ann.	ASNMOSU	Money supply	Slovenia	Post Ann.
BSNTRBA	Trade balance	Slovenia	Pre Ann.	ASNTRBA	Trade balance	Slovenia	Post Ann.
BSNEXCH	Exchange rate	Slovenia	Pre Ann.	ASNEXCH	Exchange rate	Slovenia	Post Ann.

Notes: Ann. refers to Announcement of EU accession
Industrial Prod. refers to industrial production

Appendix 6C Acronyms related to dependent return variables in regression models

Acronym	Market	Time Period	Currency
BCZRTLC	Czech Rep.	Pre Ann.	Local
BESRTLC	Estonia	Pre Ann.	Local
BHURTLC	Hungary	Pre Ann.	Local
BLARTLC	Latvia	Pre Ann.	Local
BLIRTLC	Lithuania	Pre Ann.	Local
BPLRTLC	Poland	Pre Ann.	Local
BSKRTLC	Slovak Rep.	Pre Ann.	Local
BSNRTLC	Slovenia	Pre Ann.	Local
ACZRTLC	Czech Rep.	Post Ann.	Local
AESRTLC	Estonia	Post Ann.	Local
AHURTLC	Hungary	Post Ann.	Local
ALARTLC	Latvia	Post Ann.	Local
ALIRTLC	Lithuania	Post Ann.	Local
APLRTLC	Poland	Post Ann.	Local
ASKRTLC	Slovak Rep.	Post Ann.	Local
ASNRTLC	Slovenia	Post Ann.	Local

Notes: Ann. refers to Announcement of EU accession

Appendix 6D Acronyms related to market volatility and return tests

Acronym	Market	Time Period	Currency
PLPRANLC	Poland	Pre Ann.	Local
PLPOANLC	Poland	Post Ann.	Local
HUPRANLC	Hungary	Pre Ann.	Local
HUPOANLC	Hungary	Post Ann.	Local
CZPRANLC	Czech Rep.	Pre Ann.	Local
CZPOANLC	Czech Rep.	Post Ann.	Local
LTPRANLC	Lithuania	Pre Ann.	Local
LTPOANLC	Lithuania	Post Ann.	Local
LVPRANLC	Latvia	Pre Ann.	Local
LVPOANLC	Latvia	Post Ann.	Local
ESPRANLC	Estonia	Pre Ann.	Local
ESPOANLC	Estonia	Post Ann.	Local
SVPRANLC	Slovenia	Pre Ann.	Local
SVPOANLC	Slovenia	Post Ann.	Local
SKPRANLC	Slovak Rep.	Pre Ann.	Local
SKPOANLC	Slovak Rep.	Post Ann.	Local
ALPRANLC	All Markets	Pre Ann.	Local
ALPOANLC	All Markets	Post Ann.	Local
PLPRANUS	Poland	Pre Ann.	USD
PLPOANUS	Poland	Post Ann.	USD
HUPRANUS	Hungary	Pre Ann.	USD
HUPOANUS	Hungary	Post Ann.	USD
CZPRANUS	Czech Rep.	Pre Ann.	USD
CZPOANUS	Czech Rep.	Post Ann.	USD
LTPRANUS	Lithuania	Pre Ann.	USD
LTPOANUS	Lithuania	Post Ann.	USD

(continued)

Appendix 6D (continued)

Acronym	Market	Time Period	Currency
LVPRANUS	Latvia	Pre Ann.	USD
LVPOANUS	Latvia	Post Ann.	USD
ESPRANUS	Estonia	Pre Ann.	USD
ESPOANUS	Estonia	Post Ann.	USD
SVPRANUS	Slovenia	Pre Ann.	USD
SVPOANUS	Slovenia	Post Ann.	USD
SKPRANUS	Slovak Rep.	Pre Ann.	USD
SKPOANUS	Slovak Rep.	Post Ann.	USD
ALPRANUS	All Markets	Pre Ann.	USD
ALPOANUS	All Markets	Post Ann.	USD

Notes: Ann. refers to Announcement of EU Accession

FSC
www.fsc.org
MIX
Papier | Fördert gute Waldnutzung
FSC® C083411

Kolibri 360 GmbH
Ferdinand-Jühlke-Straße 7
99095 Erfurt, Deutschland
produktsicherheit@kolibri360.de